CANADIAN CASES IN FINANCIAL ACCOUNTING

CANADIAN CASES IN FINANCIAL ACCOUNTING

Joan E. D. Conrod

Carol E. Dilworth

Both of The Faculty of Management,
University of Toronto

Homewood, IL   60430
Boston, MA   02116

© RICHARD D. IRWIN, INC., 1989

Sponsoring editor: *Roderick T. Banister*
Project editor: *Rita McMullen*
Production manager: *Carma W. Fazio*
Cover Designer: *Maureen McCutcheon*
Compositor: *Bi-Comp, Incorporated*
Typeface: *10/12 Times Roman*
Printer: *R. R. Donnelley & Sons Company*

ISBN 0-256-06595-0

Library of Congress Catalog Card No. 88–83341

Printed in the United States of America

2 3 4 5 6 7 8 9 0 DO 6 5 4 3 2 1 0

Preface

Canadian Cases in Financial Accounting is a text that may be used either on its own or as a supplement to an intermediate or advanced financial accounting text. The book is the result of course development that was done in response to the direction of the accounting profession's accreditation examinations and, therefore, in response to student demand. The current textbooks do a commendable job of blending technical material and decision problems; however, due to length constraints, they are not able to provide cases that have the degree of depth and breadth that we hope you will find herein.

Many of the cases in this text are multisubject. We realize that not all courses cover the same material and that not all students have the same course prerequisites. However, we believe that the cases may be adapted for specific purposes, and we have provided guidance for this in the solutions manual, which is available to the instructor.

We have not reproduced sections of the *CICA Handbook* or relevant pronouncements to any great extent. Instructors may wish to place selected items on reserve in their campus library or to leave the library research to the student.

We are very fortunate in being permitted to adapt material from the Canadian Institute of Chartered Accountants, the Society of Management Accountants, the Atlantic Provinces Association of Chartered Accountants, and the Institute of Chartered Accountants of Ontario. The copyright for all these cases remains with the relevant institute/society. We also wish to warmly thank our colleagues Mike Longworth, John R. E. Parker, Tim Sutton, and Manfred Schneider, who generously gave us permission to use their material. Credit is also due to numerous Canadian public corporations whose accounting policy and disclosure decisions gave us so many ideas for our cases.

Our pride in the finished product is due to the feedback and support we had from our reviewers, our colleagues, our students, and our editors. Some very special people deserve mention.

Our reviewers read the drafts carefully and conscientiously; their comments were most insightful and constructive. Thanks for this time-consuming job goes to Professors Bruce Densmore, Mount Saint Vincent University; Michael Gibbins, University of Alberta; Irene M. Gordon, Simon Fraser University; Morton Nelson, Wilfred Laurier University; and Barbara Trenholm, University of New Brunswick, Fredericton.

The cases were extensively class-tested by ourselves and our colleagues at the University of Toronto and by Professor Barbara Trenholm. We humbly thank these people for their bravery and apologize to the students who occasionally groped to uncover something that we, in our enthusiasm, had mistakenly thought was obvious.

To our supporter and friend Mary Pacy, many thanks for the quality of the finished manuscript.

To Jim Evans, managing director of Richard D. Irwin Canada, who had the prescience to sign us—good work! To Rita McMullen, project editor, and Nancy Lanum, developmental editor, who have had to translate our jargon and shortforms—it was a pleasure! And now to Rod Banister, sponsoring editor. With Rod we have lived through a cross-country move (his), a new baby (Joan's), and a new computer (Carol's). For two years Rod has kept us on time, on track, on the telephone, and still laughing.

Joan E. D. Conrod
Carol E. Dilworth

Contents

CANADIAN CASES IN FINANCIAL ACCOUNTING

Introduction to Case Analysis

Case analysis provides an opportunity to apply technical knowledge in a specific situation and to appreciate how the environment will affect this application. Case analysis begins the process of developing professional judgement, an integral part of financial accounting.

A financial report can be viewed as a communication device from one group (e.g., a business owner) to another (e.g., a chartered bank). The person who receives this information is expected to base decisions on it (e.g., lend money, change interest rates). If financial accounting is seen as having the power to affect behavior, it is only natural to expect the preparers to wish to present it in such a way as to increase the likelihood of getting the behavior they want. This is neither good nor bad, it is merely a factual observation. Professional accountants have to understand the potential biases in a situation in order to be useful.

In financial accounting, generally accepted accounting principles (GAAP) exist to establish the basic ground rules. In some instances, they are specific, rule-oriented pronouncements that leave little room for the exercise of professional judgement. For example, the *CICA Handbook* section on leases is very specific. In other areas, the standards themselves require that the environment be carefully considered when establishing an accounting policy. For example, the accounting policy chosen to translate the accounts of a foreign subsidiary into Canadian dollars depends on individual circumstances. In other areas, there are a variety of accounting policies that are acceptable under GAAP, with few indications of the factors that should dictate choice. For example, inventory costing methods (FIFO, LIFO, weighted average, etc.) and depreciation methods (straight line, declining balance, etc.) are not narrowed down in any directive manner.

How does a professional make decisions when there is choice? If application of certain policies produces statements that are more suitable for the purpose for which they are intended, then their choice seems obvious. But "suitability" is subjective. The professional accountant must guard against biasing the statements to attempt to ensure a given outcome. Fair presentation is an overriding concern.

The value of accounting information is partly a function of the information's reliability, of which a major component is neutrality.[1] Accounting information would soon lose its credibility if it were biased, or expected to be biased.

We describe the role of the professional accountant as follows: First, to understand the environment, circumstances, and motivations of the preparers (and receivers) of accounting information who produce (or use) an accounting policy or a desired policy. Second, to judge on the acceptability of the policy in relation to the established standards, a combination of technical knowledge and judgement. Usually, the standards are GAAP and fair presentation, but in some cases all parties are better served by tailor-made standards. Third, the accountant must have the ability to implement the policy—the application of technical knowledge.

There are few black and white areas in the practice of accounting. Case analysis is meant to introduce the various shades of gray.

APPROACH TO CASE ANALYSIS

The following steps are offered to help in case preparation:

1. **Skim**
   a. Read all material quickly.
   b. Determine your role.
   c. Read the required.
   d. See what information is available.

2. **Read**
   a. Read all material carefully.
   b. Understand all information.
   c. Work through numeric exhibits.
   d. Gather information for steps 3 and 4.

3. **Identify problem areas, issues**

4. **Recognize situational variables, as applicable**
   a. Environment analysis—Identify the industry, state of the economy, the competitive factors that help this organization succeed, and so forth.

---

[1] FASB *Statement of Financial Accounting Concepts No. 2*, "Qualitative Characteristics of Accounting Information" (Stamford, Conn., May 1980).

  b. Organization analysis—Identify planning and control systems, including incentive schemes, reporting structure, and so on.
  c. Financial statement analysis—Identify financial strengths and
  weaknesses.
  d. Statement uses analysis—Identify users, types of decisions to be
  made, and motivation of the key players.
5. **Analysis**
  For each problem:
  a. Identify alternatives.
  b. Analyze each alternative:
    (1) Qualitative, both sides of argument.
    (2) Quantitative.
    (3) Sensitive to situational variables.
6. **Recommendation**
  Consistent with analysis.

KELOWNA WOODWORKERS ASSOCIATION

The Kelowna Woodworkers Association is a group of amateur woodworkers which was formed by 10 people in the mid-1960s. Membership
had grown to approximately 120 by 1989. The association holds monthly
meetings from September to May in a meeting room of a local church;
most meetings feature either a speaker (a professional craftsperson) or a
"mini-workshop" (members teaching each other). The one exception is in
May when the annual general meeting is held. At this meeting a financial
statement is presented and members are asked to vote on issues such as a
proposed increase in dues (currently $25 per year payable in September—
new and renewing members have all paid by the December meeting),
changes to the by-laws and constitution, and activities for the following
year. Each November the association rents a historic schoolhouse and
offers handmade wooden items for sale to the public; the sale extends
from Friday evening to Sunday afternoon and has been held for five years.
The association merely acts as an agent for the members, who bring their
items to the schoolhouse on Friday afternoon. It takes a percentage of the
proceeds and returns the balance to the members whose work was sold.
In addition, the association mounts an exhibition of members' work approximately every second year.
  The association owns eight lathes of various sizes which may be rented
by members for a $50 refundable deposit plus $15 per month. It also owns
hand tools for woodworking which rent for several dollars a month. The
only other asset of the association is a library collection of approximately
200 books and 15 subscriptions to periodicals; there is no charge to borrow these items, but the fine for overdue items is $1 per month per item.

All library items must be returned in May so the librarian can update and organize the collection over the summer. In fact many items are kept by members over the summer and are either returned or classified as lost in September. The lathes seldom need summer storage by the association as members are anxious to produce items for the fall sale during the summer months and begin to sign the lathes out as early as March.

The association's financial statement has traditionally been prepared on a cash flow basis. An example of the information sent to members is attached (Exhibit 1). You have just accepted the appointment as the association's accountant (the previous accountant has retired and moved to California) and have been approached by the incoming president who wonders if the members are receiving enough information on the statement. The association's books are open to scrutiny by any member but no one has ever requested this. The president is particularly concerned that

---

EXHIBIT 1

KELOWNA WOODWORKERS ASSOCIATION
Statement of Receipts and Disbursements
For the Year Ended April 30, 1989

Receipts:	
Memberships	$ 3,000.00
Sale income	6,124.58
Equipment rentals and deposits.	474.00
Interest income	156.14
Library income	119.00
Miscellaneous	337.50
Total receipts	$10,211.22
Disbursements:	
Memberships	$ 157.72
Exhibition expense	40.32
Equipment expense	458.67
Library expense	607.20
Program expense	54.79
Correspondence and bulletin	943.20
Room rental	200.00
Administration	579.98
Bank charges	65.69
Sale expense	5,582.68
Speaker expense	486.60
Miscellaneous	65.84
Total disbursements	$ 9,242.69
Excess of receipts over disbursements . .	$ 968.53

the statement can be used to convince the members that an increase in dues is unavoidable this year; increases are always met with resentment and the loss of some members.

Required

Respond to the requests of the president by suggesting appropriate reporting practices for the association.

KELOWNA WOODWORKERS ASSOCIATION
SUGGESTED APPROACH TO ANSWERING

OVERVIEW

The Kelowna Woodworkers Association is a small group of people who meet in order primarily to share and further their knowledge of and interest in woodworking. A secondary activity of the group is an annual sale; there is also an exhibition held every two years.

The only assets of the association are eight lathes and a library collection of about 200 books and 15 subscriptions to periodicals; therefore, asset valuation is not a concern when preparing financial statements.

The group is facing another increase in annual dues, and the president wants to present financial statements that reflect the need for the increase. In the past the members have been given a statement of receipts and disbursements for the year ended April 30 prepared on a cash flow basis. The adequacy of this presentation must be examined.

Because of the nature of the organization and because the group does not appear to have a bank loan or require an audit or an unqualified audit report, there is no need to adhere to generally accepted accounting principles.

ISSUES

1. Adequacy of cash flow statements.
    a. Refundable deposits.
    b. Library lending.
    c. Dues.
    d. Expenses.
2. Year-end.
3. Presentation of statement.
4. Additional information.

ANALYSIS AND RECOMMENDATIONS

1. Adequacy of Cash Flow Statements

a. Refundable Deposits. For an organization of this type, cash flow statements are usually representative of the activities. There are several aspects of the association's operations which may be misrepresented by cash flow statements based on an April year-end. For example, refundable deposits of $50 are required on each lathe rental. The deposits are included in the statements when received as no balance sheet is being prepared. The refund (assuming the lathe is returned in good condition) and the rental charge would be recorded in the month the equipment is returned. The busiest time for lathe rental is immediately prior to the summer months; therefore, the deposit is reflected in one set of statements and the refund and rental proceeds appear in a subsequent set.

Given the current deposit and rental charges, the impact does not appear to be material. Assuming that all lathes are rented during the summer, deposits of $400 are contained in the 1989 statement, and rental income of $480 (four months at $15 for the eight lathes) less the deposits will be recorded in the fall. Assuming the same level of rental activity and rates each year, the current policy closely approximates the earnings process as each statement will include a set of deposits from the end of the year and the net rental revenue from the previous fall. However, if the rental were increased and/or deposits were not refunded because of damage to the equipment, the difference could be material. Since the president wants to show statements which will help justify a dues increase, removing the deposits from 1989 receipts would help meet this objective.

b. Library Lending. The other activity of the association which straddles the summer is the library lending. Books and periodicals are due in May but are frequently kept over the summer or permanently. The receipts from fines are recorded as the items are returned. Again the difference may not be material as the 1989 statement includes fines from the previous fall and omits fines on the items which are out over the summer. However, at the extreme the misstatement is material. Assume that no items were overdue in September 1988 and assume that all the books in the library were taken out in April 1989 and not returned in May. The total fines due in September would be $1,000 (five months on 200 items at $1). In the context of the 1989 figures this is a material amount although presumably unlikely to occur to this extent. The problem with accrual of fines is that it is impossible to estimate in advance which volumes are permanently gone and which will be returned with an overdue penalty. Thus, the cash basis should be maintained.

c. Dues. The annual dues are not payable until September; therefore the April year-end does not mismatch cash flow and activities in this respect. However, since May is when the annual general meeting is held, it would be good cash management if members were encouraged to renew their memberships at this meeting. There may be activity by executive members over the summer (e.g., the cataloguing of the library) and expenditures may be necessary at this time in preparation for the new year.

d. Expenses. A prime concern in cash flow statements is whether expenses incurred but not paid are reflected in the results. If the level of payables is fairly constant, omission thereof will not greatly affect the assessment of results by the members. Usually, an organization this size operates on a cash basis and has few unpaid bills. However, if this norm is violated, the commitments of the organization are not disclosed to the members, and severe bias is introduced into the statements. For this reason, it is recommended that payables be accrued at year-end.

2. Year-End

An alternative to analyzing the impact of the differences between timing of the cash flow and the related activity described above would be to consider changing the year-end of the association. A September year-end would reduce the problems of lathe rental and library fine receipts recognition. However, annual dues paid in September would be mismatched with the previous year's expenditures. A December year-end could be considered, particularly because it is after the sale; however, a material amount of the expenditures relating to the sale may still be pending. An August year-end would enable the recognition of four months' receivables on the lathes and overdue books; the association's annual general meeting would end up being the first meeting of the new season and would probably not be preferable. Thus, the year-end should remain at April 30.

3. Presentation of Statement

The statement now being presented to the members could provide more information which would help demonstrate the need for the dues increase. There is no breakdown at the moment between equipment repairs and replacement. The 1989 expense of $458.67 indicates that it is unlikely that a new lathe was purchased during the year; members should be reminded of the age of the equipment and how soon it will need to be upgraded. The library expense does not distinguish between new acquisitions and those which were replacements for items not returned the previous September. In fact, if an item is stolen and not replaced, its cost may not be appearing on the statement at all. Members are unaware at the moment of the magnitude of replacement and the extent to which acquisitions are an expansion of the collection. If the executive is also unaware of how many items are not being returned, the president would be well advised to have the library inventory counted and compared to the card catalogue. In addition to a more detailed statement, the president may wish to consider a change in format to highlight how expenditures are being covered. For example, the net proceeds of the sale are $541.90, and of equipment rental are $15.33. Therefore, the membership dues must cover the cost of the library (net disbursements of $488.20) and the bulletin and correspondence (presumably the majority of this amount is attributable to the bulletin). The data could be presented in a way which demonstrates the projects or purchases which would not be possible, such as the acquisition of a new lathe, without the increase in dues. At the moment members may just be focusing on the bottom line showing an excess of receipts over disbursements and concluding that no increase is justified.

4. Additional Information

Balance sheet information, including liability for lathe deposits and accounts payable, as well as asset values for equipment and library books, would aid in assessing the association's commitments.

A key disclosure for justifying fee increases would be a budget for the coming year which could highlight expenditures the fee increase will finance (a new lathe, for instance, or library books). The members can then decide if these projects justify a fee increase.

In summary, the president should consider the following policies and disclosures:

1. Refundable deposits should not be recorded as revenue or expense.
2. Payables should be accrued at year-end.
3. Presentation of items on the statement should be reconsidered.
4. A balance sheet should be prepared.
5. Budget information for the coming year should be disclosed.

Numbers 3 and 5 will likely help the president's request for higher dues the most.

SAMPLE RESPONSE 1

Description

Kelowna Woodworkers Association is a small, private organization consisting of 120 members, a president, and a newly appointed accountant. The president has asked the accountant to comment on the amount and extent of the information presented to the members in the financial statements and to change the statement to provide ample reason for a membership fee increase. In the past, the association has depended on cash based accounting, and thus their disclosure presently consists of a receipts and disbursements statement.

Objectives

The objectives of the president are first to minimize net income while still maintaining a favourable standing. He feels that the present net receipts in excess of disbursements of $969 are too high to convince members that a fee increase is necessary. However, he does not want there to be an unfavourable position of a net loss or zero profit, for fear that his position or the operations of the organization may be questioned. Second, he wonders whether the members are receiving enough information from the present statement regarding the association's activities.

One must also keep in mind the objectives of the members. They want to be sure that their fees are being used to improve the association as a whole and that there is truly a need for a fee increase.

Issues/Alternatives

1. Adjust the statement so that results of operations, not cash transactions, are shown. The method of adjustment would be to convert from a cash basis to an accrual basis of accounting.
2. Provide the members with better disclosure, by giving them more explanations for key figures and more organized grouping of items on the income statement.
3. If converting to the accrual method, set accounting policies in accordance with GAAP.
4. Disclose next year's budget, highlighting the proposed uses for the fee increase.

Analysis

1. The major reason to switch to the accrual method is to provide proper representation of revenue earned and all expenses incurred to earn that revenue. Revenues would be recorded as earned, and expenses as incurred, regardless of time of payment. Matching would be achieved.

There is nothing really wrong with the result of the policy used now for revenue recognition, recording it as received. Technically, there is some "unearned" portion over the summer months, but since the association is not active over that period, adjustment is unnecessary. Their policy would be misleading if monthly statements were prepared, as September and December would be the only months with revenue. However, although the policy is flawed, it produces a satisfactory result for 12-month statements.

Deposits on lathes do not represent revenue and should not be recorded as such. Deposits are a liability.

Fines on overdue books should be accrued as books are outstanding and overdue. Better records should be kept to reduce the number of books that are stolen.

It is necessary that the lathes, tools, and books be depreciated to match cost with revenue. This would increase expense and let the members know the full cost of services provided. Also, there must be an allowance for books that will not be returned. This will also decrease net income.

There are disadvantages to the accrual method, however. Since the association is small and private, there is no real need for following GAAP. It will also be time consuming to switch methods and will be disruptive to the members, because they will not be able to compare past statements with the new income statement. Moreover, since the association deals mainly with cash and very little with credit (as is assumed from the statement presented), it is not really necessary for the cash basis to be discarded for the accrual method. Their primary measure of fiscal "success" is the cash receipt and disbursement record.

2. Even if an income statement is not prepared, and the current statement is used, there are only advantages to providing notes with the statement explaining policies, activities represented by expenses, and so forth. The more information the better, since this will help the members understand the statement and any changes in methods of accounting.

Additionally, the items on the statement should be organized more logically, putting related items together, so that the results of specific activities are more obvious (see Exhibit A).

3. GAAP is desirable because it makes the statements more comparable, and members will find it easier to understand. It also should result in fair presentation and give the credibility needed to justify a fee increase. As previously stated, GAAP does not have to be followed by an organization this size.

4. The president could disclose next year's cash budget, showing a cash shortfall caused by the acquisition of new lathes, or books, or some other project the members will want. They would be more willing to approve a fee increase if they saw what their money would be used for. On the other hand, it may be expensive to produce a budget, or the president may be reluctant to disclose this information. The benefits should outweigh the costs, though.

EXHIBIT A

KELOWNA WOODWORKERS ASSOCIATION
Income Statement
For the year ended April 30, 1989

Revenues:
Memberships $3,000.00

Expenses:
Memberships	$ 157.72	
Exhibition expense	40.32	
Program expense	54.79	
Correspondence and bulletin . .	943.20	
Room rental	200.00	
Administration	579.98	
Speaker expense	486.60	
Miscellaneous	65.84	2,528.45
		471.55

Operating income:
Activities:
Library
Income	119.00	
Expense	607.20	
Book depreciation*	100.00	
Book theft*	100.00	(688.20)

Equipment rental:
Income	474.00	
Expense	458.67	
Equipment depreciation* . .	200.00	(184.67)

Sale:
Income	6,124.58	
Expense	5,582.68	541.90

Other:
Interest income	156.14	
Bank charges	(65.69)	
Miscellaneous income . . .	337.50	427.95
Net income		$ 568.53

* Figures assumed.

Recommendations

From the analysis, and keeping in mind the objectives of the president and members, it is advisable that Kelowna switch to an accrual method and provide an income statement at the next meeting (see Exhibit A). It is also suggested that notes are provided and that there are better explanations of activities.

All expenses incurred to earn income should be included. Budgets for the coming year should be given to members to show them what their money will be used for.

Comments

Note that in the *Objectives* section, there is an incorrect emphasis on the importance of net income. Members will not be "tricked" into a fee increase if they see low net income when cash balances are increasing.

This response is a reasonable attempt at the case situation. Note that the motives of the president and the members are addressed throughout the response, and their needs addressed in a substantive way.

SAMPLE RESPONSE 2

Description

Kelowna Woodworkers Association is privately held by a growing group of amateur woodworkers. It is not large enough to require a statutory audit and, therefore, GAAP is not a constraint. The association receives its income from membership dues, sales of handmade wooden items, equipment rentals, interest income, and library income. The main function of this association is to acquire and learn new woodworking skills and knowledge. Profits are not very important, but it should at least break even in order to survive.

Objectives

The president wants the year-end financial statement to help convince the members that an increase in dues is unavoidable this year. The president may want more relevant information to be disclosed or he may even want a lower profit shown on the financial statement. Another objective is that of the many members. They would like the statement to show that the association is well managed, so that dues will not increase and the association may expand since there is more money on hand to buy new equipment.

Constraints

Since Kelowna is small and has no audit, GAAP should not be a constraint. But fairness and accuracy are ethical constraints. Consistency is also important so that different annual statements may be compared to each other. The statement should also try to match revenue to the costs that generated them.

Alternatives and Analysis

1. Status quo—The year-end statement should stay as is because it is accurate, fair, and easy to produce and understand. Also, it will be consistent with previous years' statements. The president's objective will not be solved, though.

2. Accrual basis—The revenue from the memberships should be recognized evenly during the nine months from September to May. This way, revenue is recognized as it is earned. The sale income, equipment rentals, interest income, and library income should be recognized when it is earned also, on the accrual basis. This results in revenue being fairly matched with the expenses that generated it.

    All expenses incurred must be recognized in this period. A Depreciation Expense account should replace the Equipment Expense account.

3. In order for the president to convince the members that an increase in dues is needed, more information must be disclosed on the statement.

    The equipment and tools may be very old and may need replacing. Library books may be old and "out of date" and therefore many new books may be bought. New magazine subscriptions may be required. Many costs may have risen because of reasons such as inflation. The problem with this is that it is much more complicated and requires much more detail.

    Books and magazines which are extremely overdue should be written off as an expense since they will probably never be returned.

Recommendations

Kelowna Woodworkers Association must switch to the accrual basis instead of using the cash flow basis. The accrual basis is much more fair and accurate. Also, cash basis financials do not conform with GAAP, but GAAP is not a constraint in this case.

In order for the president to convince the members that an increase in dues is needed, much more information such as the age of assets and replacement costs must be disclosed.

Comments

This is a weak response to the case. Little analysis was done, and there is only a recommendation, unsupported by any analysis, for many issues (e.g., see Point 2, accrual basis). The first part of the case considers the motives of the individuals, but this is integrated into the analysis superficially. While GAAP is not a legal constraint, the fairness of presentation it represents may well be desirable.

Note that monthly revenue recognition (Point 2) only has impact if statements are prepared for periods of less than 12 months.

Acme Construction Ltd.

Bob Bothwell had started Acme Construction Ltd. early in 1986 after working for several years as a supervisor for a local construction company. An inheritance from his parents had provided the start-up capital. Bob's wife, Susan, did all of the bookkeeping on weekends without pay to help conserve cash.

For the 1986 and 1987 year-ends, the firm where you are employed as a student-in-accounts had performed a review of the financial statements and prepared the tax returns for the company. In late December 1988, Bob Bothwell phoned the partner in charge of the engagement to arrange a meeting in Bob's office on December 30, 1988. The partner asked George Cathcart, chartered accountant, the senior on the engagement in 1986 and 1987, to represent him at the meeting and asked that you accompany George.

At the meeting, Bob explained that business was booming, and that he was considering privately raising additional equity capital to undertake some very large projects. He wanted to retain control of the company but was willing to relinquish sole ownership instead of increasing his bank loan. However, the preliminary draft statements for 1988 did not look as impressive as he had expected.

He handed George and you a copy of the income statement (Exhibit 1), along with a summary of contracts undertaken (Exhibit 2). He shook his head and said, "I didn't bring the balance sheet because I don't think it is correct. The materials in inventory are worth $200,000 now, not the $150,000 I paid for them. The same thing applies to the temporary investments. My broker assures me that they are worth twice what I paid. I also don't see anything reflected in the financial statements about the lawsuit that I'm involved in. My lawyer says that when we go to court next week,

Institute of Chartered Accountants of Ontario adapted.

I'll be sure to win the $27,000 from the subcontractor that delayed the curling rink project.''

"My biggest problem is with the income figure," he continued. "I don't seem to get credit for the projects that are in progress, even though my costs are usually in line, and I know I'm making money. Is there any way to improve my net income without paying any additional income tax?''

Required

Prepare a memo to George Cathcart. The memo is to include a revised net income figure for both 1988 and 1987 assuming that the company changes its revenue recognition policy from completed contract to percentage-of-completion, but continues to calculate taxes on the completed contract basis. You should also include your thoughts on the best way to deal with the problems Bob raised. Cathcart will be using your work as a basis for his report to the partner.

EXHIBIT 1

ACME CONSTRUCTION LTD.
Statement of Income (Draft)
For the year ended December 31

	1988	1987
Net revenue from completed contracts . . .	$365,000	$136,000
General and administrative expenses	172,000	100,000
Income before taxes	193,000	36,000
Income taxes.	48,250	9,000
Net income for the year	$144,750	$ 27,000

Significant Accounting Policies

Revenue recognition: the company follows the completed contract method of recognizing revenue from construction projects.

EXHIBIT 2   Summary of Contracts Undertaken

STARTED IN 1986

Mainline Apartments

The contract price was $600,000, and costs were estimated at $450,000. The project was one-half complete at the end of 1986, and costs were on target at

---

EXHIBIT 2 *(concluded)*

$225,000. In 1987 the project was completed but costs were $14,000 higher than estimated. The customer was billed $600,000 and all but $90,000 was received in 1987. The balance was collected in 1988.

STARTED IN 1987

Harbour View Apartments

The contract price was $940,000 and costs were originally estimated at $800,000. At the end of 1987, the project was 80 percent completed, but price declines on materials resulted in costs of only $600,000. Progress billings were sent out for $470,000, of which $310,000 had been received at the year-end.

In 1988 the project was completed with additional costs of $150,000. The customer paid the full contract price by November 1988.

Sunnyside Curling Rink

The contract was awarded at $1,425,000 and costs were estimated at $1,250,000. At the end of 1987, the project was 20 percent completed, and costs were on target at $250,000. Progress billings had been sent for $200,000 and one half had been received by December 31, 1987.

The contract was completed in 1988. Costs were higher than estimated because of a subcontractor that delayed the project. Completed contract income of $148,000 is included in income, and all of the contract price was received from the customer before December 31, 1988.

STARTED IN 1988

Victoria Mall

This contract for a three-unit mall was completed in 1988. The contract price of $450,000 has been billed, but $70,000 has not been received. Total costs of $423,000 were incurred.

DaVinci Apartments

The contract price was $1,825,000 and costs were estimated at $1,500,000. At the end of 1988, the project was 15 percent completed and actual costs included in construction in progress were $225,000. Although progress billings were sent out for $150,000 nothing had been received by December 31, 1988.

Discount Don's Department Store

The contract was awarded in November of 1988, but no construction has started. The cost of preparing the bid was $9,000 and this has been included in general and administrative expenses.

Case 2

Adelaide Ltd.

Adelaide Ltd. is a medium-sized Canadian real estate company. It was incorporated in the early 1960s by Joan Chaisson who had inherited considerable wealth from her father's estate. By the 1970s the company had profitability and expansion plans which made a public share issue very attractive. Joan now owns 17 percent of the voting shares; the other shares are widely held.

In 1978 Adelaide purchased a parcel of land for $800,000 near Ottawa. The company intended to use this land for condominium development. During the following years this area became a very popular location for the head offices and plants of high-tech industries; it was close to the government and the airport and was an easy commute for employees. Rather than develop the property, Adelaide held it for eventual resale. In October 1990 the property was sold to Longfellow Land Development Ltd. for $3 million. No cash changed hands; Adelaide took back a 20-year mortgage at 10 percent, the current market rate. Longfellow Land Development Ltd. is a private company, 75 percent of whose shares are owned by William Hillman, a cousin of Joan Chaisson. In February 1991 Longfellow sold the property for $3,050,000 and discharged the mortgage held by Adelaide.

Attached are the draft financial statements of Adelaide Ltd. and Longfellow Land Development Ltd.

Required

Determine the appropriate disclosure on both Adelaide Ltd.'s and Longfellow Land Development Ltd.'s 1990 financial statements for the sale and purchase of the land. Is this anything other than a regular business transaction between two companies?

ADELAIDE LTD.
Balance Sheet
December 31, 1990
(in thousands)

	1990	1989
Assets		
Cash and short-term investments	$ 5,867	$ 3,385
Receivables	15,717	21,685
Residential units	2,772	6,028
Land, developed and under development . . .	7,446	9,711
Land held for future development	28,091	41,141
Rental properties	16,930	21,384
Deferred financing costs and other assets . . .	1,530	931
Total assets	$78,353	$104,265
Liabilities		
General bank indebtedness.	$19,971	$ 23,515
Payables and accruals	10,309	7,020
Income taxes payable	1,046	1,092
Bank project loans	25,279	29,366
Other secured debt	17,572	24,132
Debentures payable	8,729	8,729
Deferred income taxes.	1,416	3,398
Total liabilities	$84,322	$ 97,252
Owners' Equity		
Share capital	$14,941	$ 14,941
Deficit	(20,910)	(7,928)
Total owners' equity	($ 5,969)	$ 7,013
Total liabilities and owners' equity	$78,353	$104,265

ADELAIDE LTD.
Income Statement
For the Year Ended December 31, 1990
(in thousands)

	1990	1989
Revenue:		
Residential lots	$ 2,343	$ 2,924
Residential units	6,583	1,563
Commercial and undeveloped property	10,758	15,963
Rental income	1,297	1,636
	$20,981	$22,086

(*continued*)

	1990	1989
Expenses:		
Cost of real estate:		
Residential lots	$ 1,011	$ 2,560
Residential units	4,918	1,495
Commercial and undeveloped property	10,995	16,054
Property valuation write-downs	9,817	7,693
Interest	5,716	7,411
General and administrative	1,793	2,559
Provision for doubtful accounts	1,311	1,876
Depreciation and amortization	384	275
	$35,945	$39,923
Net loss before income taxes	($14,964)	($17,837)
Income tax recovery	1,982	3,597
Net loss	($12,982)	($14,240)
Loss per common share	($ 7.66)	($ 8.40)

LONGFELLOW LAND DEVELOPMENT LTD.
Balance Sheet
December 31, 1990
(in thousands)

	1990	1989
Assets		
Cash and short-term deposits	$ 71	$ 259
Accounts receivable	120	112
Income taxes receivable	13	—
Deposits on land purchases	54	—
Mortgages and other secured receivables	164	85
Inventory of land and construction in progress	7,673	5,332
Rental properties:		
Buildings and equipment	2,619	2,306
Land	242	247
Total assets	$10,956	$8,341
Liabilities and Owners' Equity		
Bank indebtedness, partially secured by an assignment of certain amounts receivable	$ 665	$ 221
Accounts payable and accrued liabilities	803	579
Income taxes payable	—	281
Mortgage advances on construction	112	142
Deferred profit on land sales	—	16
Mortgages payable	4,131	1,998
Other long-term debt	1,160	1,399

(continued)

	1990	1989
Deferred income taxes	$ 441	$ 344
Capital stock	798	798
Retained earnings	2,846	2,563
Total liabilities and owners' equity.	$10,956	$8,341

LONGFELLOW LAND DEVELOPMENT LTD.
Income Statement
For the Year Ended December 31, 1990
(in thousands)

	1990	1989
Revenue:		
Land development and construction	$3,349	$5,641
Rental properties	966	871
Interest and sundry	70	62
	$4,385	$6,574
Expenses:		
Cost of land and houses sold	$2,883	$4,884
Rental property operating expenses	517	405
Depreciation	60	61
Interest	332	300
General and administrative	316	391
Gain on sale of rental properties	(267)	—
	$3,841	$6,041
Net income before income taxes	$ 544	$ 533
Income taxes—current	106	333
—deferred	96	(76)
Net income	$ 342	$ 276

Azzip Limited

Azzip Limited is a medium-sized, successful public Canadian company started in 1963 which is engaged in natural resources exploration and production in several of the Canadian provinces. The officers, directors, and one "friendly" financial group control 35 percent of the company. The remainder of the outstanding shares are widely held in Canada, the United States, and the United Kingdom. Azzip Limited's shares are not listed in the United States nor does the company plan to obtain any financing there in the future.

The company purchases exploration rights and carries out exploration and development activities. On approximately 10 percent of its successful properties, it undertakes production and sale of the minerals and hydrocarbons which have been discovered. Production rights associated with the remainder of the successful properties are sold.

You have recently been retained as a consultant to the audit committee of the board of directors to help resolve a dispute which has arisen. The president, the two vice presidents, one of finance and the other of exploration and development, as well as two of the directors on the audit committee, disagree strongly among themselves about the most appropriate approach for reporting the firm's asset values. Through discussion with these officers and directors, you realize that a major concern of theirs is that they believe Azzip Limited may be a potential target for a takeover bid within the next two years. In fact, they see signs that some anonymous small share accumulation may be getting under way right now. This, in their view, is not in the best interests of the company, or of its other shareholders.

Adapted, with permission from the *Uniform Final Examination Handbook,* 1979, © The Canadian Institute of Chartered Accountants, Toronto. Changes to the original question and/or suggested approach to answering are the sole responsibility of the authors and have not been reviewed or endorsed by the Canadian Institute of Chartered Accountants.

Two of the officers and one director, while understanding the basics of certain technical accounting requirements, believe that the company may be unwittingly contributing to the possibility of its own takeover by refusing to recognize as assets the discovery (exit) values of the firm's undoubtedly successful activities. This is of major concern, they suggest, because other shareholders may not be fully aware of the firm's success, and might easily be convinced to sell their shares at low prices to individuals or groups seeking control.

The third officer shares the concern about a potential takeover but believes that the firm's assets should be valued on a replacement cost basis rather than on either the present historical cost or on the suggested discovery-value basis.

The remaining director also readily acknowledges the possibility of a takeover. He believes, however, that conservative accounting policies and historical cost valuation are in the best interests of the firm and its shareholders. He argues that the management group should be able to explain the real situation to the shareholders, solicit their proxies, and obtain support for present policies. At an appropriate time in the future the entire firm would be sold at prices representing real economic value substantially in excess of the market and what may be offered in a takeover.

Upon returning to the office, you received a telephone call from the president. The president asked you to prepare a position paper which would be discussed at the next audit committee meeting. In the position paper, you are to analyze the subject of the disagreement among the officers and directors, explain the financial impact which may be expected from possible approaches, and recommend a preferred approach for Azzip Limited.

Required

Prepare the requested position paper.

Case 4

Black Corporation I

Black Corporation is a widely held public company. The company has suffered a recent decline in earnings due to general economic conditions. In an effort to improve performance, the company introduced an executive compensation plan last year. The plan provides that bonuses to management be paid out of a bonus pool. The excess, if any, of audited net income before extraordinary items over 20 percent of average total assets employed during the year, goes to the bonus pool.

The company has a $52 million, 8% debenture issue outstanding that has 15 years to maturity. Five years ago, the debentures were issued at par. They are not publicly traded, and are neither convertible nor callable. There is no provision in the debt agreement for either the early extinguishment of debt or the maintenance of a sinking fund.

Interest rates are significantly higher now than at the time of the original issue of the debentures. The company's management is contemplating an early extinguishment of the debt.

Their plan is referred to as "in-substance extinguishment." The company would need to invest $32 million in Government of Canada bonds with a coupon rate substantially higher than the rate on its issued debentures. The annual interest revenue and principal at maturity of the government bonds would be sufficient to fund both the annual interest expense and principal at maturity of the debentures. The bonds would be placed in an irrevocable trust solely for use in satisfying the debenture liability and interest payments. The company would finance the Government of Canada bond investment with the proceeds of a new equity issue.

Adapted, with permission from the *Uniform Final Examination Report*, 1984. © The Canadian Institute of Chartered Accountants, Toronto. Changes to the original question and/or suggested approach to answering are the sole responsibility of the authors and have not been reviewed or endorsed by the CICA.

Management proposes the following journal entries to record the contemplated transaction:

Cash.	$31,900,000	
Share issue costs (legal expense and		
commissions).	100,000	
Common stock		$32,000,000
To record new common share issue.		

Investment in Government of Canada bonds .	$32,000,000	
Legal expenses and commissions	100,000	
Cash.		$32,100,000
To record purchase of Government of		
Canada bonds.		

Debentures payable	$52,000,000	
Investment in Government of Canada		
bonds		$32,000,000
Gain on in-substance extinguishment of		
debt		20,000,000
To record the in-substance extinguishment		
of corporate debenture liability.		

Management believes that the proposed accounting treatment properly reflects the substance of the transaction and is justified by the facts. The managers argue that the debenture liability is extinguished in substance even though there is no legal discharge. In addition, they argue that since the company is currently in a strong financial position it is unlikely that there will be a breach of debt covenants or corporate bankruptcy. Therefore, the face value of any corporate debt would not become due prior to maturity. They point out that accountants are supposed to attach more importance to the economic substance of a transaction than to the legal form.

The gain would dramatically reduce the drop in earnings per share. Management proposes that the gain be included in "miscellaneous income" accompanied by a note explaining the transaction and the accounting treatment. They assert that an efficient market is indifferent between separate line-item disclosure of the gain (ordinary or extraordinary) on the income statement and complete note disclosure.

To support its views, management points out that reflecting debentures at current replacement value would allow recognition, as unrealized holding gains, of the gains which would be recorded in the contemplated transaction. They contend that this would be more realistic than recording the debentures under historical cost accounting.

The auditor in charge of the Black Corporation engagement has expressed concern about management's proposed treatment of the gain for the transaction. He points out that the company's liability for the face amount of the debt still exists after the transaction. He also points out that, if the stock market is efficient as management suggests, the market will not be fooled by management's efforts to bolster earnings. Finally, he has reminded management of its stewardship responsibilities to shareholders, since the advance refunding of corporate debt normally takes place in order to secure lower interest rates.

Required

Prepare a memo to the board of directors of Black Corporation which discusses the accounting and business issues of the proposed transaction. The memo should also address whether any economic effects would result for the company.

Black Corporation II

Black Corporation is a widely held public company. The company has suffered a recent decline in earnings due to general economic conditions. In an effort to improve performance, the company introduced an executive compensation plan last year. The plan provides that bonuses to management be paid out of a bonus pool. The excess, if any, of audited net income before extraordinary items over 20 percent of average total assets employed during the year, goes to the bonus pool.

The company has a $52 million, 8% debenture issue outstanding that has 15 years to maturity. Five years ago, the debentures were issued at par. They are not publicly traded, and are neither convertible nor callable. There is no provision in the debt agreement for either the early extinguishment of debt or the maintenance of a sinking fund.

Interest rates are significantly higher now than at the time of the original issue of the debentures. The company's management is contemplating an early extinguishment of the debt.

This would be achieved through a debt-equity swap arrangement. Common shares of Black Corporation would be issued to the debenture holders in exchange for cancellation of the debt. Using discounted cash flow analysis, management appraised the fair value of the debt at $30 million. Management has proposed the following journal entry to record the contemplated transaction:

Adapted, with permission from the *Uniform Final Examination Report*, (1984). © The Canadian Institute of Chartered Accountants, Toronto. Changes to the original question and/or suggested approach to answering are the sole responsibility of the authors and have not been reviewed or endorsed by the CICA.

Legal expenses and commissions . . . . . . $ 200,000
Debentures payable   52,000,000
    Common stock (management's appraised
       value) $30,000,000
    Gain on extinguishment of debt. $22,000,000
    Cash.   200,000
To record the debt-equity swap and related
extinguishment of corporate debenture
liability.

Management believes that this treatment simply recognizes a realized holding gain, which is analogous to the gain resulting from the routine disposal of land or a fixed asset.

The gain resulting from this transaction would dramatically reduce the drop in earnings per share. Management proposes that the gain be included in "miscellaneous income" accompanied by a note explaining the transaction and the accounting treatment. They assert that an efficient market is indifferent between separate line-item disclosure of the gain (ordinary or extraordinary) on the income statement and complete note disclosure.

To support its view, management points out that reflecting debentures at current replacement value would allow recognition, as unrealized holding gains, of the gains which would be recorded in the contemplated transaction. They contend that this would be more realistic than recording the debentures under historical cost accounting.

The partner in charge of the Black Corporation engagement has expressed concern about management's proposed treatment of the gain for the transaction. One of his concerns is whether the discount rate used to determine the fair value of the debt is appropriate. He also points out that, if the stock market is efficient as management suggests, the market will not be fooled by management's efforts to bolster earnings. Finally, he has reminded management of its stewardship responsibilities to shareholders, since the replacement of corporate debt normally takes place to secure lower financing costs.

Required

Prepare a memo to the board of directors of Black Corporation which discusses the accounting and business issues of the proposed transaction. The memo should also address whether any economic effects would result for the company.

Black Corporation III

Black Corporation is a widely held public company. The company has suffered a recent decline in earnings due to general economic conditions. In an effort to improve performance, the company introduced an executive compensation plan last year. The plan provides that bonuses to management be paid out of a bonus pool. The excess, if any, of audited net income before extraordinary items over 20 percent of average total assets employed during the year, goes to the bonus pool.

The company has a $100 million, 14% debenture outstanding that has 18 years to maturity. Two years ago, the debentures were issued at par. At the same time, an interest rate swap was entered into.

The swap agreement is with another Canadian public company that has $100 million in floating-rate debt outstanding, at a rate of prime plus 2 percent. Black had access to fixed rate financing but, believing interest rates were due to fall, wanted a floating-rate instrument. The other company preferred the security of fixed rate financing. Accordingly, Black agreed to pay the other company prime plus 2 percent each year; the other company pays Black $14 million each year. This, in essence, turns Black's fixed rate financing into variable rate financing.

The interest rate swap was arranged through a financial intermediary, who guaranteed all payments in exchange for an up-front fee. The two companies signed an agreement which outlined their responsibilities, and agreed to continue the swap for the entire 20-year life of Black's debenture.

Adapted, with permission from the *Uniform Final Examination Report,* (1984). © The Canadian Institute of Chartered Accountants, Toronto. Changes to the original question and/or suggested approach to answering are the sole responsibility of the authors and have not been reviewed or endorsed by the CICA.

Black has, in accordance with industry practice, continued to show their legal liability (14 percent long-term, fixed rate debt) on the balance sheet. The existence of the swap is clearly described in the notes to the financial statements.

As the management of Black had predicted, prime rates fell subsequent to the issuance of the debenture, from 12 percent to 8 percent. As a result, throughout this year, Black has had a 10 percent (prime plus 2) cost of debt financing.

The other company in the swap, burdened with 14 percent financing, has approached the management of Black with a view to ending the swap arrangement. They are willing to pay Black a $5 million fee to end the contract.

Management at Black has examined the interest rate market, and believes that interest rates will climb back to their previous level, or higher. They are willing to accept the deal.

Management has proposed that the $5 million fee be included as an "unusual item" on the current year's income statement. They argue that, because there are no remaining cash flows or risks associated with the agreement, any gains or losses should be recognized immediately in income. This treatment also parallels the cash flow to Black.

The auditors, on the other hand, have suggested that the $5 million should be deferred and amortized as an interest adjustment over the remaining life of the debenture. They argue that the $5 million represents a payment in advance for future interest rate reductions, and is properly accounted for as such.

FASB, in *Statement No. 80, Accounting for Futures Contracts,* has concluded that deferred exchange gains and losses on hedges should become part of the carrying value of the hedged asset or liability. On termination of the hedge, the cost or carrying value of the hedged asset or liability is not to be adjusted by writing off the deferrals. They are to be linked continuously to the hedged item, and the accounting for them should be consistent with the accounting for the hedged item.

The auditors argue that the "defer and amortize" treatment of the payment is consistent with this rationale, while the "immediate recognition" alternative violates the logic.

The auditors have also questioned the "unusual item" classification suggested by management. They have asked management to clarify why the item should not be classified as extraordinary.

Management is not pleased with the view the auditors have taken. They point out that a deferred item such as this adds "clutter" to the balance sheet, and the credit does not require any "future sacrifice of economic benefits" by the corporation.

The auditors have performed their own review of the interest rate market and have concluded that interest rates are expected to stay low for the next few years, subject to various fluctuations.

Required

Evaluate the position taken by management and the auditors. Conclude with a recommendation on the proper accounting treatment for the transaction.

Brampton Brick Limited

Brampton Brick Limited is a manufacturer of clay bricks with plants located in Toronto and Quebec City. The company was founded more than 120 years ago. It became Brampton Brick Limited, a private company, in the late 1940s, and in 1986 a public share offering was made on the Toronto and Montreal Stock Exchanges.

Demand for clay bricks has exceeded Brampton Brick's and the Ontario industry's capacity for the past several years and the trend is expected to continue. To satisfy the demand, industry members imported over 80 million clay bricks into Ontario in 1986. In addition, producers of cement bricks reported increased sales and now service 15 percent to 20 percent of the Ontario brick market. Because of the forecast strong demand, Brampton Brick Limited increased its production capacity at the Quebec City plant by approximately 15 percent in 1986 and was able to generate 31 million of its 116 million total brick sales from this location. The projected sales from the Quebec plant are 48 million in 1987. Also during the past year the company announced plans to open a new state-of-the-art plant in 1988. The new plant will have a production capacity of 120 million bricks annually and will be able to manufacture the bricks at an estimated 60 percent of current production costs.

The Quebec City plant, Brique Citadelle Ltee., became a part of Brampton Brick Limited's operations at the beginning of 1986. In addition, Brampton Brick acquired an interest in Roxy Construction Company Limited during the past year. Roxy provides trucking services to the parent company and has no other customers or operations. Details of the two acquisitions and extracts from Brampton Brick Limited's 1986 financial statements are presented below.

Required

Assume the role of a financial analyst and comment on the accounting treatment of the two companies acquired by Brampton Brick Limited in 1986.

BRAMPTON BRICK LIMITED
Consolidated Balance Sheet
December 31, 1986
(in thousands)

	1986	1985
Assets		
Current assets:		
Cash and short-term investments	$ 9,321	$ 2,019
Accounts receivable	4,793	3,423
Inventories	4,013	1,353
Other current assets	390	63
Total current assets	18,517	6,858
Fixed assets, at cost	27,265	10,683
Less: accumulated depreciation	14,577	7,817
	12,688	2,866
Other noncurrent assets:		
Deferred property development costs	756	934
Investments and other	49	17
	805	951
Total assets	$32,010	$10,675
Liabilities and Shareholders' Equity		
Current liabilities:		
Bank indebtedness	$ —	$ 239
Accounts payable and accrued liabilities	4,029	2,848
Income taxes payable	2,093	824
Dividends payable	420	—
Long-term debt, current portion	305	836
Total current liabilities	6,847	4,747
Long-term debt, less current portion	3,911	738
Loans from shareholders (Note 6)	—	1,195
Minority interest	120	100
Deferred income taxes	906	786
	4,937	2,819

(continued)

	1986	1985
Shareholders' equity:		
Capital stock (Note 7)	$13,244	$ 3
Retained earnings	6,982	3,106
Total shareholders' equity	20,226	3,109
Total liabilities and shareholders' equity	$32,010	$10,675

BRAMPTON BRICK LIMITED
Consolidated Statement of Income
Year Ended December 31, 1986
(in thousands)

	1986	1985
Net sales	$29,220	$19,079
Costs and expenses:		
Cost of sales.	17,264	12,775
Selling, general, and administrative expenses (Note 8).	3,227	2,121
Depreciation.	1,021	918
Interest on long-term debt.	347	154
Other interest expense (income)	(153)	(8)
Other income	(233)	(40)
	21,473	15,920
Income before management bonuses and income taxes	7,747	3,159
Management bonuses (Note 8).		600
Income before income taxes.	7,747	2,559
Income taxes (recovery):		
Current	3,529	1,025
Deferred	(123)	60
Net income for the year	$ 4,341	$ 1,474

BRAMPTON BRICK LIMITED
Extracts from the Notes
December 31, 1986

Note 2: Acquisitions

A. Brique Citadelle Ltee.

On February 11, 1986 Brampton Brick Limited acquired the outstanding shares of Brique Citadelle Ltee., a manufacturer of bricks and other ceramic products, at Beauport, Quebec, for $3.9 million cash. The acquisition has been

(continued)

accounted for as a purchase. A summary of the net assets acquired is as follows:

	(000s)
Current assets.	$3,168
Fixed assets (net)	1,596
	4,764
Less: liabilities	815
Net assets acquired . . .	$3,949

The excess of the net assets over the purchase price ($49,000) has been applied to reduce the cost of fixed assets. The results of operations and changes in financial position of the acquired company have been included in the consolidated financial statements of Brampton Brick Limited from the acquisition date.

B. Roxy Construction Company Limited

On November 12, 1986, the company acquired 80 percent of the outstanding shares of Roxy Construction Company Limited ("Roxy") the sole business of which is providing trucking services to Brampton Brick Limited. The purchase price was satisfied by the issuance of 101,531 Class A Subordinate Voting Shares and 15,381 Class B Multiple Voting Shares of Brampton Brick Limited with an aggregate value of approximately $994,000. The holders of the Roxy shares acquired are or are related to the shareholders of Brampton Brick Limited, and therefore the acquisition has been accounted for as a pooling of interests. Accordingly, the consolidated financial statements reflect assets and liabilities of Roxy at their book values and the results of its operations and changes in financial position as if the acquisition had occurred effective January 1, 1985. The 1985 consolidated financial statements have been restated appropriately.

At December 31, 1985 the net assets of Roxy were as follows:

	(000s)
Total assets	$620
Total liabilities	121
	499
Minority interest . . .	100
	$399

Revenue of Roxy for the year ended December 31, 1985 amounted to $1,105,000 and net income, after deduction of minority interest, amounted to $60,000.

In 1986, prior to the acquisition by Brampton Brick Limited, Roxy paid a dividend to shareholders of $56,000, including related taxes ($45,000 after minority interest).

(continued)

Note 6: Loans from Shareholders

Loans from shareholders amounting to $1,195,000 were repaid on November 10, 1986. The shareholders used these funds to subscribe for 140,588 Class A Subordinate Voting Shares (see Note 7).

Note 7: Capital Stock

Prior to 1986 the capital stock of the company consisted of 1,500 authorized and issued common shares. By Articles of Amendment dated October 30, 1986, the company reorganized its capital structure so that its authorized capital consists of an unlimited number of Preference Shares, Class A Subordinate Voting Shares and Class B Multiple Voting Shares. The 1,500 existing issued common shares were converted to 5,242,500 Class B Multiple Voting Shares on the basis of 3,495 Class B Multiple Voting Shares for each common share.

The Class B Shares are convertible to Class A shares on a share-for-share basis at any time. Class A shares may be converted to Class B shares in certain circumstances in connection with a takeover bid. Class A shareholders are entitled to 1 vote and Class B shareholders are entitled to 10 votes at any meeting of the shareholders.

The following summarizes the changes in issued capital stock during the year ended December 31, 1986:

	Class A Shares (Number of Shares) Stated Capital	Class B Shares (Number of Shares) Stated Capital
Conversion of existing common shares to Class B shares		(5,242,500) $3,000
Conversion of Class B shares into Class A shares.	(15,381) $9	(−15,381) $−9
Issue of Class A shares for cash (Note 6).	(140,588) $1,195,000	
Issue of Class A and B shares for purchase of 80% of shares of Roxy [Note 2(b)].	(101,531) $71	(15,381) $9
Issue of Class A shares pursuant to public offering on November 14, 1986.	(1,500,000) $12,046,000	
Outstanding at December 31, 1986.	(1,757,500) $13,241,080	(5,242,500) $3,000

The public offering of 1.5 million Class A shares was for a price of $8.50 per share. The stated capital is net of underwriters' commission of $828,750 and expenses of issue and share reorganization of $481,254, less the related income tax reduction of $606,004.

(continued)

Note 8: Management Bonuses

The statement of income for the year ended December 31, 1985 reflects substantial management bonuses. The amount of these bonuses in excess of 1986 management compensation levels has been excluded from selling, general, and administrative expenses and disclosed separately.

Case 8

CCB

"You can't have a system where you pay more for deposits, and you have higher operating costs, and you charge less on loans and take less security in order to grow faster than other institutions. Life isn't that way."

Richard Thompson, *chairman and CEO of the Toronto Dominion Bank,* commenting on the CCB in May 1985.

The Canadian Commercial Bank (CCB) was created in the mid-1970s as an Alberta-based operation, lending to small- and medium-sized businesses that needed loans in the $1 million to $10 million range. It was strictly commercial, and had no retail outlets. Most deposits were short term, from institutions and corporations, attracted by higher interest rates. Under CEO Howard Eaton, the bank loaned aggressively. Profits, $13,000 in 1978, reached $8.5 million in 1982, while assets, loans mostly, totaled $1.9 billion by 1982.

The National Energy Policy and the recession in the western provinces had disastrous effects on the CCB. Land prices in Alberta and British Columbia fell as much as 50 percent. Oil properties and drilling equipment plunged in value. More than 40 percent of the CCB's loan base was in real estate and construction, or energy and drilling rigs. Eaton's goal had been growth: when Alberta had failed to deliver the targeted $5 billion asset base, he began oil industry lending in the United States as well. He also masterminded the CCB's purchase of 39 percent of the Westland Bank in 1981. Eaton was fired on January 24, 1983, partially due to his links with Leonard Rosenburg, of Crown Trust fame. Rosenburg had been attempting to accumulate, illegally, a 27 percent interest in the CCB. Gerald McLaughlan was installed as the new CEO.

Between 1982 and 1983, net income slumped 88 percent, and there was a before-tax loss of $7 million in 1984 (see financial statements, Exhibit 1). Return on assets declined from 0.88 percent in 1981 to 0.03 percent in 1984. (On average Canadian Chartered Banks earn 0.50 percent to 0.55 percent on assets.) Even these income figures were optimistic due to various accounting methods adopted by the bank.

Throughout 1984, the CCB continued aggressive lending practices, trying to diversify its loan portfolio away from real estate and energy. Assets grew almost 30 percent. The audit report for the 1984 fiscal year was unqualified, with loan losses of approximately $70 million on a $3 billion asset base. This, despite the fact that most of the loans which eventually were determined uncollectible were already on the books. Indeed, McLaughlan claimed that less than 2 percent of the bad loans were booked after Eaton left.

In early 1985, a decline in OPEC oil prices placed the CCB's oil drilling loan portfolio, both in Canada and the United States, in grave jeopardy, and prompted a call from the U.S. Federal Reserve Board to the Canadian Inspector of Banks concerning the CCB's U.S. loan portfolio. Although the Canadian Inspector had been closely monitoring the CCB since Eaton's firing in 1983, neither they, nor the auditors, nor the investment community sounded any alarms during the 1983–84 period. The CCB even sold stock in a subsidiary, CCB Realty Trust, in February of 1985.

On March 14, 1985, McLaughlan notified the Inspector General's office that approximately $544 million of the CCB's loans were bad, and that the bank would require assistance or have to fold. On March 22, a private bailout proposal, to be financed by the six major Canadian chartered banks, was refused by those banks. On March 24, a package involving the federal government ($165 million), the Alberta and B.C. governments ($18 million each) was announced, that would provide additional capital to the CCB.

Despite public assurances of the bank's stability, 30 percent of the bank's $2.8 billion of deposits were withdrawn over the next six weeks. By July, $1.6 billion had been removed, as even the chartered banks involved in the bailout had removed their deposits, and the CCB was little more than a shell. Bad loan estimates, $70 million in the 1984 audited financial statements, escalated to $544 million in March of 1985, and finally to the $800 million to $1 billion range by August. During this period, the CCB was permitted to draw on the Bank of Canada to cover its cash requirements. By the end of August, they had drawn more than $1.3 billion.

A final bailout or merger package found no takers at the end of August, and on September 1, 1985, a formal announcement was made. Canada had its first bank failure since 1923. The cost to the Canadian taxpayer at the federal level has been estimated at $1.5 billion.

THE FALLOUT ON THE ACCOUNTING PROFESSION

Many reasons have been suggested for the bank's failure:

the recession, the vulnerability of the western economy, the mischievous over-expansion of the chartered banking system in the name of more regionalism and variety, the willingness of politicians to spend taxpayers' money on a cynical vote-buying adventure; or else a board of directors that had failed in its clear duty, auditors who didn't signal irregular practices, an inspector general who could have moved sooner and with more force, the chartered bankers who said one thing and did another.
(*Canadian Business,* December 1985.)

Whatever the actual reason or combination of reasons, the federal enquiry into the bank collapse, chaired by Mr. Justice Willard Estey, served to focus attention on the role of the auditors, Peat Marwick Mitchell & Co. and Clarkson Gordon. One can suggest that a purpose of the enquiry was to deflect criticism from the federal government and focus on the other players.

A series of headlines in the financial press illustrates the tone of Estey's (and others') open criticism:

"Estey shows impatience at methods of auditors" (*Globe and Mail,* November 23, 1985).

" 'Bank management, the auditors and the Government's bank inspection system must share the blame for the collapse,' Bouey says" (*Globe and Mail,* December 14, 1985).

"Bank failures put auditors under fire" (*Financial Post,* November 23, 1985).

"Glare of spotlight reveals warts in auditing system" (*Globe and Mail,* December 7, 1985).

"Auditors didn't blink at bank's poor loans" (*Toronto Star,* September 25, 1985).

ACCOUNTING POLICIES

The following accounting policies of the CCB were examined and criticized at the hearings:

1. When a loan initially went into arrears, overdue interest would be added to the amount owed (i.e., capitalized) and brought into income regardless of the fact it had not been paid. In addition to that, however, the bank would charge a flat fee to the client, which was also capitalized and brought into income. Income from such loan fees alone totaled $16.8 million in 1984. This was not disclosed in the notes. The

now higher loan balance would, of course, be subject to loan loss review.

2. In the loan loss review, loans in arrears were evaluated against the security lodged against them. In many cases, the current value of real estate or oil properties was nowhere near the loan value. However, CCB management apparently valued much of the real estate security at theoretical prices that might be fetched years in the future. Presumably, these were values following recovery of the western economy. The bank was also getting into novel oil exploration agreements to create work for the rigs on which it had lent money. The auditors commented that the bank's credit officers continued to demonstrate "creative and imaginative" workout capabilities.

3. Loans in arrears on principal and interest payments were often "sold" to a third party who was willing to speculate on recovery of collateral. The CCB would replace the "loan" asset with a "note receivable" asset, making no write-down. If the third party made a profit, the note was repaid. If not, the bank's only recourse was against the original security. These nonrecourse loans are more like equity, and very risky. The $350 million of such notes were not separately disclosed in the 1984 financials.

4. "The 1984 [loan reserve, on the audited financial statements] was only 0.68% of total loans, which suggested a reasonably healthy position. . . . The Bank Act did not permit the CCB to take a larger reserve, since that would have given it negative retained earnings. Management and the auditors suggested to the Inspector General of Banks that a larger reserve be taken . . . this was rejected." (*Financial Post,* November 23, 1985). In their annual report, the CCB claimed that the 0.68 percent "continues to compare favorably with industry averages." Even though bound by the Bank Act, the additional reserve requested could have been disclosed in the notes.

5. Part of the bank's compensation for a loan deal would often include an up-front fee. Common with industry practice, this fee would be included in income when the loan was booked. Since many of the loans which involved up-front fees went sour, and may not have even paid the fee, the revenue recognition policy appears, in retrospect, questionable.

For Discussion

1. Evaluate the accounting policies outlined, including an evaluation of the adequacy of disclosure in the 1984 financial statements.
2. Evaluate the content of the 1984 auditors' report (Exhibit 1), which states that the CCB's financial statements present fairly the financial position of the bank . . . in accordance with prescribed accounting principles (the Bank Act).

EXHIBIT 1   Financial Statements

CANADIAN COMMERCIAL BANK
Consolidated Statement of Assets and Liabilities
As at October 31
(in thousands)

	1984	*1983*
Assets		
Cash resources:		
Cash and deposits with Bank of Canada	$ 55,406	$ 36,132
Deposits with other banks.	196,004	18,726
Cheques and other items in transit, net	—	25,292
	251,410	80,150
Securities:		
Issued or guaranteed by Canada	66,197	107,447
Other securities	205,885	88,801
	272,082	196,248
Loans:		
Day, call and short loans to investment dealers and		
brokers, secured	71,000	170,000
Mortgage loans.	70,471	25,691
Other loans	2,274,456	1,810,540
	2,415,927	2,006,231
Other:		
Customers' liability under acceptances	20,600	43,900
Land, buildings, and equipment	22,819	12,206
Other assets	103,778	58,538
	147,197	114,644
	$3,086,616	$2,397,273

	1984	*1983*
Liabilities		
Deposits:		
Payable on demand	$ 137,324	$ 8,897
Payable after notice.	7,802	—
Payable on a fixed date	2,693,297	2,165,061
	2,838,423	2,173,958
Other:		
Cheques and other items in transit, net	735	—
Acceptances	20,600	43,900
Liabilities of subsidiaries, other than deposits . . .	1,303	815
Other liabilities.	55,019	39,422
	77,657	84,137

EXHIBIT 1 *(continued)*

	1984	1983
Liabilities		
Subordinated debt:		
Bank debentures	$ 49,000	$ 33,800
Capital and Reserves		
Appropriations for contingencies	16,596	23,947
Shareholders' equity:		
Capital stock:		
Class A preferred shares	30,000	—
Common shares	49,148	48,725
Contributed surplus	25,680	25,334
Retained earnings	112	7,372
	121,536	105,378
	$3,086,616	$2,397,273

CANADIAN COMMERCIAL BANK
Consolidated Statement of Income
For the Year Ended October 31
(in thousands)

	1984	1983
Interest income:		
Income from loans, excluding leases	$252,335	$208,841
Income from lease financing	2,071	2,606
Income from securities	18,176	7,638
Income from deposits with banks	11,546	2,502
Total interest income, including dividends	284,128	221,587
Interest expense:		
Interest on deposits	251,253	188,402
Interest on bank debentures	5,016	2,867
Interest on liabilities other than deposits	614	150
Total interest expense	256,883	191,419
Net interest income	27,245	30,168
Provision for loan losses	14,832	9,024
Net interest income after provision for loan losses . . .	12,413	21,144
Other income	21,698	24,040
Net interest and other income	34,111	45,184

EXHIBIT 1 *(continued)*

	1984	1983
Non-interest expenses:		
Salaries	$ 18,209	$ 17,252
Pension contributions and other staff benefits	1,785	1,781
Premises and equipment expenses, including depreciation	9,739	8,220
Other expenses	11,306	9,706
Total non-interest expenses	41,039	36,959
Net income (loss) before provision for income taxes	(6,928)	8,225
Provision for (recoverable) income taxes.	(7,732)	1,720
Net income for the year	$ 804	$ 6,505
Net income (loss) per common share	$ (0.22)	$ 1.57
Net income (loss) per common share fully diluted	$ (0.22)	$ 1.55

CANADIAN COMMERCIAL BANK
Consolidated Statement of Appropriations for Contingencies
For the Year Ended October 31
(in thousands)

	1984	1983
Balance at beginning of year:		
Tax allowable	$22,849	$20,992
Tax paid.	1,098	1,438
Total	23,947	22,430
Changes during the year:		
Loss experience on loans	(25,183)	(14,507)
Provision for loan losses included in consolidated statement of income	14,832	9,024
Transfer from retained earnings	3,000	7,000
Net change during the year	(7,351)	1,517
Balance at end of year:		
Tax allowable	13,555	22,849
Tax paid.	3,041	1,098
Total	$16,596	$23,947

EXHIBIT 1   *(continued)*

CANADIAN COMMERCIAL BANK
Consolidated Statement of Changes in Shareholders' Equity
For the Year Ended October 31
(in thousands)

	1984	*1983*
Capital stock:		
Balance at beginning of year	$48,725	$38,560
Issued during the year:		
Class A preferred shares	30,000	—
Common shares	423	10,165
	30,423	10,165
Balance at end of year	$79,148	$48,725
Contributed surplus:		
Balance at beginning of year	$25,334	$15,225
Addition from common share issues	346	10,109
Balance at end of year	$25,680	$25,334
Retained earnings:		
Balance at beginning of year	$ 7,372	$ 7,395
Net income for the year	804	6,505
Dividends paid	(4,065)	(2,894)
Transfer to appropriations for contingencies	(3,000)	(7,000)
Income taxes related to the above transfer	—	3,444
Expenses of capital stock issues, net of deferred income taxes of $924 (1983—$76)	(999)	(78)
Balance at end of year	$ 112	$ 7,372

Notes to Consolidated Financial Statements
October 31, 1984 (*All dollar amounts displayed in tabular form are in thousands of dollars.*)

1. Prescribed Accounting Principles

The consolidated financial statements of banks in Canada follow accounting principles prescribed by the Bank Act, 1980, and the related rules issued by the Inspector General of Banks under the authority of the Minister of Finance. The significant accounting policies are as follows:

a. Basis of Consolidation

The consolidated financial statements include the accounts of all subsidiaries after eliminating intercompany transactions and balances. The Bank accounts for the

EXHIBIT 1   *(continued)*

acquisition of subsidiaries using the purchase method; any difference between the cost of the investment and the proportionate share of the fair value of assets acquired is amortized on a straight-line basis over 40 years. See the Schedule of Subsidiaries for a listing of subsidiary companies.

Investments in corporations of which the Bank owns between 20 percent and 50 percent of the voting shares are accounted for using the equity method and are included in "Other securities" in the Consolidated Statement of Assets and Liabilities. The Bank's share of earnings of such corporations is included in "Income from securities" in the Consolidated Statement of Income for the period of such percentage ownership.

b. Securities

Securities include both investment account and trading account securities.

Debt securities held in the investment account are carried at amortized cost. Realized gains and losses relating thereto are amortized on a straight-line basis in the Consolidated Statement of Income over five years. Unamortized balances of realized gains and losses are carried in "Other liabilities" and "Other assets" on the Bank's Consolidated Statement of Assets and Liabilities.

Other securities held for investment purposes are carried at cost, with due provisions for losses in value which are other than temporary. Gains and losses are reported in the Consolidated Statement of Income in the year in which they occur.

All securities held in the trading account are carried at market value. Gains and losses are reported in the Consolidated Statement of Income in the year in which they occur.

Realized gains and losses on Government of Canada Treasury bills are reported in the Consolidated Statement of Income in the year in which they occur.

c. Translation of Foreign Currencies

Assets and liabilities denominated in foreign currencies are translated into Canadian dollars at rates prevailing at the balance sheet date. Revenue and expenses in foreign currencies are translated into Canadian dollars at the average of the prevailing month-end exchange rates. Realized and unrealized gains and losses from foreign currency translation are included in "Other income," with the exception of unrealized gains and losses in respect of net investment positions in foreign operations, which are included in retained earnings, net of applicable income taxes, in the Consolidated Statement of Changes in Shareholders' Equity together with any gains and losses arising from economic hedges of these net investment positions.

Prior to November 1, 1983, unrealized gains and losses in respect of net investment positions in foreign operations and related economic hedges of these net investment positions were reported in "Other income" in the Consolidated Statement of Income. In accordance with instructions issued under the authority of the Minister of Finance, this change in accounting policy has been applied prospectively and the prior year's financial statements have not been adjusted. The effect of this change is not material in relation to the prior year's financial statements.

EXHIBIT 1   *(continued)*

d. Loans

Loans are carried at their principal amount less any specific provisions for anticipated losses. The actual net loss experience on loans for the year comprises the amount of loans written off, recoveries on loans previously written off and net changes in provisions. This amount is charged to the Consolidated Statement of Appropriations for Contingencies.

The provision for loan losses is based on a formula designed to average the loss experience on loans over a five-year period as prescribed by the Minister of Finance. This provision is included in the Consolidated Statement of Income and that amount is carried to the Consolidated Statement of Appropriations for Contingencies.

Loan income is recorded on the accrual basis. Accrued but uncollected loan income is generally reversed whenever loans are placed on a nonaccrual basis. The accrual of loan interest income is discontinued where interest or principal is contractually past due 90 days unless senior credit management determines that there is no reasonable doubt as to the ultimate collectibility of principal and interest. Interest payments received in respect of nonaccrual loans are first applied to the recovery of specific provisions, if any, and secondly, to income.

e. Appropriations for Contingencies

In addition to provisions against specific loans, the Bank maintains appropriations for contingencies to provide for unforeseen future losses in respect of loans.

The appropriations for contingencies consists of two portions, tax-allowable and tax-paid. The tax-allowable portion includes the net loss experience on loans and the provision for loan losses charged to the Consolidated Statement of Income in respect of the Bank itself, together with tax-allowable transfers from retained earnings, which are subject to a cumulative limit prescribed by the Minister of Finance.

The tax-paid portion includes the net loss experience on loans net of related income taxes, if any, and the provision for loan losses charged to the Consolidated Statement of Income in respect of subsidiaries of the Bank, together with transfers from retained earnings in excess of the prescribed limit.

f. Land, Buildings, and Equipment

Land, buildings and equipment are recorded at original cost and depreciated over their estimated useful lives, using primarily the straight-line method of depreciation. Gains and losses on disposals are included in "Other income."

g. Provision for Income Taxes

The Bank follows the tax allocation method of providing for income taxes. The cumulative difference between tax calculated on such basis and that currently payable is essentially a timing difference and results in deferred income taxes included in "Other assets" or "Other liabilities."

EXHIBIT 1   *(concluded)*

Auditors' Report

To the Shareholders of Canadian Commercial Bank

We have examined the Consolidated Statement of Assets and Liabilities of Canadian Commercial Bank as at October 31, 1984 and the Consolidated Statements of Income, Appropriations for Contingencies and Changes in Shareholders' Equity for the year then ended. Our examination was made in accordance with generally accepted auditing standards, and accordingly included such tests and other procedures as we considered necessary in the circumstances.

In our opinion, these consolidated financial statements present fairly the financial position of the Bank as at October 31, 1984 and the results of its operations for the year then ended, in accordance with prescribed accounting principles applied on a basis consistent with that of the preceding year.

Edmonton, Alberta   Clarkson Gordon   Peat, Marwick, Mitchell & Co.
December 4, 1984   Chartered Accountants   Chartered Accountants

Case 9

CNR

Canadian National Railway Company (CNR) is the largest railway in North America. Included in its assets are 45,000 kilometers of track and 1,845 diesel electric locomotives. The railway is one of the 40 companies controlled by the Canadian National Railway System, a company wholly owned by the government of Canada. In addition to the railway, "System" controls firms in the hotel, telecommunications, steamship, delivery, and technology marketing industries, and has joint venture arrangements with numerous American companies involved in land and sea transportation. In 1986 System employed approximately 57,000 people (a drop of 10,000 from the level five years earlier). That same year Railway provided 74.8 percent of System's revenues.

CNR is a Crown corporation. A Crown corporation is one that is wholly or majority owned by the federal government or by a provincial government, or one where the majority of members of the board of directors are appointed by the government. CNR is wholly owned by the government of Canada. Under the requirements of the Financial Administration Act, CNR must provide an annual report, including audited financial statements and a capital and operating budget, to the Minister of Transport. The Minister of Transport presents the annual report and the capital budget to parliament.

The railway operates coast to coast, although 70 percent of the work load is located in western Canada. The major items transported by the railway include lumber, grain, and fuel from the West, potatoes from Prince Edward Island, potash from Saskatchewan, and newsprint, steel, and automobiles from central Canada. In 1986 responsibility for passenger services was transferred by legislation to Via Rail.

Among the competitive pressures the railway faces are:

Lower world demand for Canadian resource products.

Increased competition in international markets.

Protectionist moves affecting lumber exports to the United States.

Alternative modes of transportation.

Protective measures ensuring that rates are fair and nondiscriminatory.

In addition, other components of System are contending with lower world oil prices and new products in the telex market.

The following article appeared in the *Globe and Mail* on May 2, 1987:

CN Loses $86.3 Million after Taking Writedowns

Canadian National Railway Co. of Montreal took writedowns of $110 million in 1986 to be rid of a money-losing trucking division and to whittle down its work force.

An operating profit of $281 million on revenue of $4.7 billion was turned into a loss of $86.3 million after the writedowns and losses for services provided for the federal Government. The corporation paid $382 million in interest on long-term debt of $3.5 billion.

This compares with an operating profit of $440 million in 1985 on revenue of $5 billion. Final profit was $117.6 million in 1985. The Crown corporation also lost $41.3 million on TerraTransport in Newfoundland, the passenger and freight service that it runs for the federal Government.

CN sold its trucking company last year for $23 million to a group of Toronto business people. In recent years, the division consistently lost about $50 million annually.

To get rid of the trucking company, CN took a writedown of $71 million, including a shut-down cost of $26.9 million. It also took a loss of $9.4 million for a Newfoundland dockyard that was spun off by the company. In addition, CN wrote off $41 million in severence pay to employees last year.

Chief executive Ronald Lawless said the overall loss reflected one-time expenses and that 1987 results should be better. For one thing, Ottawa is expected to pay a bigger share of the cost for TerraTransport.

One of the worst turnarounds last year was in the rail division, which accounts for the bulk of the company's revenue. It had a loss of $11.2 million, compared with a profit of $105.5 million a year earlier.

This resulted from receiving lower payments from Via Rail Inc. of Montreal for the use of its facilities and from carrying reduced volumes for companies in the automotive and natural resources sectors.

Grand Trunk Corp., the U.S. rail division, and the CN Hotels chain, which has been put up for sale, also posted losses. Grand Trunk had a loss of $14.2 million, compared with a profit of $13.6 million. CN Hotels reduced its loss to $659,000 from $3.4 million.

The communications group had a profit of $36.2 million compared with $43 million in 1985. Profit at the exploration division dropped to $4.5 million from $30.6 million, and the real estate arm increased profit to $18.8 million from $14.7 million.

The write-downs were disclosed after operating results but before extraordinary items. With regard to TerraTransport, the annual report said,

TerraTransport, which manages CN's rail, highway freight and inter-city bus services in Newfoundland, experienced a 5 percent drop in freight tonnage in 1986, mainly because of a Canadian Transport Commission decision requiring increases in CN's freight rates for containerized traffic, increases which served to favor competing carriers.

The future of rail services in Newfoundland has been under consideration for some years and, in June of 1986, the federal government decided that services will be continued at least until 1990 and that government will provide some funding during this four-year period.

The government's decision did not provide for compensation to CN Rail for an inevitable operating deficit with the result that the company has been obliged to carry out this imposed public duty without adequate financial compensation. CN will pursue resolution of this matter with the government.

Extracts from the 1986 financial statements of Canadian National Railway System follow in the exhibits.

Required

Discuss the importance of accounting policy selection and disclosure alternatives for Canadian National Railway System.

EXHIBIT 1

CANADIAN NATIONAL RAILWAY SYSTEM
Consolidated Statement of Income
Year Ended December 31
(in millions)

	1986	*1985*
CN Rail:		
Revenues	$3,652,655	$3,753,190
Expenses	3,663,826	3,647,658
Income (loss)	(11,171)	105,532
Grand Trunk Corporation:		
Revenues	531,399	551,782
Expenses	545,556	538,200
Income (loss)	(14,157)	13,582
Enterprises Group:		
CN Communications:		
Revenues	303,384	303,930
Expenses	267,145	260,882
Income (loss)	36,239	43,048

EXHIBIT 1   *(concluded)*

	1986	1985
CN Hotels:		
Revenues	$ 146,911	$ 129,846
Expenses	147,570	133,289
(Loss)	(659)	(3,443)
CN Exploration:		
Revenues	33,869	56,730
Expenses	29,368	26,123
Income	4,501	30,607
CN Real Estate:		
Revenues	35,157	29,582
Expenses	16,330	14,885
Income	18,827	14,697
Other:		
Income (loss)	1,822	(489)
Total Enterprises	60,730	84,420
Total CN Rail, Grand Trunk, Enterprises	35,402	203,534
Imposed public duty:		
TerraTransport:		
(Loss)	(41,291)	(39,908)
Total continuing operations	(5,889)	163,626
Discounted operations:		
CN Route		
(Loss)	(70,961)	(42,590)
Dockyard		
(Loss)	(9,430)	(2,933)
Total discontinued operations	(80,391)	(45,523)
Income (loss) before income taxes and		
extraordinary item	(86,280)	118,103
Income taxes	—	57,823
Income (loss) before extraordinary item	(86,280)	60,280
Reduction in income taxes on application of		
prior years' losses		57,359
Net income (loss)	(86,280)	117,639

EXHIBIT 2

CANADIAN NATIONAL RAILWAY SYSTEM
Consolidated Balance Sheet
December 31
(in millions)

	1986	*1985*
Assets		
Current assets:		
Accounts receivable.	$ 494,597	$ 486,922
Material and supplies	377,132	406,184
Other	252,915	234,849
Total current assets	1,124,644	1,127,955
Insurance fund	8,905	9,176
Investments	75,270	380,011
Properties	6,248,505	6,193,468
Other assets and deferred charges	385,290	428,171
Total assets	$7,842,614	$8,138,781
Liabilities		
Current liabilities:		
Bank indebtedness	$ 106,894	$ 152,719
Accounts payable and accrued charges	899,189	954,235
Current portion of long-term debt.	305,812	223,885
Other	186,273	155,732
Total current liabilities.	1,498,168	1,486,571
Provision for insurance	8,905	9,176
Other liabilities and deferred credits.	274,097	271,891
Long-term debt	3,052,486	2,948,347
Minority interest in subsidiary companies	4,345	4,345
Shareholders' Equity		
Capital stock	2,278,867	2,606,425
Retained earnings	725,746	812,026
Total liabilities and shareholders' equity	$7,842,614	$8,138,781

EXHIBIT 3   Extracts from the Notes to the Consolidated Financial Statements, December 31, 1986

Note 1: Summary of Significant Accounting Policies

Introduction

All references in these Notes to the "Company" refer to Canadian National Railway Company which is wholly owned by the Government of Canada and, unless the context otherwise requires, its consolidated subsidiaries, and all references to the "System" mean Canadian National Railway Company and its consolidated subsidiaries together with the lines of railway, telecommunications, and other property entrusted by the Government of Canada to the Company for management and operation. A division designated in the Consolidated Statement of Income as an "Imposed public duty," as is TerraTransport, is one whose operations are continued by the Company in accordance with directions from the Government of Canada despite the fact that such continued operations are contrary to the economic interests of the Company.

a. Principles of Consolidation

With the exception of Coastal Transport Limited, the consolidated financial statements include the accounts of all subsidiaries and the Company's share of the assets, liabilities, revenues, and expenses of CNCP Telecommunications which is accounted for by the proportionate consolidation method; CN's share in the activities of CNCP Telecommunications represents slightly less than 60 percent of the activities of CN Communications. Also, consistent with the legislation governing the System, the accounts of the Canadian Government Railways entrusted to the Company by the Government of Canada are included in the consolidated financial statements. Coastal Transport Limited and the net assets of the Company's dockyard operation in Newfoundland, which formerly formed part of the consolidation, have been included in investments in anticipation of their forthcoming divestiture.

Investments in entities in which the Company has less than a majority interest are accounted for by the equity method, where appropriate.

*   *   *   *   *

d. Properties

Accounting for railway and telecommunications properties is carried out in accordance with rules issued by the Canadian Transport Commission and the Canadian Radio-television and Telecommunications Commission, respectively (Canadian properties), and the Interstate Commerce Commission (U.S. properties). Generally, major additions and replacements are capitalized and interest costs are charged to expense.

The cost of depreciable railway and telecommunications assets retired or disposed of, less salvage, is charged to accumulated depreciation in accordance with the group plan of depreciation. Other depreciable assets retired or disposed of are accounted for in accordance with the unit plan whereby gains or losses are taken into income as they occur.

EXHIBIT 3   (*continued*)

The Company follows the successful efforts method of accounting for its oil and gas operations whereby the acquisition costs of oil and gas properties, the costs of successful exploratory wells, and the costs of drilling and equipping development wells are capitalized.

e. Depreciation

Depreciation is calculated at rates sufficient to write off properties over their estimated useful lives, generally on a straight-line basis. For railway and tele-communications properties, rates are authorized by the Canadian Transport Commission, the Canadian Radio-television and Telecommunications Commission, and the Interstate Commerce Commission. The rates for significant classes of assets are as follows:

	Annual Rate (percent)
Ties	2.89%
Rails	1.87
Other track material.	2.23–2.83
Ballast.	2.76
Road locomotives.	5.23
Freight cars	1.73–3.18
Commercial communication systems . . .	6.40
Hotel properties	1.00–10.0

Acquisition costs of oil and gas properties are amortized on a straight-line basis over the term of the lease until such time as they are determined to be productive or judged to be impaired. Acquisition costs of productive properties and costs of successful exploratory drilling and of drilling and equipping development wells are charged against income on the unit-of-production method based upon proven reserves of oil and gas. Exploratory dry hole and acquisition costs judged to be impaired are charged against income in the current period. Other exploratory expenditures are charged against income as incurred.

f. Transportation Revenues

Transportation revenues are generally recognized on completion of movements, with interline movements being treated as complete when the shipment is turned over to the connecting carrier. Costs associated with uncompleted movements are generally deferred.

Note 2: Special Charge and Discontinued Operations

a. Special Charge

CN Rail expenses include a special charge of $60.2 million (1985—$40.4 million) relating to a provision for rationalization costs in connection with an ongoing program to reduce the size of the CN Rail work force.

EXHIBIT 3   *(continued)*

---

b. Discontinued Operations

During 1986 the Company disposed of its former division CN Route and its investment in CN Marine Inc. (see Note 6*a*) and entered into negotiations for the disposition of its dockyard operations in Newfoundland. Details of the charges (income) incurred on these operations are as follows:

Year Ended December 31 (000s)

	1986	1985
CN Route:		
Operating loss	$25,641	$42,590
Loss arising from disposal	45,320	—
	70,961	42,590
Dockyard:		
Operating loss	4,530	2,933
Provision for loss arising from disposal	4,900	—
	9,430	2,933
Total discontinued operations	$80,391	$45,523

Note 4: Properties

December 31, 1986 (000s)

	Cost	Accumulated Depreciation	Net
CN Rail	$7,978,729	$2,869,139	$5,109,590
Grand Trunk Corporation	557,864	153,150	404,714
Enterprises Group:			
CN Communications	742,175	312,045	430,130
CN Hotels	236,247	75,551	160,696
CN Exploration	85,728	25,261	60,467
CN Real Estate	63,279	13,861	49,418
TerraTransport	89,919	56,429	33,490
	$9,753,941	$3,505,436	$6,248,505

December 31, 1985 (000s)

	Cost	Accumulated Depreciation	Net
CN Rail	$7,755,679	$2,766,643	$4,989,036
Grand Trunk Corporation	561,570	153,718	407,852
Enterprises group:			
CN Communications	708,538	288,916	419,622
CN Hotels	217,059	72,351	144,708
CN Exploration	74,947	12,211	62,736
CN Real Estate	72,750	18,221	54,529
Other	17	4	13
TerraTransport	95,484	52,430	43,054

EXHIBIT 3 (*continued*)

	Cost	Accumulated Depreciation	Net
Discontinued operations:			
CN Route	$ 95,284	$ 55,257	$ 40,027
Dockyard	34,555	2,664	31,891
	$9,615,883	$3,422,415	$6,193,468

Amounts included above with respect to Canadian Government Railways entrusted to the Company by the Government of Canada:

1986	$1,060,097	$ 569,633	$ 490,464
1985	$1,037,108	$ 556,142	$ 480,966

At December 31, 1986 the gross value of assets under capital leases included above was $119.4 million (1985—$108.4 million) and related accumulated amortization thereon amounted to $9.3 million (1985—$5.5 million).

Note 6: Shareholders' Equity

a. Capital Stock

The capital stock of Canadian National Railway is as follows:

Common shares of no par value authorized, issued and outstanding, December 31, 1985	6,523,902	$2,606,425
Less: Shares canceled in December 1986 in consideration of transfer of all the common shares of CN Marine Inc. and certain assets held by the Company to the Government of Canada pursuant to the enactment on June 27, 1986 of the Marine Atlantic Inc. Acquisition Authorization Act which act also changed the name CN Marine Inc. to Marine Atlantic Inc.	655,116	327,558
	5,868,786	$2,278,867

b. Retained Earnings

Under its governing legislation, the Company is required to pay to the Receiver General for Canada a dividend equal to 20 percent of net income for the year or such greater percentage as the Governor in Council may direct.

*   *   *   *   *

EXHIBIT 3 *(concluded)*

Note 8: Subsidies

Revenues include the following subsidies:

December 31 (000s)

	1986	1985
Payments under the Railway Act paid under authority of that act and the related Appropriation Act in respect of certain uneconomic operations, services, and pre-scribed rates which railways are required by the Railway Act to maintain	$39,641	$37,151
Maritime Freight Rates Act and Atlantic Region Freight Assistance Act subsidies	18,735	20,460
Sundry	2,502	6,074
Other assistance	163	167
	$61,041	$63,852

* * * * *

Note 13: Other Matters

a. The Company carries on ordinary business transactions with various entities controlled by the Government of Canada on the same terms and conditions as current transactions with unrelated parties.

In addition, the Company provides, under contractual arrangements, rail transportation and maintenance services to the Government of Canada and to entities controlled by the latter. The revenue derived from such services rendered in 1986 aggregated $203.0 million (1985—$320.0 million).

b. Following enactment of the Western Grain Transportation Act, which became effective on January 1, 1984, the Government of Canada, in order to minimize the cost to grain shippers, pays a portion of the cost of shipping grain. Amounts received from the Government of Canada under the Western Grain Transportation Act amounted to $378.0 million in 1986 (1985—$278.9 million), a reflection of the volume of grain handled.

c. Commencing in 1977, the Government of Canada has agreed to pay to the Company, by way of capital grants not exceeding $557.9 million, certain amounts with respect to expenditures incurred in carrying out rehabilitation programs for branch lines in Western Canada. Total payments received up to December 31, 1986 amounted to $431.4 million of which $34.5 million was received in 1986 (1985—$43.7 million).

d. As part of a program commenced in 1981 for the testing and evaluation of railway operations in Newfoundland, the Government of Canada reimbursed CN for certain costs. Total billings under this program amounted to $5.3 million in 1986 (1985—$7.6 million).

Canada Northwest Energy Ltd.

In September 1986 the Canadian Institute of Chartered Accountants issued a Guideline entitled "Full cost accounting in the oil and gas industry." The accounting policy change in the Guideline could be applied retroactively or prospectively. The same year, oil prices fell by more than 50 percent.

The following item appeared in the *Globe and Mail* in December 5, 1986:

Northwest Shows a Loss on Writedown

Canada Northwest Energy Ltd. of Calgary has "reservations with respect to the methodology" of an accounting change that forced it to write down oil and gas properties by $124 million in its most recent fiscal year.

Following accounting changes recommended by the Canadian Institute of Chartered Accountants, oil and gas companies have taken huge writedowns on producing assets.

Canada Northwest said in its Sept. 30 year-end report that the change—which limits the net carrying cost of an asset to future revenue based on proved reserves calculated at current prices—makes no provision for future price rises. The new accounting "is not intended to reflect the underlying value of producing assets," it said.

Combined with another $9 million writedown, the $124 million accounting writedown, both of which the company described as "unusual items," turned a profit from operations of $17.5 million into a final loss of $115.5 million for the year-end Sept. 30.

But the writedown has a bright side. Reduced depletion flowing from the asset writedown will have "a significant positive impact" on future profit, the company said.

Canada Northwest also said it has arranged an $80 million (U.S.) corporate loan with the Royal Bank of Canada, to be used to meet fiscal 1987 capital spending plans. This includes the first phase off-shore Vega oil field near Sicily. Production will begin in July, 1987.

Required

Discuss the options which were available to the company's management with regard to the disclosure of the writedown and the reasons for their choice.

Canadair Limited

Canadair Limited is a Crown corporation, acquired from General Dynamics Corporation of St. Louis in 1976 for $46.6 million. The company had developed to serve the needs of the Canadian Military, but when military spending began to deteriorate in the 1960s, Canadair began to evolve into something closer to a maintenance center than a development company. Acquisition by the Canada Development Investment Company was meant to reverse this.

Work on the *Challenger* jet program began in the mid-1970s. The jet was plagued with problems from the very beginning. Canadair had little expertise in this area. Their engineering staff was at an all-time low of 150 at the inception of the project. They selected an unproven engine. They committed to a design and certification schedule they could not meet. Their prototype had a shorter range and needed a longer runway than called for in the original design.

These design problems cost the company money for development costs, and their rising cash needs were met entirely by borrowing at a time when interest rates were high. The debt issued was all government guaranteed.

As costs escalated, the viability of the jet program was continually questioned. In March 1980, the company predicted that it would break even with sales of 255 planes by mid-1984. In December 1982, the number had become 389 planes by the end of 1992. As the number of planes required for break-even increased, so did the optimism of management, who were confidently predicting required sales targets would be met.

In 1983, the aircraft was in commercial production. However, most aircraft delivered to that date had been sold at a loss. The company was so anxious to hold orders and compensate for shortfalls in performance that it was willing to sell at low prices. This encouraged buyers to turn around and resell at a profit, competing with Canadair's own marketing efforts.

By spring 1983, however, the bubble burst. Management finally acknowledged that the *Challenger* program would never break even. They were requesting a $240 million injection of capital from the government in order to stay afloat until the end of the year. Senator Jack Austin was appointed to investigate.

Concurrently, the financial statements for fiscal year 1982 were released with an audit report dated May 18, 1983. These showed a $1 billion write-off of deferred development expenses relating to the *Challenger* program. The write-off left the company with assets of $267,024, and a shareholders' deficit of $1,160,000. (See Exhibit 1.) The loss made headlines in the financial press.

Like many other aviation companies, Canadair had followed a policy of deferring costs associated with new aircraft development. The costs would be amortized to net income when the aircraft started commercial production. This would match the costs to the revenues generated by the project. This method of accounting recognizes the unique nature of an industry that makes huge investments at the beginning of an aircraft program and realizes a profit only after many years.

According to the description of their deferral policy contained in the notes to the financial statements, Canadair treated all costs which were in any way related to the *Challenger* program as costs of the program and eligible for deferral. These included materials, labour, factory overhead, development, tooling, interest, marketing, after-sales support, and general administration. The cumulative interest charges alone on the *Challenger* program were $440 million by the end of 1982.

In 1982, the company had made a chain of decisions that resulted in the write-offs. First, they designated January 1, 1982 as the date for accounting purposes on which the *Challenger* came into commercial production. Second, they came to the realization that the company "could never reasonably hope" to break even; that is, they became more realistic in their sales estimates. Finally, and most importantly, they decided to more closely follow the accounting policies of the other North American aviation companies. Interest, marketing, after sales-support, administrative overhead and ongoing development, and tooling costs were no longer considered appropriate for deferral.

Questions for Discussion

1. At the inception of the program, management faced three basic alternatives for their accounting treatment of the *Challenger* program costs:

   a. Defer all costs.

   b. Defer only those costs direct to the program (as other aviation companies chose to do).

   c. Expense all costs.

Canadair chose alternative (1). Were they in error? Your answer should include a complete analysis of all alternatives.

2. Do you think that the write-down was properly treated in the 1982 financial statements? Your answer should include a review of the alternative treatments. Why do you think they chose the alternative they did?

EXHIBIT 1

CANADAIR LIMITED
(Incorporated under the laws of Canada)
Consolidated Balance Sheet
As at December 31, 1982 and 1981
(in thousands)

	1982	1981
Assets		
Current assets:		
Cash	$ 5,497	$ 3,012
Accounts receivable	43,045	65,516
Contracts in process and inventories, less advances and progress billings (Notes 3 and 4).	127,651	1,031,619
Prepaid expenses.	5,040	3,322
	181,233	1,103,469
Property, plant and equipment.	118,353	110,401
Less accumulated depreciation.	60,174	54,600
	58,179	55,801
Other assets:		
Note receivable, net of current portion	5,129	—
Deferred charges, net.	22,483	(1,443)
	27,612	(1,443)
Total assets	$ 267,024	$1,157,827
Liabilities		
Current liabilities:		
Bank loans	$ 10,575	$ 322,087
Accounts payable and accrued liabilities	352,949	117,019
Customer deposits	2,620	13,186
Principal due within one year on long-term debt	86,062	50,212
	452,206	502,504
Long-term debt	975,605	601,160

EXHIBIT 1   *(continued)*

	1982	1981
Shareholders' Equity (Deficit)		
Capital stock:		
251,700 Preferred shares, Class B	$ 25,170	$ 25,170
3,102,206 Common shares, Class A	17,244	17,244
	42,414	42,414
Contributed surplus (Note 2).	200,000	—
Excess of appraised value of land over cost . . .	10,760	10,788
Retained earnings (deficit)	(1,413,961)	961
	(1,160,787)	54,163
Total liabilities and shareholders' equity	$ 267,024	$1,157,827

CANADAIR LIMITED
Consolidated Statement of Income
and Retained Earnings (Deficit)
Years Ended December 31, 1982 and 1981
(in thousands)

	1982	1981
Sales	$ 429,379	$285,662
Expenses (Note 3):		
Cost of sales	500,971	273,991
Selling, general, and administrative	57,311	3,363
Research and development	16,189	1,800
Interest and other financing (Note 12)	215,477	3,430
	789,948	282,584
Income (loss) before unusual items and income taxes	(360,569)	3,078
Unusual items relating to *Challenger* program (Note 3)	(1,054,327)	—
Income (loss) before income taxes	(1,414,896)	3,078
Income taxes (Note 11).	26	43
Net income (loss) for the year.	(1,414,922)	3,035
Retained earnings (deficit) at beginning of year . . .	961	(2,074)
Retained earnings (deficit) at end of year	$(1,413,961)	$ 961

EXHIBIT 1 *(continued)*

Note to Consolidated Financial Statements
Years Ended December 31, 1982 and 1981

---

1. Summary of Significant Accounting Policies

b. Accounting for long-term contracts and programs

Under long-term contracts and programs, the company does not recognize earnings until such time as sufficient production has been accomplished to minimize the risk in estimating total contract earnings. At such time, earnings are recorded as they have been earned to date. Estimated losses are recorded in full as soon as they are identified. Earnings and losses recorded in the current year may include the cumulative effect of adjustments to prior years' estimates.

Estimated earnings or losses on contracts and programs are determined from projected revenues and manufacturing costs taking into account factors such as expected sales, price levels, production costs and other variables which are beyond the company's control. Because these factors cannot be measured with precision, the estimates are subject to periodic revisions. If future assessments indicate that any unamortized costs are not recoverable, the excess will be charged to earnings immediately.

Development costs which qualify for deferral are inventoried and amortized over the number of units to be produced. When the recovery of amounts deferred to future periods becomes uncertain, such costs are written off as a charge to earnings in the year.

Title to work performed under certain contracts in process and to related inventories is vested in the customer in accordance with contract provisions.

Costs relating to claims by Canadair arising out of contractual disputes are included in contracts in process when management is of the opinion that the amount of such costs does not exceed the net realizable value of the claims. Losses on claims are recorded in full as soon as they are identified.

2. Government Guarantees and Financing Requirements

The government of Canada has the authority to guarantee certain financial arrangements of the company with financial institutions to a maximum of $1.350 million. On December 30, 1982, the government of Canada contributed $200 million to the company's equity account.

The company's forecast cash requirements indicate that, without additional financing arrangements, the total debt for which the company expects to need government guarantees will exceed the authorized limit of $1.350 million in 1983. Additional capital subscriptions or an increase in the guarantee limit, or both, will be necessary to provide the company with the working capital required to ensure that the company will continue as a going concern, the basis on which these financial statements have been prepared.

EXHIBIT 1   *(continued)*

The government of Canada, through an item in supplementary estimates introduced in the Parliament of Canada on May 18, 1983, has requested Parliamen-
tary authority for additional government equity financing of $240 million for
the company.

3. *Challenger* Program—Commercial Production and Unusual Items

The *Challenger 600* program commenced in late 1976 with first flight in November 1978 and type certification in November 1980. Modifications developed through the certification process were incorporated in the aircraft in
production during 1981. As a result of continual review and monitoring of
production throughout 1982, management has determined that the program
development process was completed by December 31, 1981 and that commercial production commenced in 1982. Type certification of the *Challenger 601*
was received in March 1983. At December 31, 1982, 67 aircraft had been
delivered under the program.

Prior to 1982, costs such as development, finance, marketing, product support,
and general and administrative expenses had been included as part of contracts
in process inventory as the management of the company believed at the time
that all such inventoried costs would be recovered in the future. Concurrently
with the commencement of commercial production, the company ceased
charging these costs to contracts in process inventory and such costs incurred
since January 1, 1982, have been expensed in the year. Before the commencement of commercial production, the cost of each aircraft delivered was removed from contracts in process and charged to cost of sales in an amount
which equaled the selling price of the aircraft delivered.

Management no longer believes that there is reasonable assurance that the
inventoried costs discussed in the preceding paragraph will be recovered from
future sales. Thus, these costs have been written off to 1982 earnings as unusual items. Unusual items written off in the amount of $1,054.3 million also
include estimated excess early production cost, development costs incurred in
1982 for the *Challenger 601,* provisions for claims, surplus and obsolete materials, and other related estimated losses, aggregating $361.2 million.

4. Contracts in Process and Inventories

	1982	1981
	(in thousands)	
Finished goods including aircraft, less advances and progress billings of $19.1 million (1981—nil)	$ 68,553	$ 5,820
Government contracts in process	1,749	5,461

EXHIBIT 1   *(concluded)*

	1982	1981
	(in thousands)	
Commercial programs and contracts in process, less advances and progress billings of $180.9 million (1981—$201.4 million)	$ 44,446	$1,008,766
Inventories of commercial products, materials and spare parts	12,903	11,572
	$127,651	$1,031,619

Auditor's Report

To the Shareholders of
Canadair Limited

We have examined the consolidated balance sheet of Canadair Limited as at December 31, 1982 and 1981 and the consolidated statements of income and retained earnings (deficit) and changes in financial position for the years then ended. Our examination was made in accordance with generally accepted auditing standards, and accordingly included such tests and other procedures as we considered necessary in the circumstances.

In our opinion, these consolidated financial statements present fairly the financial position of the company as at December 31, 1982 and 1981 and the results of its operations and the changes in its financial position for the years then added in accordance with generally accepted accounting principles applied on a consistent basis.

Montreal, Canada   Thorne Riddell
May 18, 1983   Chartered Accountants

Case 12

Canadian Conglomerate

Canadian Conglomerate (CC) is one of Canada's largest and oldest public companies, with controlling interests in the tobacco industry, drugstores, and financial services. At the end of 1989, CC's total assets amounted to $3 billion; the 1989 revenue was $4.3 billion and net income was $242 million.

In November 1990 the vice president of accounting met with the company's audit partner to discuss the procedures for the year-end audit and the presentation to be adopted in this year's statements. There were two items in particular that the Vice President, Jacques Anthony, wanted to review with the auditors. One concerned the $17.5 million gain on the sale of the company's interest in an oil and gas exploration company. This investment had been in preferred shares only (there had been no vote attached to the shares), and the holding represented an insignificant portion of the outstanding preferreds. The other issue to be discussed was a provision made in August relating to an early retirement program which had been announced by CC in 1989. By coincidence the provision had also amounted to $17.5 million. The provision included estimated company pension contributions for the employees electing early retirement, as well as an extra months' salary upon retirement, vacation pay owing, and in some cases career counseling. It was CC's hope that by the end of 1993 almost 500 employees would take advantage of the program so that layoffs during the forecast downturn in the next 18 months would not be necessary.

Anthony had several ideas concerning the treatment of the two items. With regard to the gain on the sale of the investment he would be delighted to show it in this year's income statement included with the other sources of revenue; operating revenues were down from the previous year and the gain would help offset this drop. Anthony suggested that the related tax of $4.75 million could either be netted against the gain (although this was not his preference as he wanted to maximize the revenue subtotal) or be included in the tax expense at the bottom of the statement.

Regarding the provision for the early retirement program, Anthony felt that there were a number of possible alternatives. Because the program had actually been announced the previous year, Anthony suggested that the majority of the provision could be charged retroactively to 1989. Another possibility would be to spread out the charge over the succeeding four years, with a minimal charge to 1990 as the program had just started and the smallest number of retirements were forecast to have occurred during this past year. The third possibility arose due to the fortunate coincidence of the two items being identical amounts; the gain on the sale of the investments and the provision for early retirements could be offset on the income statement so that in fact no reference to either would be necessary as the total was zero. Expensing the entire $17.5 million provision in 1990 would have the worst effect on net income of all the alternatives. However, there would be a benefit to the company's employee relations if the provision were treated this way (i.e., fully expensed and netted against the gain from the sale of the investment) in that the employees and the public would not see the extent of the downsizing forecast by the company.

Required

Assume the role of the auditor and respond to Anthony's ideas.

Carleton Company

Carleton Company is a major Canadian producer of high-quality glass and plastics packaging. The company's customers include most of the leading consumer-products companies in North America. Carleton operates 12 manufacturing facilities—5 glass-container plants in Canada and 7 plastics packaging plants, 5 in Canada and 2 in the United States.

Carleton Company was founded by Montreal's deGruchy family in 1917. A deGruchy grandson is now one of the company's vice presidents; otherwise the family is only a minor shareholder. The company is federally incorporated, and its common shares are traded on the Montreal and Vancouver stock exchanges.

The company operated a single glass-container plant near Montreal until 1954 when a second glass-container facility was constructed in Orillia, Ontario. This was followed by the acquisition of a plant in the Montreal area in 1967 and construction of plants in British Columbia and Alberta. Carleton Company has a long-established policy of keeping all its plants well maintained and technologically efficient, and each year most of the company's profit is reinvested in implementing this policy.

In 1966 Carleton Company expanded its range of packaging products beyond glass containers by entering the plastics packaging industry. Since then, it has grown to become a major fabricator of thermoformed, injection-molded, extrusion and injection blow-molded plastic packaging and of complete filling machine systems. The company holds licensing agreements with several of the world's most technologically advanced packaging companies.

Carleton Company has always rewarded its senior executives well. The compensation includes a generous salary and benefits package, as well as a share purchase plan. The share purchase plan permits the president and selected vice presidents to buy preferred shares of Carleton with the assistance of interest-free loans from the company. These loans have a 10-year term, and 75 percent of all dividends received on the shares must be applied to the outstanding loans.

Extracts from Carleton's draft 1990 financial statements are included as Exhibit 1.

Required

Evaluate Carleton's valuation and disclosure policies for the loans receivable.

EXHIBIT 1   Extracts from the Draft Financial Statements of Carleton Company

	December 31	
	1990	*1989*
Current assets:		
Accounts receivable.	$ 37,132,000	$ 30,553,000
Loans receivable from senior executives. . .	12,860,000	12,630,000
Inventories.	58,016,000	50,274,000
Prepaid expenses	3,568,000	2,621,000
Total current assets	$111,576,000	$ 96,078,000
Total assets	$253,588,000	$210,904,000
Shareholders' equity (Note 4):		
Preferred shares	$ 14,920,000	$ 13,780,000
Common shares.	50,883,000	50,883,000
Retained earnings	67,167,000	60,520,000
	$132,970,000	$125,183,000

Note 4: Capital Stock

Authorized

Unlimited numbers of common and preferred shares.

Issued

770,000 preferred shares
12,759,504 common shares

The preferred shares are redeemable in certain circumstances and, at the option of the holders, are convertible into an aggregate of 1.470 million common shares. They have been treated as common share equivalents for purposes of computing earnings per share since they participate equally with the common shares as to dividends.

At the beginning of 1990 the company issued 70,000 convertible redeemable preferred shares for consideration of $1.140 million.

	1990	*1989*	*1988*	*1987*	*1986*
Net income ($ millions) . . .	16.2	21.1	23.8	27.2	27.5
Dividends paid	9.6	10.7	11.3	11.6	12.1

Case 14

Carlyle Construction Corporation

The Carlyle Construction Corporation (CCC) is incorporated under the Ontario Business Corporations Act. It is a private company, controlled by Cyd Carlyle. Members of Cyd's immediate family and a few close business associates are also shareholders.

In the past, CCC has had its financial statements prepared by the company's head bookkeeper, and the bank and other creditors have accepted these statements without serious question. For the year ended July 31, 1990, however, the bank would like to have some assurance that the statements have been prepared in accordance with generally accepted accounting principles (GAAP). The bank's concern has arisen from the increase in the bank's lending to CCC; the operating loan increased from $1 million at the end of fiscal 1989 to $5 million at the end of fiscal 1990. In particular, the bank is concerned that the cash flow statement that CCC has been presenting does not coincide with its own analysis of CCC's cash flows.

Therefore, Cyd has approached you to review the financial statements for compliance with GAAP, in order to satisfy the bank. The draft statements as prepared by the head bookkeeper are attached. After some investigation, you learn the following information:

1. The net revenue shown on the income statement is the gross margin on the construction contracts, determined by use of the percentage of completion method. The costs incurred on contracts during fiscal year 1990 totaled $32.9 million.

Institute of Chartered Accountants of Ontario adapted.

2. The contracts in progress as shown on the balance sheet are the total costs incurred to date on unfinished contracts, plus the gross margin earned to date, less amounts billed. For some contracts, CCC bills in advance, so that the billings are in excess of costs plus profit to date. The $6.6 million shown on the balance sheet therefore is the excess of underbilled contracts less the overbilled (or advance billed) contracts.

3. The note receivable arose from the sale of fixed assets during the year and represents the gross sales price. The note is due on March 5, 1991, at which time the gain on the sale will be taxable at a 46 percent rate. The note is noninterest-bearing.

4. The current note payable is the bank operating loan. There are two long-term notes. One is a bank term loan of $5 million (1989—$6 million) that is the remaining principal amount of the loan that helped to finance the fixed assets. This loan is being paid down at the rate of $1 million per year plus interest at prime plus 1.2 percent. The second long-term note is a loan of $8 million (1989—$7 million) from Cyd Carlyle. This note is payable on call with 60 days' notice, but Cyd has no intention of calling the loan.

5. CCC uses the same rate for depreciation as for capital cost allowance for income tax purposes. The depreciation expense is included primarily in the contract costs, with some depreciation included in administrative expenses.

6. CCC's fixed assets are low because the company rents most of its construction equipment on a short-term basis as it is needed for contracts.

7. In 1990 a major customer went into bankruptcy. The construction project that CCC was engaged in for this customer was 18 percent completed; the bankruptcy trustee suspended construction and canceled the contract. In view of the bank's refusal to include the costs incurred in the normal formula for operating loans and in view of the unlikely prospects of ever collecting the amounts owed, the outstanding billings and costs of $1.2 million were written off as a special charge.

Required

a. Review the draft statements and comment on any inappropriate presentation or disclosure and any apparent lack of conformity with GAAP. Briefly describe the more appropriate presentation or disclosure. Pay special attention to statement presentation.

b. Redraft the Cash Flow Statement, taking into consideration the points raised in part (*a*), so it is in accordance with GAAP.

CARLYLE CONSTRUCTION CORPORATION
Balance Sheet (draft)
July 31
(in thousands)

	1990	1989
Current assets:		
Cash	$ 200	$ 100
Term deposits	1,300	1,000
Note receivable	1,600	—
Accounts receivable	18,000	16,600
Less bad debt allowance	(900)	(830)
Contracts in progress, net of billings	6,600	4,000
	26,800	20,870
Furniture and equipment, net	11,000	13,000
	$37,800	$33,870
Current liabilities:		
Accounts payable	$ 7,000	$ 6,240
Accrued expenses	500	630
Bank loan	5,000	1,000
	12,500	7,870
Long-term notes payable	13,000	13,000
	25,500	20,870
Shareholders' equity:		
Common shares	1,000	1,000
Retained earnings	11,300	12,000
	$37,800	$33,870

CARLYLE CONSTRUCTION CORPORATION
Income Statement (draft)
July 31, 1990
(in thousands)

Net construction revenue	$4,100
Gain on assets disposal	600
Total revenue	4,700
Administrative expenses	1,100
Interest expense	2,100
Income tax expense	700
Total operating expenses	3,900

(continued)

Net income before extraordinary item	$	800
Extraordinary loss: write-off of contract costs . . .		1,200
Net income (loss)	$	(400)

CARLYLE CONSTRUCTION CORPORATION
Cash Flow Statement (draft)
July 31, 1990
(in thousands)

Sources of cash:

Operations, before extraordinary item . . . $	800
Recovery of cost of fixed assets sold	1,000
Increase in operating bank loan	4,000
Depreciation.	1,000
Total inflows	6,800

Uses of cash:

Dividends	300
Investment in working capital items	5,200
Contract costs written off.	1,200
Total outflows	6,700
Increase in cash during the year . . . . $	100

Notes to Financial Statements

Note 1: These statements are prepared in keeping with widely acceptable accounting practices and are unchanged from the preceding year.

Note 2: The $5 million bank loan carries interest at prime plus 1 percent.

Note 3: There are 1,000 common shares outstanding.

Note 4: The extraordinary item will not recur and therefore is not an operating expense and should not be considered when reviewing these financial statements.

Note 5: For the next fiscal year, the company will have to pay income tax of $276,000 on the gain on the fixed asset sale, once the company has collected the note receivable.

Note 6: The retained earnings reflects the payment of dividends to the owners and the shareholders.

Case 15

Cheer Radio

You are the assistant controller at Cheer Radio, an FM and AM operation in a large urban center. Your boss has just asked you to consider their policy for barter transactions. The station often enters into such barter arrangements with radio advertising time it cannot sell. It trades advertising time in exchange for gifts to be awarded to its listeners. (For example, the radio station will mention a store's products, services, hours, and so on in exchange for a dishwasher donated by the store as a "Jackpot" prize for a lucky listener.) To this point in the company's history, these barter transactions have not been recorded in the accounts, although they represent about 20 percent of the commercial air time.

Your boss has pointed out that the transaction could be recorded at:

1. The market value of the air time.
2. The market value of the prizes.
3. The cost (to the client) of the prizes.
4. The cost (to Cheer) of the air time.
5. A nominal amount (e.g., $1.00).

He has also told you that, on the whole, he likes the current system the best, as it is simple and a change would involve a lack of consistency. He is troubled, though, by the increasing volume of the transactions and, anyway, he does not think you are all that busy at the moment. He has asked you for a memo dealing with the issue, including your recommendations.

Required

Prepare the memo.

Cineplex

Cineplex Odeon Corporation (Cineplex) is a Canadian public company which owns movie theatres throughout North America. The company commenced operations in 1979 and was established by Garth Drabinsky, who is the company's chairman of the board, president and chief executive officer. At January 1, 1988 Cineplex operated almost 500 theatres in six Canadian provinces and 20 of the United States. Common stock of the company was initially offered on the Toronto Stock Exchange; common shares began trading on the New York Stock Exchange in May 1987.

Cineplex's growth has been spectacular. At the end of 1985 the company's total consolidated assets were Can. $142,660,000; one year later the balance was Can. $885,408,000. From April to December of 1986 Cineplex directly or through a subsidiary acquired the majority of the shares or net assets of six companies in Canada and the United States, for total consideration of almost Can. $400 million. The 1986 expansion was partially financed through an increase in long-term debt of Can. $243,219,000 (U.S. $173,315,000).

In 1987 Cineplex's financial statements were stated in U.S. dollars; therefore the remaining figures are in U.S. currency. The comparative 1986 total consolidated assets were $631,876,000. The 1987 figure was $925,676,000. Approximately $85 million of this increase was due to the acquisition in the latter half of the year of the shares or net assets of two companies located in the United States. Moreover, $137,345,000 was spent on the acquisition of property, equipment, and leaseholds. An addition of $129,187,000 in long-term debt helped finance this year's activities.

At the end of 1985 Cineplex revised its estimates of the useful lives of certain fixed assets and of goodwill. The Summary of Significant Accounting Policies notes in 1986 and 1987 described the change as follows (amounts are in U.S. dollars):

Property, Equipment, and Leaseholds: Property, equipment, and leaseholds are stated at cost. Depreciation and amortization was calculated using the following methods and annual rates for all the periods ending on or prior to December 26, 1985:

Buildings. . . . .   5% straight-line
Projection equipment . . . . . .   5% straight-line
Other equipment . . . .   10% straight-line
Leaseholds . . . .   Straight-line over the lease term, plus all
                                   optional terms specified by the lease.

Effective December 27, 1985, after a detailed study and analysis of the estimated lives for buildings and other equipment, which was supported by professional evaluations, the Corporation revised its depreciation rates on buildings and other equipment. The annual rates for these categories are:

Buildings. . . . . . .   2.5% straight-line
Other equipment . . .   6.7% straight-line

As a result of this change in accounting estimate, depreciation expense was reduced by approximately $3,859,000 for the year ended December 31, 1987 ($2,183,000 for the fifty-three weeks ended December 31, 1986) and net income increased by approximately $1,929,000 ($1,098,000 in 1986) and fully diluted earnings per share by 4 cents (3 cents in 1986).

Goodwill: Goodwill represents the excess of the purchase price of certain subsidiaries over the fair value of the net assets acquired and was being amortized over a period of twenty years for all periods ending on or prior to December 26, 1985. Effective December 27, 1985, after reviewing the appropriate estimated life for goodwill, the Corporation revised its amortization rate and as a result goodwill is now being amortized over forty years. This change in accounting estimate reduced amortization expense for the year ended December 31, 1987 by approximately $1,158,000 ($661,000 for the fifty-three weeks ended December 31, 1986) and increased net income by approximately $579,000 ($379,000 for 1986) and fully diluted earnings per share by 1 cent (1 cent for 1987).

Extracts from Cineplex's 1987 consolidated income statement and balance sheet, exclusive of the related notes, are presented in Exhibits 1 and 2. (The income statement dates are the 52 weeks ended December 31, 1985, the 53 weeks ended December 31, 1986, and the year ended December 31, 1987. The 1987 balance sheet contained only two years' comparative figures.)

Required

What impact did the change in estimates described above have on the comparative results of Cineplex Odeon Corporation? Present your evaluation of the changes.

EXHIBIT 1

CINEPLEX ODEON CORPORATION
Extracts from the Consolidated Statement of Income
(in thousands of U.S. dollars, except per share figures)

	1987	1986	1985
Revenue	$520,153	$356,989	$124,300
Expenses except for depreciation and			
amortization.	430,291	299,080	103,884
Depreciation and amortization.	23,998	14,266	3,678
	454,289	313,346	107,562
Income before the undernoted	65,864	43,643	16,738
Other income	—	—	(330)
Interest on long-term debt and bank			
indebtedness.	27,026	16,195	3,961
Income before income taxes, equity			
earnings, preacquisition losses and			
extraordinary item	38,838	27,448	13,107
Income taxes	4,280	6,310	5,032
Income before equity earnings,			
preacquisition losses and extra-			
ordinary item	34,558	21,138	8,075
Add back: preacquisition losses attribut-			
able to 50% interest of Plitt not owned			
by the corporation	—	1,381	—
Equity in earnings of 50% owned			
companies.	—	—	1,021
Income before extraordinary item	34,558	22,519	9,096
Extraordinary item	—	—	1,278
Net income	$ 34,558	$ 22,519	$ 10,374
Earnings per share:			
Before extraordinary item.	$ 0.81	$ 0.74	$ 0.56
Net income	$ 0.81	$ 0.74	$ 0.65
Fully diluted earnings per share:			
Before extraordinary item.	$ 0.72	$ 0.63	$ 0.44
Net income	$ 0.72	$ 0.63	$ 0.49

EXHIBIT 2

CINEPLEX ODEON CORPORATION
Extracts from the Consolidated Balance Sheet
(in thousands of U.S. dollars)

	December 31, 1987	December 31, 1986
Property, equipment, and leaseholds	$711,523	$513,411
Goodwill (less amortization of $1,878; 1986—$720)	52,596	40,838
Bank indebtedness	20,672	30
Current portion of long-term debt and other obligations	5,965	6,337
Long-term debt.	449,707	317,550
Capitalized lease obligations	14,565	15,928
Deferred income taxes	13,318	11,142
Pension obligations	4,026	3,668
Shareholders' equity:		
Capital stock.	$289,181	$212,121
Translation adjustment	1,915	(3,591)
Retained earnings.	46,791	19,113
	$337,887	$227,643

Collier Custom Jewelry Ltd.

Early in 1987, several independent Ontario jewelry retailers established Collier Custom Jewelry Ltd. (CCJL), as a private corporation under the Ontario Business Corporations Act. CCJL was formed to sell custom-made jewelry to retailers.

Retail jewelers receive orders from customers for the construction of unique pieces of jewelry. Both the design (if needed) and the construction of the piece are normally subcontracted to independent specialists such as designers, goldsmiths, silversmiths, and so on.

CCJL was formed to provide the owner retailers with a reliable, centralized source of design and construction, with profits being returned largely to the retailers. In addition to doing individual custom work, CCJL would hold design competitions and select outstanding designs for multiple production. These products would be distributed exclusively through the owner retailers, supported by regional cooperative advertising by CCJL and the retailers.

Once CCJL was established and operating satisfactorily, additional business would be accepted from retailers who are not owners of CCJL to the extent that capacity permits. This additional outside business would help to even the work load and to maintain full employment of the staff of skilled experts.

The pricing of the outputs of CCJL would differ for each of the three lines of business. For the owner retailers' custom business, the price to the retailer would be equal to the direct cost of the item of jewelry plus a fixed percentage margin to cover overhead and to provide a modest profit margin. The percentage would be set annually by CCJL's board of directors.

Institute of Chartered Accountants of Ontario adapted.

For the exclusive product lines, production levels would be based on sales estimates of the participating retailers. The production set would ensure CCJL would have adequate inventory throughout the year. The prices to the owner retailers would be the wholesale prices for comparable products. Custom work for outside retailers would be charged at normal market rates.

At any one time there would be finished goods, work-in-process and raw materials inventory of precious metals and gems on hand. In determining the level of raw materials to carry, CCJL's management would have to consider such factors as the availability of gold, silver, and diamonds. The factors would include fluctuations in the commodities markets and the foreign currency exchange rates.

In establishing CCJL, each of the eight founding retailer owners purchased between one and five shares of common stock for $50,000 per share. The founders' intention was that the initial investment should be sufficient to maintain the company's productive capacity without additional injections of capital. A shareholders' agreement was drawn up that included the following points:

- The CCJL board of directors was to be comprised of one representative from each of the owner retailers, regardless of the number of shares held.
- New shares would be sold to existing or new shareholders only upon approval of two thirds of the board of directors.
- Existing shareholders who wished to sell part or all of their shares must first offer the shares to CCJL for repurchase, and then to the remaining shareholders before any offers could be solicited from outside retailers.
- The price of all share transactions would be based on CCJL's net asset value per share at the end of the most recent quarter.

The top managers of CCJL had been selected prior to the official incorporation of the company, and many of the leading artisans for the company had been identified as well. Once CCJL was established, management quickly moved to find suitable quarters to house the operations and to equip and adapt the space to CCJL's needs. Loft space in a partially renovated building on Toronto's Duncan Street was obtained at reasonable rental rates, although a substantial one-time signing payment was required at the beginning of the 10-year lease to compensate the lessor for adapting the space to CCJL's needs. The lease also contained renewal options (at the lessee's option). Only about four months would be needed before the company was ready to begin full operation. During that time the managers and artisans would be engaged in a full range of start-up activities including equipping and stocking the leased space and hiring and training staff.

The board of directors established a defined contribution pension plan for the company's permanent skilled staff; the plan was based on compulsory employee and employer contributions and was fully vested from the outset. The board also approved a profit sharing plan for the managers.

Any additional financing that the company may need is to be arranged by the managers through normal bank financing. Interest costs are to be excluded, however, in determining the managers' profit sharing.

As a part of the start-up activity, the managers of CCJL are seeking expert assistance in selecting appropriate accounting policies for the company. The proposed policies will be submitted to the board of directors' newly formed audit committee for approval. It is anticipated that CCJL's fiscal year-end will be January 31, and that quarterly statements will be prepared for submission to the owner retailers and to the bank.

Required

Assume that you have been retained as the accounting adviser. Prepare a report in which you recommend suitable financial accounting policies, consistent with CCJL's reporting objectives. Include the reasons for your specific recommendations.

Consolidated Holdings Inc.

Andrew Fleming, president and chief executive officer of Consolidated Holdings Inc. (CHI), has quickly risen to prominence in the business community. Known as a shrewd dealmaker capable of spotting good quality opportunities in start-up and turnaround situations, he has recently built an impressive holding of investments.

Fleming started his career in 1976 with XL Corp. (XL), the Canadian subsidiary of a major U.S. multinational. As a manufacturer of precision components such as timing chains and cam shafts for the automotive industry, XL encountered difficult times during the late 1970s and early 1980s. These problems were created primarily by a decline in the demand for less fuel-efficient six- and eight-cylinder engines, for which XL's products were targeted. Sensing a desire on the part of the U.S. parent to cut its losses, Fleming orchestrated a leveraged management buyout in 1983, that resulted in his ownership of 53 percent of XL's 6 million common shares outstanding.

Since that time, XL has invested in new product development and marketing, and is now quite successful in supplying components for the new generation of V-6 engines used by both Big Three and Japanese automakers manufacturing here in Canada. Through CHI, which he formed as a holding company, Fleming has set out to invest in other business operations capable of being rejuvenated with proper management and financing.

Fleming has recently offered John Sheridan, a partner in a regional public accounting firm, the opportunity to provide audit services to his group of companies. Sheridan and his engagement manager, Tony Fer-

Institute of Chartered Accountants of Ontario adapted.

rone, attended an initial meeting with Fleming on April 15, 1990. The following conversation took place at that time:

AF:

> As you know, XL has a March 31 year-end. The current auditors have just commenced the 1990 audit, but once they're done I'll let them know that you'll be taking over the engagement from 1991 onward. Of course, I want you to take on the CHI audit right away.

JS:

> That sounds fine to me. I understand that you have been busy turning CHI into far more than just a holding company for your investment in XL.

AF:

> It has been a very exciting and challenge-filled year. We successfully outbid the competition for 100% control of Elliot Lake Mining Limited (EL), a former Crown corporation engaged in the uranium industry. EL was spun off by the federal government as part of its privatization program. We also acquired the lease financing subsidiary of PC Corp. Further details are contained in the notes prepared by my corporate controller [attached as Exhibit 1].

JS:

> I'll have Tony review these notes in detail, and we'll get back to you on any significant implications they may have for our June 30 audit of CHI. Is there anything else we should know?

AF:

> Given the substantial changes in CHI's operations that have taken place recently, it is important that CHI's financial statements reflect the unique nature of its holdings. I have had my controller draft a set of statements in the form we would like to see, based on March 31, 1990 figures [Exhibit 2]. A public offering of CHI is not more than two years down the road, so I'll be using the actual June 30 statements to attract interest in the investment community. Let me know if there is anything about the draft statements that you will not be able to live with.

Required

Assume the role of Tony Ferrone. Prepare a memorandum to John Sheridan that discusses the major accounting issues to be resolved with this new client.

ELLIOT LAKE MINING LIMITED (EL)

EL is involved in the mining and refining of uranium for such nonmilitary uses as nuclear-powered generating stations and submarines. A federal Crown corporation since its inception in 1959, EL has had its share of ups and downs due to the political and social pressures which have shaped government policies directly affecting its marketplace.

The $10 million acquisition price for EL was financed by a term loan from XL Corp.'s bankers, bearing interest at a floating rate of prime plus 2 percent. For consolidation purposes, book values have been picked up directly from EL's internal statements, with the excess of EL's book value over the purchase price being recorded as additional accumulated depletion on EL's mining properties.

Uranium prices worldwide are established in U.S. dollars. EL's management regularly enters into U.S. dollar-denominated forward sales contracts covering approximately 50 percent of the total uranium refined each month. All defined uranium inventories are carried at the average realizable value established by these forward contracts, and are translated into Canadian dollars at the exchange rate prevailing at the end of the month in which refining is completed. Subsequent price and currency fluctuations are taken into income as incurred.

EL's year-end is June 30.

EQUINOX FINANCE INC. (EFI)

Previously owned by PC Corp. (PC), a major publicly traded conglomerate, EFI provides long-term direct financing leases covering large-scale manufacturing equipment to various industrial customers, including XL Corp.

Under the terms of the EFI acquisition, CHI obtained 100 percent of EFI's common shares from PC in exchange for 1,200 common shares of CHI and 10-year noninterest-bearing notes payable. The common shares issued were recorded in CHI's books at $4,094,000, representing the amount by which the book value of EFI's net assets exceeded the $4 million face value of the notes payable.

Due to favourable income tax treatment of its leases, EFI has built up significant deferred income tax credits. CHI has booked on consolidation an adjustment of these deferred tax balances to reflect lower tax rates expected in the period of reversal. Income tax expense has been credited by the amount of this adjustment.

EFI's year-end is June 30.

XL CORP.

A major new production line is currently under construction at XL's Brampton facility. During the period of construction, all associated direct and indirect costs, such as interest and administrative overhead, will be capitalized as deferred start-up costs. XL's current intention is to amortize the deferred start-up costs on a straight-line basis over 10 years, commencing with the end of construction and the start of commercial production (expected to occur in the fall of 1990).

For consolidation purposes, CHI has historically picked up XL's March 31 year-end results.

EXHIBIT 1   CHI Corporate Structure

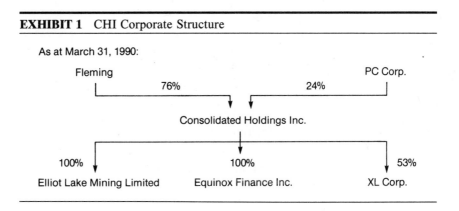

EXHIBIT 2

CONSOLIDATED HOLDINGS INC.
Balance Sheet
As at March 31, 1990
(in thousands)

Assets

Cash and short-term deposits	$ 2,348
Receivables (Note 2)	41,369
Inventories (Note 3)	28,741
Investments	4,676
Fixed assets (Note 4)	29,505
Other assets (Note 5)	6,732
Total assets	$113,371

Liabilities and Shareholders' Equity

Trade payables and accrued expenses	$ 23,758
Secured creditors (Note 6)	63,214
Deferred credits (Note 7)	16,257
Share capital (Note 8)	4,474
Retained income	5,668
Total liabilities and shareholder's equity	$113,371

EXHIBIT 2   (*continued*)

CONSOLIDATED HOLDINGS INC.
Statement of Income and Retained Earnings
For the nine months ended March 31, 1990
(in thousands)

Sales	$125,985
Cost of sales	111,509
Operating income.	14,476
Finance income	727
Investment income	875
	16,078
Selling, general, and administrative expenses . . .	5,522
Interest expense	5,689
	11,211
Net income before tax	4,867
Income taxes: current.	1,856
deferred	(841)
	1,015
	3,852
Less: minority interest	727
Income available to all common shareholders . . .	3,125
Retained income, beginning of period	2,543
Retained income, end of period	5,668

See accompanying notes to financial statements.

Notes to Financial Statements
For the nine months ended March 31, 1990
(*all amounts expressed in thousands of dollars*)

Note 1. Significant Accounting Policies

The accompanying financial statements have been prepared in accordance with the Recommendations of the Accounting Standards Committee of the Canadian Institute of Chartered Accountants. Where such Recommendations are incomplete, management has applied those accounting principles which it considers to result in the most meaningful portrayal of the activities of the company.

Consolidation

The following majority-owned subsidiaries have been consolidated herein: XL Corp., Elliot Lake Mining Limited, and Equinox Finance Inc. All material intercompany transactions and balances have been eliminated.

EXHIBIT 2   *(continued)*

Revenue Recognition

Revenue is recognized upon substantial completion of the earnings process.

Inventories

Manufacturing inventories are valued at the lower of cost and net realizable value. Refined minerals are valued at realizable value as established by forward sales contracts.

Note 2: Receivables

Trade receivables.	$21,708
Lease receivables, net of unearned finance income	21,661
	43,369
Less doubtful accounts	(2,000)
	$41,369

Note 3: Inventories

Manufacturing inventories	$24,436
Refined materials	4,305
	$28,741

Note 4: Fixed Assets

	Cost	Accumulated Depreciation and Depletion	Net Book Value
Land.	$ 2,500	$ —	$ 2,500
Buildings	6,000	2,986	3,014
Machinery and equipment . . .	41,581	35,556	6,025
Mining properties	38,434	20,468	17,966
	$88,515	$59,010	$29,505

Depreciation and depletion expense for the period totaled $2,951.

Note 5: Other Assets

Goodwill	$3,623
Deferred start-up costs	2,220
Prepaid expenses	889
	$6,732

EXHIBIT 2   *(concluded)*

Note 6: Secured Creditors

Consolidated Holdings Inc.:
  Noninterest-bearing notes payable to a shareholder,
    due February 1, 2000 . . . . $ 4,000
XL Corp:
  Revolving bank line of credit, at prime plus 1/2%   1,214
  10-year debentures bearing interest at 12 3/4%, due
    April 1, 1995, convertible after April 1, 1991 into
    common shares of XL Corp. at the rate of 50 common
    shares per $1,000 debenture 48,000
Elliot Lake Mining Limited:
  Bank term loan, bearing interest at a floating rate
    of prime plus 2%; principal due in five equal annual
    installments commencing October 1, 1990 10,000
                                                            $63,214

Note 7: Deferred Credits

Deferred income taxes $13,887
Minority interest in a subsidiary   2,370
                                                            $16,257

Note 8: Share Capital

Common stock, with no par value
  10,000 shares authorized
  5,000 shares issued and outstanding $4,474

During the period, 1,200 common shares were issued in conjunction with the acquisition of Equinox Finance Inc. These shares have been recorded at a stated value of $4,094.

Note 9: Pension Plans

There are no significant unfunded liabilities in the defined benefit pension plans covering employees of the various subsidiaries consolidated herein.

Case 19

Constant Equipment Ltd.

Constant Equipment Ltd. is a heavy equipment dealer, selling road construction equipment, backhoes, bulldozers, and all types of farm equipment. Much of their volume is in construction equipment, a cyclical industry, and Constant accordingly suffers from volatile earnings and cash flows.

In 1988, such a cyclical downswing prompted the Charter Bank, Constant's primary secured creditor, to appoint a receiver. The receiver negotiated the sale of the company to Husky Equipment Ltd., a large equipment dealer in another province. The bank made some compromises, and a debt/equity financing package was structured to keep Constant in business. Husky Equipment Ltd. made some significant changes at Constant, reducing support staff positions considerably and replacing most of the top management. The new general manager, Walter Strong, has been charged with the responsibility to make the operation profitable as quickly as possible. He is paid a certain base salary, plus a bonus of 10 percent of operating income before tax. If the company has a loss, no bonus is paid, but future years' bonuses are unaffected. That is, each year stands on its own.

It is now July 17, 1989, and you are part of the audit team doing the fieldwork for the fiscal year ended June 30, 1989, Mr. Strong's first year as president. Preliminary results indicate that Constant will show an operating loss of $120,000 in fiscal year 1989. This loss position was expected both by the bank and by Husky, as 1989 was a rebuilding and restructuring year. Everyone has high hopes for 1990, however, as the company seems to be running efficiently and the construction industry is "heating up."

You have been put in charge of the current liabilities portion of the audit, and have collected the information in Exhibit 1. The chartered accountant in charge of the fieldwork has asked you to analyse Constant's accounts and policies and make any adjusting journal entries that are required. He has warned you to watch for overstatement of expenses, as he suspects Strong is trying to accrue as much as possible this year, as the company is already in a loss position.

Required

Carry out the assignment.

EXHIBIT 1

Accounts Payable and Accrued Liabilities

Balance, June 30, 1989 . . . $337,974 cr

A review of invoices on and around June 30 reveals the following:

1. Two invoices for heavy equipment, for $71,200 and $47,900, were recorded on June 29. The equipment was received on July 4. Constant keeps a perpetual inventory system.
2. The following invoices were received and recorded in July 1989 and pertained to June 1989 or before:

Advertising	$ 1,200
Repairs and maintenance	4,120
Shop supplies	720
Parts inventory (periodic inventory) . . .	34,200
Miscellaneous	300

Accrued Wages Payable

Balance, June 30, 1989 . . . $17,400 cr

This amount relates to June 30, 1988. There was a weekly payroll on July 4, 1989, for $24,750, one fifth of which related to 1989. All payroll costs are charged to "Compensation Expense."

Demand Bank Loans

Balance, June 30, 1989 . . . $2,474,000 cr

This amount has been confirmed by the bank. While it is due on demand, or on 30 days' notice, there is a repayment schedule requiring $10,000 of principal, plus interest, each month. All parties seem to consider this debt to be long-term in nature, and management of Constant feel it should be disclosed as long-term debt.

EXHIBIT 1   *(concluded)*

Warranty Liability

Balance, June 30, 1989 . . . $52,000 cr

This amount represents the expected warranty costs associated with new machinery sales, which carry a 24-month warranty on parts and a 12-month warranty on labour.

In the past, the warranty liability has been set up based on a percentage of sales, which would have resulted in a liability balance of $35,000 at June 30, 1989.

This year, Strong had his staff prepare an analysis of all equipment with warranties still outstanding and an estimate of cost per machine, which totaled the $52,000 above. You have checked this list and it appears accurate, although the cost estimate per machine is highly subjective.

You have checked with staff at your office who have done audits of other heavy equipment dealers, and all of them seem to set up a warranty liability based on sales, not specific identification.

Strong argues that, in their special circumstances, an average percentage based on sales is "not good enough," and specific identification is "much more accurate."

Coupon Liability

Balance, June 30, 1989 . . . $10,000 cr

In April of 1989, Constant published an ad in a construction industry journal that gave customers a 5 percent discount if they mentioned the ad when buying new equipment. The journal is circulated to 70,000 subscribers, only 2 percent of which might be in the market for new equipment. Of these, only 10 percent might buy from Constant, and only half of them might mention the ad.

An average sale is $22,000. To June 30, 1989, 65 customers have mentioned the ad.

The $10,000 balance in this account was set up to be "on the safe side." This amount has been charged to Promotions Expense.

This is the first year this type of campaign has been undertaken by Constant.

Case 20

D'Eon Corporation

The president of D'Eon Corporation had just been discussing the December 31, 1987 financial statements with Jane Wylie, the chartered accountant in charge of the fieldwork for the annual audit. For the past six years, the company had been involved in a cost-based pension plan but had switched to a benefits-based plan in 1987. Although D'Eon Corporation was family controlled, the president was considering a public issue of the company's shares in the near future to finance much needed capital expenditure programs. Consequently, he was anxious to avoid a qualified audit report.

The change in pension plans, from cost to benefits, was the result of a new agreement with the union in January of 1987. The new plan was independently administered, and benefits were calculated as a flat benefit of "pension per year" multiplied by the years of employment, calculated from the date of commencement of service.

The pension fund contributions were to be made by the company, and employees were to acquire a vested interest in these payments after five years of employment. However, the union contract did not provide for full funding of the past-service benefits.

At the end of 1987, the president had engaged a firm of actuarial consultants to perform an evaluation of D'Eon Corporation's pension plan. They reported that, as of December 31, 1987, unfunded past service costs aggregated $14 million and that an annual provision of about $1.5 million would be required to fully cover both continuing current service costs and unfunded past service costs over a 30-year period. Unfunded vested bene-

Adapted, with permission from the *Uniform Final Examination Handbook*, (1978) ©. The Canadian Institute of Chartered Accountants, Toronto.

Changes to the original question and/or suggested approach to answering are the sole responsibility of the authors and have not been reviewed or endorsed by the CICA.

fits, included in the $14 million, aggregated $2 million. A projected benefit actuarial cost method was used in this evaluation.

In his discussion with Jane, the president had pointed out that the actuarial evaluation did not reflect an anticipated 20 percent reduction in the work force when the modernization plan was implemented. The president also felt that the 6 percent rate of interest used by the actuary in his evaluation was not realistic and 7 percent more fairly represented the rate of return that could be expected on the fund contributions. If the 7 percent rate of return were used, the annual provision would need to be $1.2 million as opposed to the $1.5 million at the 6 percent rate. Moreover, D'Eon Corporation's legal liability under the pension plan was limited by the provision of the union contract which was due to expire in two years, and the existing contract did not provide for full funding of past service costs. In view of these points, the president felt that a $1.5 million annual provision based on the actuarial evaluation was excessive. Finally, the president insisted that the firm simply would not have sufficient cash resources to pay a $1.5 million annual contribution. (See Exhibit 1.)

The president asked Jane to prepare a report concerning the actuarial report and his concerns, and whether the actuary's numbers can be used for external reporting. He would also like to know how the pension plan would be reflected in the 1987 financial statements, including the notes.

Required

Assume the role of Jane Wylie and prepare the report to the president of D'Eon Corporation.

EXHIBIT 1

D'EON CORPORATION
Operating Statistics
(in thousands)

	Net Income (Loss)	Year-End Cash	Balance of Retained Earnings
1981 . . .	$3,500	$2,000	$12,000
1982 . . .	4,000	2,500	12,500
1983 . . .	1,800	1,900	10,100
1984 . . .	(600)	1,500	8,000
1985 . . .	(200)	1,300	7,800
1986 . . .	1,500	1,400	7,000
1987 . . .	2,000	900	6,500

Case 21

Dartmouth Enterprises Ltd.

Dartmouth Enterprises Ltd. adopted a defined benefit pension plan early in 1989. You, as a member of the accounting department, have been assigned the task of determining the effect the pension plan will have on the 1989 financial statements. Dartmouth Enterprises has a December 31 year-end.

The plan is administered by an insurance company, and Dartmouth Enterprises Ltd. agreed to make annual payments to the insurance company in two parts:

1. Annual payments of $10,000 beginning January 2, 1989 and ending on January 2, 1998, covering past service cost for qualified employees. These payments are to be adjusted periodically on the basis of an actuarial valuation to reflect any changes in benefits to be paid to employees or because of termination of employees whose rights are forfeited, and so forth. An interest rate of 7 percent was used to compute the payments.

2. Annual payments for the current service of employees, payable June 30 each year. This calculation, performed by the actuary, is based on the number of employees, their birthdates, the earnings rate that the insurance company is able to achieve on pension fund assets (expected to be 7 percent), and so on. In 1989, this payment was $48,750. The actuary used a projected benefit actuarial cost method, prorated on services.

In 1989, the insurance company paid $7,920 to retired employees.

The estimated remaining working lives for all employees was 25 years at the end of 1989.

From the insurance company, you learn that the inventory of fund assets was $52,100 at the end of 1989. According to the actuarial valuation, accrued benefits were $126,000 at the end of 1989.

Required

Determine the effect of the pension on the 1989 financial statements of Dartmouth Enterprises Ltd., including the notes, in accordance with Section 3460 of the *CICA Handbook*.

Denison Mines Limited

Recently, a business acquaintance, knowing of your expertise in the accounting area, presented you with the 1970 financial statements for Denison Mines Ltd. (Exhibit 1) plus the material she had gathered on normal accounting practices around that time (Exhibit 2).

"Look at this!" she exclaimed, "I bet you can't explain this one! Denison Mines changed its accounting policy for marketable securities in 1970, from 'cost' to 'market', as the carrying value. Why didn't they do it in 1969, when market was also lower than cost? Would they be allowed to carry at market value if it was *higher* than cost?

"Anyway, look at what they did with the write-down. It's all in retained earnings. Does that make it a prior period adjustment? If so, why didn't they change 1969, doing it retroactively? Should the write-down be there at all?

"Where were the auditors in all this? Why don't they make the company do it right?

"Now, don't tell me all this happened a long time ago. I want an explanation!"

Required

Respond to the issues raised.

EXHIBIT 1   Extracts from Denison Mines Ltd. 1970 Financial Statements

DENISON MINES LIMITED AND ITS SUBSIDIARIES
Consolidated Statement of Income and Retained Earnings
For Year Ended December 31, 1970

	1970	1969
Net income items shown below	$ 8,834,985	$ 7,142,318
Revenue from investments	1,270,419	7,045,918
	10,105,404	$14,188,236
Deduct:		
Provision for Ontario mining tax	660,000	900,000
Provision for depreciation and depletion	1,498,071	1,133,718
	2,158,071	2,033,718
	7,947,333	12,154,518
Share of net earnings of the unconsolidated		
subsidiary	292,289	562,304
Net income for the year.	8,239,622	12,716,822
Balance of retained earnings at beginning		
of year	73,837,026	67,384,788
	82,076,648	80,101,610
Deduct:		
Dividends	6,264,584	6,264,584
Adjustment resulting from change in basis of		
valuation of marketable securities (Note 2). . .	15,651,278	—
	21,915,862	6,264,584
Balance of retained earnings at end of year	$60,160,786	$73,837,026
Net income per share	$ 1.84	$ 2.84

Notes to Consolidated Financial Statements

Note 2: Marketable Securities

Marketable securities at December 31, 1970 are carried at market value; marketable securities carried at December 31, 1969 at $32,614,414 had a market value at that time of $22,649,118.

The company commenced during the year to carry its portfolio of marketable securities at the lower of cost or market value. This change in valuation basis resulted in a charge to retained earnings of $15,651,278 after adjusting for subsequent gains on sales and changes in market value to December 31, 1970. The company believes that the presentation adopted provides a clearer statement of its income for the current year than the recommendations of the Canadian Institute of Chartered Accountants which, if adopted, would have resulted in a loss of

---

EXHIBIT 1   *(continued)*

$7,411,656 for the year ended December 31, 1970 instead of the net income of $8,239,622 reported. Had the above change in valuation basis not been made net income for 1970, computed on the same basis as for 1969, would have been $1,945,000. In future, realized gains and losses on marketable securities and changes in market value not in excess of cost will be reflected in income.

Note 5: Income Taxes

It is estimated that the company has available for tax purposes deductions sufficient to eliminate current income taxes payable. The company has not adopted the tax allocation basis of accounting for taxes and therefore the accounts do not reflect deferred income taxes to date of $5,030,000 of which $2,270,000 is applicable to 1970 ($2,130,000 to 1969).

   The company has received Federal and Ontario income tax reassessments for the years 1961 to 1963 which claim income taxes in the aggregate amount of $6,273,722 plus interest. The federal reassessment for 1961 has been appealed to the Exchequer Court of Canada and the company has filed notices of objection with respect to the other reassessments. In the opinion of special counsel, the company should be substantially successful in its appeal and objections. Accordingly, no provision has been made in the accounts for any tax liability which may be exigible as a result of the above reassessments or for the fiscal years subsequent to 1963 due to transactions similar to those in respect of which reassessments have been received. Certain assets of the company have been assigned to the tax authorities as security for the outstanding reassessments pending settlement.

Opinion of Independent Chartered Accountants

Eddis & Associates
Chartered Accountants

To the Shareholders,
Denison Mines Limited

We have examined the consolidated balance sheet of Denison Mines Limited and its subsidiaries as at December 31, 1970 and the consolidated statements of income and retained earnings and source and application of funds for the year then ended. Our examination of the financial statements of Denison Mines Limited and those subsidiaries of which we are the auditors included a general review of the accounting procedures and such tests of accounting records and other supporting evidence as we considered necessary in the circumstances. We have relied on the reports of the auditors who have examined the financial statements of the other subsidiaries.

   As outlined in Note 2, the adjustment of $15,651,278 resulting from a change in the basis of valuation of marketable securities has been charged to retained earnings instead of being charged against the net income for the year.

   In our opinion, except that no provision has been made for deferred income taxes (see Note 5), these consolidated financial statements present fairly the

EXHIBIT 1 *(concluded)*

financial position of the companies as at December 31, 1970 and, except for the significant effect on net income and retained earnings for the year of the matter referred to in the preceding paragraph, the results of their operations and the source and application of their funds for the year then ended, in accordance with generally accepted accounting principles. Further, in our opinion, except for the change in the basis of valuation of marketable securities (with which we concur), such accounting principles are applied on a basis consistent with that of the preceding year.

Toronto, Canada, January 11, 1971
Eddis & Associates

EXHIBIT 2   Extracts from Financial Reporting in Canada, 9th Ed.[1]—Marketable Securities

Basis of Valuation and Market Value of Marketable Securities

The committee's recommendations on disclosure of the basis of valuation and market value of marketable securities included in current assets are included in paragraphs 3010.03–.04:[2]

The basis of valuation should be clearly indicated.

Where there are significant holdings of marketable securities, their quoted market value as well as their carrying value should be disclosed.

The statistics set out in Table 3 summarize the extent of disclosure followed by the survey companies and show that the common practice among the survey companies is to provide both the basis of valuation and market value.

Table 3   Basis of Valuation and Disclosure of Market Value of Marketable Securities

	Number of Companies				Percentage			
	1970	1969	1968	1967	1970	1969	1968	1967
Basis of valuation:								
Cost	82	92	103	107	67	73	75	76
Market/cost and market/lower of cost and market	13	6	8	9	11	5	6	6
Miscellaneous	5	5	4	6	4	4	3	4
Basis not disclosed.	22	23	23	20	18	18	16	14
Total	122	126	138	142	100	100	100	100
Disclosure of Market Value								
Market disclosed	95	102	109	113	78	81	79	80
Market not disclosed	27	24	29	29	22	19	21	20
Total	122	126	138	142	100	100	100	100

[1] *Financial Reporting in Canada* is now in its 17th edition. However, the ninth edition is appropriate to the time frame of the case.
[2] *CICA Handbook,* Section 3010.03–.04

EXHIBIT 2   *(concluded)*

Adjustment of Carrying Value to Lower of Cost and Market

That the carrying value of marketable securities included in current assets should be adjusted to reflect a current decline in market value below cost is supported by recommendations made by the American and English Institutes as well as by the Canadian Institute.

In paragraph 3010.05, the Accounting and Auditing Research Committee of the Canadian Institute recommends that:

> *Where the market value has declined below the carrying value by a significant amount, the securities should be carried at market value.*[3]

A ruling in 1953 by the American Institute of Certified Public Accountants suggested that, in circumstances where the market value was less than cost for marketable securities, the disclosed amount of a current asset should not exceed the market value, provided the decline in market value was not a temporary nature.[4]

Similarly, in 1958, the Council of the Institute of Chartered Accountants in England and Wales agreed that a provision should be included in the statements for those occasions when the market value of marketable securities was lower than cost.[5]

To get some idea of Canadian practice in this respect, a comparison was made of the relationship between the carrying value and disclosed market value of marketable securities classified as current assets in the balance sheet. The following sets out the results of this comparison:

	Percentage of Companies			
	1970	*1969*	*1968*	*1967*
Market value:				
Either greater than or at least 95% of carrying value . . .	56%	60%	63%	66%
Below 95% of carrying value	22	21	16	14
Not disclosed	22	19	21	20
	100%	100%	100%	100%

The second category of the above schedule, where market value was below 95 percent of carrying value, shows an increasing percentage of companies where a problem of adjustment did exist but was not made in the accounts. Unfortunately, it was not possible to determine the reasons why no adjustment was made but perhaps it could be taken as an indication that management did not anticipate the liquidation of these securities in the immediate future or that the decline in market value was a temporary condition.

[3] *CICA Handbook: Accounting Recommendations,* Section 3010, "Temporary Investments" (Toronto: Canadian Institute of Chartered Accountants, 1978), par. .05.

[4] *Accounting Research and Terminology Bulletins—Final Edition,* "No. 43 Restatement and Revision of Accounting Research Bulletins" (New York: American Institute of Certified Public Accountants, 1953).

[5] *Member's Handbook,* Regulation N20 (Institute of Chartered Accountants of England and Wales, 1958).

Develco

Develco Limited (DL) is a leading supplier of application software for computers used by hospitals and medical practitioners. DL went public shortly after its incorporation, and has experienced rapid growth in sales over the last several years. For 1987 (DL has a December 31 fiscal year-end), audited net income was $3.2 million. During January 1988 the company returned to privately owned status by purchasing and cancelling all those shares not held by senior management.

Under an employee profit sharing plan, which was introduced in 1986, the company distributes 10 percent of audited operating income to its employees. Labour relations improved dramatically after introduction of the plan.

Prior to bringing a new software application to market, the company incurs two types of costs:

1. Costs for design, coding, and testing.
2. Costs such as user documentation that are incurred after commercial viability is established.

Once the software application has been developed and tested, manufacturing consists of reproduction using automated copying equipment. Thus, the manufacturing costs are relatively low. The disks, tapes and diskettes produced are kept in inventory until ordered by a customer.

Promotional and selling costs include the following:

1. Preparation of salesman demonstration kits.
2. Initial media space to advertise the introduction of the application.
3. Ongoing advertising costs.

Society of Management Accountants adapted

The commercial life of a new application is difficult to ascertain, given the possibility of the development of similar software by competitors. The average life of a software product line has been five years, but this can vary by two or three years in either direction.

Now that DL is privately owned, senior management wants to take a fresh look at the company's accounting policies. As controller of DL, you recently attended a meeting with senior management to discuss the following issues related to the financial statements for 1988:

1. In prior years, DL has expensed pre-viability costs (design, coding, and testing) but has capitalized and amortized costs such as user documentation. Senior management proposes to expense all of these costs for 1988. It argues that the future benefit potential of such outlays is no longer objectively ascertainable because of the increasing threat of introduction of a competing product.

2. The company has a 90-day sales return policy. Sales returns for a new application are difficult to estimate, and vary from 1 percent to 10 percent depending on the application. A sales return provision based on 5 percent (the historical average experienced by DL) was recorded in 1987 and prior years. For fiscal 1988, senior management has proposed two alternatives: to record a sales return provision using the 10 percent figure; or to delay revenue recognition until expiry of the sales return period.

3. In 1987 and prior years, the company used the percentage of sales method to estimate bad debts which occur mainly on receivables from medical practitioners. In 1988, senior management proposes to use the aging method and to provide an allowance for all receivables outstanding more than 30 days.

4. Management is planning to purchase new computers and systems software during 1988 for the software development process. This equipment (CCA rate 30 percent) will cost $750,000. Management estimates that the equipment will be technically obsolete within five years and is considering using the CCA rate for depreciation.

5. Currently, DL is suing one competitor for $1 million for copyright infringement. As well, DL itself is being sued for $2 million by another competitor for copyright infringement. This infringement was committed early in 1988 by a DL employee who was subsequently fired. The company's lawyer has expressed the opinion that both lawsuits will be settled in 1989; the first one in favour of DL and the second against.

6. DL has had requests from several customers for financing assistance by leasing software rather than selling it. The senior management is unsure what kind of lease and what terms would be most advantageous. DL would want the lease payments to cover the costs (plus a profit) of developing the software since in many cases the applications are customized. Also, DL normally guarantees to provide mainte-

nance; for example, correcting problems and updating for a specific time period. It is difficult to estimate the cost of this service which is provided free of charge to the customer.

Senior management has asked you for a report discussing the issues considered at the management meeting. The report should include your recommendations.

Electra Corporation Limited

Electra Corporation Ltd. (ECL) is a Canadian-controlled private corporation, incorporated under the laws of New Brunswick. It manufactures, wholesales, and retails high-quality, natural fiber clothes for the high price Yuppie urban market. Clothes are sold through Electra boutiques in shopping centers in large urban centers, and also through certain retail chains in the United States.

The business was first planned as a "blue sky" project by five MBA's in an entrepreneurship class. After four years' work experience, the five pooled their personal financial resources, got government grants and bank loans, and started their business. After the first few years, which were very rocky, the business took off. Now six years later, it is a successful enterprise. After a few lean years when the owner/managers did not take much remuneration, they decided to pay themselves a substantial salary plus a bonus based on net income after taxes starting in 1984.

It is now the end of 1986. ECL took out a U.S. bank loan in 1984 to finance their U.S. operation. Sales to the U.S. retail chains were major for the first time in 1983, and it was decided that a warehouse operation, to service American orders, was called for. Accordingly, a facility was leased in New York State and stocked appropriately. All its supplies come from Canada, and it is run by a competent manager. There is not much to running the operation, though, as all stocking decisions and all its accounting are through the Canadian head office.

The loan and inventory are kept on ECL's books, and the operation is simply a warehouse location.

When the U.S. $500,000 five-year term loan was entered into, the U.S. dollar was worth Can. $1.24. At the end of 1984, the rate was $1.27, and in 1985, $1.25. Now, at the end of 1986, the rate is $1.39.

Atlantic Provinces Association of Chartered Accountants, adapted

In 1984 and 1985, the loan was left on the books at $620,000. ECL reasoned that they would be refinancing the loan when it came due with more debt denominated in U.S. dollars, as they could not hope to generate enough cash flow to repay it in just five years. Their U.S. bankers had indicated a willingness to take a longer term position if the company was reasonably successful in the first five years of the loan. Since the U.S. operation is booming, ECL decided that there was no effect on cash flows or risk, so there was no point in adjusting the loan balance.

In 1984 and 1985, ECL accepted a qualified audit report over this policy. Now, they have reluctantly acknowledged that the CICA is unlikely to change its position on foreign currency translation, and they have agreed to conform with Section 1650. You have been asked to calculate what effect this will have on income in 1986, given full retroactive restatement. They also want to know what will appear on the balance sheet. In addition, they would like to hear—one more time—just exactly *why* the CICA chose the method they did, and what was wrong with ECL's rationale.

When discussing the loan, the senior management considered making the U.S. operation into a separate subsidiary. They would like to know what effect exchange fluctuations would have on income in this situation and, given their dislike of fluctuating income, what they should consider when structuring a subsidiary.

Required

Draft a response to ECL.

Case 25

Ermine Oil Limited

Ermine Oil Limited (Ermine) is a fully integrated public Canadian oil company. Ermine commenced as a petroleum exploration company and was very successful in its oil field discoveries. To attain market security and improve profits, Ermine was forced to embark on a program of vertical integration. It first acquired a refining division and then marketing and transportation divisions. From the beginning, management appreciated the integrated nature of the business, and production was transferred between divisions at standard cost. The management control system recognized the exploration, refining, and transportation divisions as cost centres and the marketing division as a revenue centre. While the exploration, refining, and transportation divisions did make external sales, historically, none of these divisions' external sales accounted for 10 percent of Ermine's total sales. However, in the last fiscal year, due to unusual world market conditions, the transportation division's sales accounted for 11 percent of Ermine's total sales. Over 90 percent of Ermine's sales were within Canada, with the balance spread over many countries worldwide. Ermine did not feel it was necessary to disclose segmented information in its annual financial statements.

Beluga Petroleum Limited (Beluga) was similar to Ermine in size and also in scope of operations except that, in addition, it had a chemical division. However, Beluga was a subsidiary of a foreign oil company and had several issues of bonds that were publicly traded in Canada. Its divisions were each organized as profit centres with products transferred between divisions at world market prices. Each division purchased and sold products extensively to outside companies. In addition, about 15 percent of Beluga's sales were export, almost exclusively to the United

Society of Management Accountants, adapted

States. In its annual financial statements, Beluga showed segmented information by the five divisions (exploration, refining, transportation, chemical, and marketing) and sales were divided between domestic and export operations.

Required

Discuss how both Ermine and Beluga could report differently with respect to disclosure of segmented information, and yet be in accordance with Section 1700 of the *CICA Handbook* (excerpts, Exhibit 1).

EXHIBIT 1   Segmented Information, Section 1700, *CICA Handbook* (excerpts)[1]

INDUSTRY SEGMENTS

Grouping of Products and Services into Industry Segments

.15 Due to the great variety of operations among enterprises, this Section sets out only general procedures for identifying industry segments. It is the responsibility of management of an enterprise to identify the products and services from which the enterprise derives its revenue and to group similar products and services into industry segments.

.16 Many enterprises may accumulate information concerning revenue and profitability on a less-than-total-enterprise basis for internal planning and control purposes. Frequently, this type of information is maintained by profit centres for individual products and services or for groups of related products and services. Existing profit centres may represent a logical starting point for determining the industry segments. However, when existing profit centres cross industry lines, it would be necessary to break them down into smaller units.

.17 When determining whether products and services are similar and, as such, would be grouped into a single industry segment, a number of factors would be considered. Included in these factors are:
  a. The nature of the product or service.
  b. The nature of the production process taking into consideration such factors as the type of raw materials involved and the sharing of common facilities.
  c. The nature of markets including such factors as the type of market, methods of marketing and sensitivity of the market to economic conditions and price changes.

[1] Reprinted with permission from the *CICA Handbook*. Canadian Institute of Chartered Accountants, Toronto, Canada.

EXHIBIT 1   *(continued)*

.18 Broad categories such as manufacturing, wholesaling, retailing, and consumer products are not, in themselves, indicative of the industries in which an enterprise operates. It would be inappropriate to use those terms without identification of a product or service to describe an enterprise's industry segments.

.19 Extension of activity in the same general line of business or expansion into supplementary, complementary or compatible products is sometimes termed horizontal integration. Integration of this type does not normally result in an enterprise operating in more than one industry.

.20 To the extent that an enterprise operates in various industries directly related to the production and distribution of its end products, it is regarded as vertically integrated. The integrated operations of such an enterprise may encompass control of the source of supply, processing, manufacturing, marketing and, sometimes, even transporting and financing its products. In such operations, although products may be sold to customers outside the enterprise at various stages, the output at each stage is primarily devoted to the production of the end products. While the portion of the enterprise's operations that is considered to be vertically integrated can often be classified by industry, such operations may properly be considered as being one industry, because of the interdependence of those activities.

.21 The Statistics Canada Standard Industrial Classification Code may provide guidance in determining the various industry segments. However, this Code would not necessarily be used by itself as a basis for determining particular segments for financial reporting; it was not designed for this purpose and does not recognize the interdependence of some products and services.

.22 It is desirable that industry segmentation of a multinational enterprise's operations be done on a worldwide basis. Occasionally this may be impracticable because financial data with respect to some foreign operations are not accumulated along industry lines. In such a situation, that portion of an enterprise's foreign operations for which presentation of disaggregated industry information is impracticable would be considered a single industry segment.

Determination of Reportable Industry Segments

.23 In determining whether an industry segment would be identified as reportable, the major factors to be considered are the extent of revenue generated by the segment, the operating profit or loss produced by the segment and the commitment of resources to the segment's operations. In the opinion of the Committee, an industry segment would usually be considered significant if any one of the following conditions is present:
   a. Its revenue is 10 percent or more of the total revenue of all industry segments (including inter-segment sales and transfers).

EXHIBIT 1 *(continued)*

---

    b. The absolute amount of its operating profit or loss is 10 percent or more of the greater, in absolute amount, of:

       i. The total operating profit of all industry segments that earned an operating profit; and

      ii. The total operating loss of all industry segments that incurred an operating loss.

    c. Its identifiable assets are 10 percent or more of the total identifiable assets of all industry segments.

.24 In order to present segmented data on a basis that would permit interperiod comparability, management needs to give consideration to reporting an industry segment that, although not currently significant to the enterprise, has been significant in previous periods and is expected to be in future periods. Conversely, it may not be appropriate to disclose an industry segment separately when it has not been previously disclosed and is currently significant to the enterprise only because its results of operations are abnormally high or the combined results of all industry segments are abnormally low. An appropriate explanation of such circumstances ought to be included in the segmented information.

.25 Management's selection and determination of industry segments ought to be such that a major portion, usually at least 75 percent, of the enterprise's total operations is disaggregated into industry segments and separately disclosed. As a practical matter, the test for determining whether a major portion of the enterprise's operations has been segmented would be based on reported revenues (i.e., revenues not including intersegment sales and transfers).

.26 When determining the number of industry segments for which financial information is to be presented, it would be necessary for management to identify enough reportable segments to provide an insight into the enterprise's operations. However, when the segmented information would be overly detailed because of the number of reportable segments, consideration would be given to grouping closely related segments into broader ones for purposes of separate disclosure.

.27 *An industry segment that is considered to be significant to the enterprise should be identified as reportable.* [June 1979]

.28 *The selection and determination of reportable industry segments should be such that they comprise a major portion of the enterprise's total operations.* [June 1979]

.29 An enterprise may have substantially all of its operations in one industry segment or operate exclusively in a single industry and, therefore, would be regarded as having a dominant industry segment. In the opinion of the Committee, an enterprise would be considered to have substantially all of its operations in one industry segment when one segment's revenue, operating

---

EXHIBIT 1   *(continued)*

---

profit or loss and identifiable assets account for more than 90 percent of the related combined totals for all industry segments and no other segment is identified as reportable.

.30 *When an enterprise has substantially all of its operations in one industry segment or operates exclusively in one industry, that industry segment should be identified as dominant and not as a reportable industry segment.*   [June 1979]

Financial Statement Presentation—Industry Segments

* * * * *

.33 *A general description of the products and services from which each report-able industry segment derives its revenue should be provided. Disclosure of the following data should be made for each reportable industry segment and, in aggregate, for the remainder of the enterprise's industry segments:*
   a. segment revenue derived from sales to customers outside the enterprise;
   b. segment revenue derived from intersegment sales or transfers and the basis of accounting therefor;
   c. segment operating profit or loss, the amount of depreciation, amortization and depletion expense, and any unusual items included in determining segment operating profit or loss; and
   d. total carrying amount of identifiable assets at the end of the fiscal year and the amount of capital expenditure for the period.
   A reconciliation of the aggregate segment revenue, aggregate segment operating profit or loss and aggregate identifiable assets to the sales, net income and total assets reported in the financial statements of the enterprise should be provided.   [June 1979]

.34 *When an enterprise has a dominant industry segment, this fact should be disclosed together with a general description of the products and services from which revenue is derived.*   [June 1979]

* * * * *

Geographic Segments

.36 Foreign countries often have significantly different business environments and, as a result, there may be levels of risk, rates of profitability and opportunities for growth that differ from those that exist in the enterprise's country of domicile. In addition to financial data concerning an enterprise's industry segments, disclosure of financial information pertaining to its operations in various geographic areas is important in assessing current performance and predicting prospects for the enterprise.

.37 When presenting segmented information concerning an enterprise's operations in various geographic areas, it is important to distinguish between foreign and domestic operations. For purposes of this Section, a multinational enterprise's domestic operations would be considered a separate geographic segment.

EXHIBIT 1   *(concluded)*

Determination of Foreign Geographic Segments

*   *   *   *   *

.42 In the opinion of the Committee, a foreign geographic segment would usually be considered significant when either of the following conditions is present:

    a. Its revenue generated from sales to customers outside the enterprise is 10 percent or more of the total revenue reported in the income statement of the enterprise; or

    b. Its identifiable assets are 10 percent or more of the total assets reported in the enterprise's balance sheet.

.43 *A foreign geographic segment that is considered to be significant to the enterprise should be identified as reportable.*   [June 1979]

Financial Statement Presentation—Geographic Segments

.44 *The location of each reportable foreign geographic segment should be disclosed. Disclosure of the following data should be made for each reportable foreign geographic segment, in total for all other foreign geographic segments when they are in the aggregate identified as significant and for the domestic geographic segment:*

    a. Segment revenue derived from sales to customers outside the enterprise;

    b. Segment revenue derived from sales or transfers between geographic segments and the basis of accounting therefor;

    c. Segment operating profit or loss or, where appropriate, some other measure of profitability (information as to after-tax profitability may be more appropriate when the tax structure applicable to the reportable foreign geographic segment is substantially different from that experienced by the enterprise's domestic operation); *and*

    d. Total carrying amount of identifiable assets at the end of the fiscal year.

A reconciliation of the aggregate segment revenue, aggregate measure of profitability and aggregate identifiable assets to the sales, net income and total assets reported in the financial statements of the enterprise should be provided.   [June 1979]

Flossy Co.

Flossy Co. is a chain of ice cream shops located in several southwestern Ontario cities. The company is 100 percent owned by its founder, Cassie O'Neill. In addition to Cassie's equity, the company has long- and short-term bank financing. The bank requires audited financial statements annually.

It is now the first week of February 1991. You are about to complete the audit work for Flossy's December 31, 1990 financial statements and are considering whether any adjustments will be required for the following items:

1. During 1990 Flossy Co. was sued by a competitor for patent infringement; the competitor charges that Flossy Co. copied one of its flavours, including the name. The competitor is claiming $30 million damages and legal fees. Unfortunately, Flossy Co.'s lawyer thinks that the suit has a good chance of succeeding. However, awards in cases of this type have typically ranged from $100,000 to $300,000, with the average settlement being $250,000 (plus legal fees).

The case is scheduled to be heard this month, but this depends on whether the judge's current case is finished. You must decide what statement presentation will be required if a judgment is rendered in the next few weeks, and what will be required if the outcome is still unknown.

2. On January 1, 1990 Flossy Co. rented a machine which makes sugar cones and made the first of four annual payments of $5,000 on the same day. Flossy Co. has the option to renew the lease for two more years at a rental of $5,000 per year and then to purchase the machine for $1. The machine has a useful life of 10 years with no salvage value. Flossy Co. could have purchased the machine on January 1, 1990 for $24,000. Flossy Co.'s incremental borrowing rate is 12 percent; Cassie O'Neill knows that the rate implicit in the lease is 10 percent. On the date the machine was rented, Cassie recorded rent expense of $5,000 for the cheque that was written. No other entries were made regarding the rental in 1990.

Required

Assume the role of Flossy Co.'s auditor. What impact, if any, will the two items above have on the December 31, 1990 financial statements of Flossy Co.? How will they be disclosed?

Case 27

Frank & William

In early 1989, Frank Williams and his half brother, William Franks, set up a limited company to invest some of their personal wealth. They chose the vehicle of a limited company for these investments for a number of reasons: both extremely wealthy, there were no tax advantages to personal ownership. They wanted to make some investments "anonymously," as their personal investment activity was closely monitored by the investment community. Finally, they were both convinced that future tax reform left their personal wealth a bit vulnerable, and wanted to "cover the bases" of legal investment vehicles.

Accordingly, South Shore Investments was incorporated in 1989. Under corporate law, the shareholders could waive the requirement for an audit, and Frank and William did this at the first shareholders' meeting, which was held in the back of Frank's limousine. Both men were directors, too.

Frank and William each contributed $4 million to the company and agreed on a certain investment portfolio balance; that is, X percent in bonds, X percent in safe, blue chip stock, X percent in risky stock, X percent in precious metals, and so on. The percentages were ranges, as holdings would be dependent on market conditions.

These parameters were communicated to two stockbrokers, each of whom was "in charge," subject to the approval of either Frank or William, of $2 million of the company's funds. The remaining $4 million is under the direct management of Frank and William, and has been invested in real estate.

The real estate bought is partially a piece of vacant land which the two men have reason to believe will be a prime development site within the next decade. They were able to buy this land privately from a business associate. They paid an amount in excess of its appraised value, but believe the appraisal did not consider the possibility of development of which they are aware. The remaining real estate is a few rental properties, apartment buildings, bought through real estate brokers. Apartment buildings are commonly valued based on their expected cash flow, discounted at the current market interest rates.

Frank and William want an annual financial report that will help them evaluate the performance of their investment decisions and the performance of the two stockbrokers. They will prepare separate accounting statements for tax purposes.

Frank is emphatic that he wants the statements to tell him if he made money—"real money—after inflation." (The high inflationary period of the 1970s left a deep impression on Frank.) William is more doubtful on this issue; he argues that inflation is low right now, so adjustments are not worth the bother. He does not really understand how the statements could be altered to reflect inflation or what items would change.

Both men agree that they want to see "relevant" information and values in the financial statements. They have asked you to discuss problems you foresee in obtaining "relevant" information. They want to know, though, where those relevant numbers would come from and what degree of reliability, especially for the real estate portfolio, could be expected.

Both also agree that they do not plan to take much out of the company, either in salaries or in dividends, over their lifetimes. They will simply reinvest company money in whatever looks like it will have the best income-earning potential in the market.

Required

Respond to the requests of Frank and William. Suggest a financial reporting system that would meet their needs. Make sure you explain it and respond to the questions they have raised.

Georgia McGuinness

Georgia McGuinness is the owner of one of Toronto's most prestigious art galleries, located in the Yorkville district of the city. Revenues and commissions approach $1 million per year.

In the spring of 1989, while visiting the Tate Gallery in London, Georgia was impressed with the work of a Spanish painter, Juan Allende, who had painted during the same period as Picasso and whose work had been greatly influenced by the master. Allende's works were included in the collections of several European royal families, further attesting to his importance, and Georgia decided to try to obtain a painting while overseas. Through her contacts in London, Georgia was introduced to an auctioneer in Paris who had recently been hired to sell an important French estate. Among the estate's possessions was a small oil painting by Allende which Georgia was able to acquire for her gallery for $75,000.

In early 1990 the art world was shaken by rumors of the discovery by the Louvre of a forgery among its Spanish collection. The rumors persisted; world news reports spoke of a sophisticated network of artists and dealers who had been able to duplicate and distribute "masterpieces" allegedly by Picasso, Dali, and El Greco, among others, which fooled even the experts.

In December 1990 Georgia met with her accountant, Katherine Dickson, to discuss the year-end financial statements. The following conversation ensued:

KD:

I've been hearing sporadic reports about a scandal involving the Louvre and its Spanish collection—something to do with forgery. Have you ever been afraid you might accidentally acquire a painting which wasn't authentic?

GM:

Well, actually the small Allende oil I bought over a year ago is the only piece in my current stock which could conceivably have been produced by this ring of forgers, but the public doesn't seem to think so—I was offered $80,000 for it last week, but I feel Allende's stature will increase so I said no. I'm sticking to my $95,000 selling price for now.

KD:

If it were a forgery, would it have any value, maybe as a collector's item of a historic event in the art world?

GM:

No—I might be able to sell it at the City Hall outdoor art sale for $400. It's a lovely painting regardless of the identity of the artist. However, this discussion is absurd! I'm paying insurance premiums based on its true market value of $95,000.

Katherine Dickson left her client's gallery feeling somewhat uneasy. She was concerned that the Allende painting should no longer be carried at cost due to the risk of a potential loss. That evening she pondered the alternatives available for the valuation and disclosure of part of Georgia's inventory and came to a decision.

Required

Should the painting be written down even if the appraisal is favourable? What disclosure, if any, would be appropriate? If it has to be written down, evaluate the following alternative treatments for the write-down: cost of goods sold, unusual item, extraordinary item, and prior period adjustment.

Case 29

Golden Co.

Golden Co. is a closed-end investment company which has been listed on the Toronto and Montreal stock exchanges since 1983. A closed-end investment company is one where the owners must deal through a stock exchange if they wish to buy or sell shares in the company, as opposed to dealing with the company directly. In addition to stock prices, an investment company's net asset value per share is public information. This value is published each week but is also available daily from the company.

Golden Co.'s investment policy requires that at all times at least 75 percent of the market value of the noncash assets are invested in gold-related investments. Cash resources of the company are invested in short-term obligations issued by the governments of Canada and the United States.

The price of gold has fluctuated widely since Golden Co. became a public company. During the same period the prices of gold shares as measured by various stock exchange gold indexes have exhibited much greater volatility than the price of gold. The political condemnation of South Africa's apartheid policies and the associated regulated disinvestment of South African assets has squeezed gold investors into smaller and less liquid markets. The prices of Canadian, American, and Australian gold shares have risen dramatically as gold investors avoided South Africa. The emergence of large North America-based gold mining companies has increased the number of gold investment alternatives for institutional investors.

In the first few weeks of 1988 the price of gold fell. The October 1987 stock market crash was causing fears of global economic recession. There was concern that the new gold production from Australia and North America would create an oversupply problem. The increasing use of gold loans and forward sales by gold producers had impacted the spot price of gold.

As is the practice for investment companies, Golden Co. carries its marketable securities at market value. It is now the third week of March 1988, and the audit of the 1987 financial statements is coming to an end. As the auditor, you are concerned about fair presentation of Golden Co.'s position at the year-end and are pondering the valuation of the marketable securities.

Golden Co.'s draft financial statements are presented in Exhibit 1.

Required

What is the impact on Golden Co.'s financial statements of carrying marketable securities at market value rather than cost? If an amount less than market value were to be used for the valuation, what would the alternatives be for calculating this amount? What is your opinion about the carrying value of Golden Co.'s marketable securities at December 31, 1987?

EXHIBIT 1

GOLDEN CO.
Consolidated Statement of Net Assets (draft)
December 31
(in thousands)

	1987	1986
Assets		
Investments at market value (cost $187,017; 1986: $167,800)	$211,450	$181,478
Cash, including Treasury bills of $10,282 (1986: $5,199)	10,719	5,494
Receivables from investments sold	662	99
Accrued income	789	491
Total assets	223,620	187,562
Liabilities		
Payables for investments purchased	1,792	1,584
Accounts payable and accruals	225	182
Income taxes payable	3,227	—
Deferred income taxes	6,186	709
Total liabilities	11,430	2,475
Net assets	212,190	185,087
Represented by:		
Share capital	183	183

EXHIBIT 1   *(continued)*

	1987	1986
Surplus:		
Contributed surplus	$171,014	$168,067
Retained income	3,286	2,216
Accumulated realized gain on sale of investments	19,460	1,653
Unrealized appreciation in the value of investments	18,247	12,968
Total surplus	212,007	184,904
Total	$212,190	$185,087
Net asset value per share	$ 12.10	$ 10.55

GOLDEN CO.
Consolidated Statement of Income (draft)
Year Ended December 31
(in thousands)

	1987	1986
Income:		
Dividends	$ 2,348	$ 2,464
Interest	1,562	613
	3,910	3,077
Expenses:		
Management fee	1,834	1,375
General and administrative	408	382
	2,242	1,757
Income before income taxes	1,668	1,320
Provision for income taxes	598	638
Net income for the year	$ 1,070	$ 682
Earnings per share	$ 0.06	$ 0.04

EXHIBIT 1   *(concluded)*

GOLDEN CO.
Consolidated Statement of Changes in Net Assets (draft)
Year Ended December 31
(in thousands)

	1987	1986
Net income for the year	$ 1,070	$ 682
Reduction of income taxes on the application of prior year's non-capital loss for income tax purposes	2,971	1,107
Purchase of shares for cancellation	(24)	(110)
Realized gain on investments for the year	17,807	1,314
Unrealized appreciation in the value of investments for the year, net of deferred income taxes	5,279	33,951
Increase in net assets	27,103	36,944
Net assets at beginning of year	185,087	148,143
Net assets at end of year	$212,190	$185,087

Case 30

Grittania Limited

You have recently completed the audit fieldwork of Grittania Limited (GL), a wholesaler of a highly specialized line of electrical components. The company commenced operations on January 1, 1987, at which time your firm was appointed auditor.

GL is a public company, although its shares are not heavily traded. To date, the company's operations have been reasonably successful. In the last year, income has increased from $2 million to $2.4 million, and sales from $20 million to $24 million. Management is convinced that they are reasonably well established in their market niche. This optimistic assessment is made with caution, however, as the market is competitive and price sensitive. GL has priced their goods based on cost, taking a lower markup than their major competitors.

The president of GL has just concluded a meeting with you and the partner-in-charge of the audit, to tie up the loose ends on the 1988 financial statements prior to an audit committee meeting next week.

During this meeting, he informed you that one of the agenda items for the audit committee meeting was current cost accounting. The president was aware that the CICA had a statement on the subject, but that it was not applicable to companies of GL's size. Instead, the president wanted to deal with the broader implications of accounting measurement models to see if GL could benefit from the information in any way.

Therefore, he plans to start a discussion in the audit committee as to the usefulness of current cost data for internal management reporting and/or external financial reporting. He has asked for your thoughts on this, including the likely limitations and problems.

Adapted, with permission, from the *Uniform Final Examination Handbook*, 1977 © The Canadian Institute of Chartered Accountants. Changes to the original question and suggested approaches to answering are the sole responsibility of the authors and have not been reviewed or endorsed by the CICA.

The president had his internal accounting staff redraft the income statement on a current cost basis, using the nominal dollar (money) as a measuring unit and productive capacity as the capital maintenance concept (Exhibit 1). These statements will also be discussed at the audit committee meeting.

He has asked you, before the meeting, to prepare a second set of financial statements, reflecting financial capital as the capital maintenance concept using the purchasing power unit as the unit of measure (round to the nearest $1,000). The president plans to compare the two statements at the meeting, and decide which is best for GL. He has indicated that he may wish to publish such a statement in the company's annual report, in order to show the company's employees and shareholders (as well as the government) what the "true" earnings of the company are. He believes this would help avoid what he considers to be excessive salary demands, excessive bonuses (based on income) and an unfair tax burden.

Required

Prepare the material requested by the president for the meeting, as well as material to aid you in the president's planned discussions.

GRITTANIA LTD.
Balance Sheets
as at December 31
(in thousands)

	Historical Cost		Current Replacement Cost	
	1988	*1987*	*1988*	*1987*
Assets				
Cash	$ 6,400	$ 3,000	$ 6,400	$ 3,000
Inventory (FIFO)	2,600	2,000	2,800	2,600
Plant and equipment (net)	4,000	8,000	5,332	9,334
	$13,000	$13,000	$14,532	$14,934
Liabilities and Shareholders' Equity				
Bond @ 10%	$ 4,000	$ 4,000	$ 4,000	$ 4,000
Share capital	9,000	9,000	9,000	9,000
	$13,000	$13,000	$13,000	$13,000

(*continued*)

	Historical Cost		Current Replacement Cost	
	1988	1987	1988	1987
Revaluation account:				
Holding gains, current year (net of backlog)	—	—	$ 2,532	$ 5,600
Balance at beginning of year . . .	—	—	5,600	—
Balance at end of year	—	—	$ 8,132	$ 5,600
Retained earnings (deficit):				
Balance beginning of year	—	—	$(3,666)	—
Net income (loss) for year	$ 2,400	$ 2,000	(534)	$(1,666)
Dividends	(2,400)	(2,000)	(2,400)	(2,000)
	—	—	$(6,600)	$(3,666)
	$13,000	$13,000	$14,532	$14,934

GRITTANIA LTD.
Income Statements
For Year Ended December 31
(in thousands)

	Historical Cost		Current Replacement Cost	
	1988	1987	1988	1987
Sales.	$24,000	$20,000	$24,000	$20,000
Cost of goods sold	12,400	10,000	14,000	13,000
Gross margin	$11,600	$10,000	$10,000	$ 7,000
Depreciation	$ 4,000	$ 4,000	$ 5,334	$ 4,666
Interest on bonds	400	400	400	400
Other expenses	4,800	3,600	4,800	3,600
	$ 9,200	$ 8,000	$10,534	$ 8,666
Net income (loss) for the year . . .	$ 2,400	$ 2,000	$ (534)	$(1,666)

Note to Current Replacement Cost Financial Statements

Principles of Valuation: The current replacement costs of inventories and of plant and equipment are shown on the balance sheet, and earnings are determined by matching current costs with current revenues. Adjustments of the historical cost of physical assets to their current replacement costs are considered as revaluations of shareholders' equity and are shown on the balance sheet.

Current replacement cost is the lowest amount that would have to be incurred

(continued)

in the normal course of business to obtain an asset of equivalent operating capacity.

You are given the following additional data related to the preparation of the current replacement cost financial statements:

1. Inventory: Inventory is valued at replacement cost at the end of the year at the following prices per unit: 1988—$700; $1987—$650. There were 4,000 units on hand at the end of years 1988 and 1987.
2. Plant and Equipment: Used plant and equipment was purchased on January 1, 1987 for $12,000,000 and had a remaining useful life of only three years. For the historical cost financial statements, Grittania Ltd. is writing off the cost on a straight-line basis over three years commencing January 1, 1987. Land is rented and the rental cost is included in other expenses.

   The current replacement cost of plant and equipment is based on independent appraisals, and the amounts are as follows:

	As at December 31	
	1988	1987
Replacement cost (new) . . .	$16,000,000	$14,000,000

   Depreciation in the current replacement cost financial statements is based on end-of-year replacement costs.

   1988 Holding Gains of $3,200,000 are shown net of backlog depreciation of $668,000, or $2,532,000.
3. Bonds: There was no change in the market rate of interest over the two-year period. The bond interest accrues evenly during the year.
4. Share Capital: Shareholders contributed $9,000,000 on January 1, 1987 when Grittania Ltd. was formed. No further contributions have been made.
5. Sales: Sales occurred evenly throughout the year. In 1988 and 1987, 20,000 units were sold at the following prices per unit (all sales are made at prices prevailing at the beginning of each year): 1988—$1,200; 1987—$1,000.
6. Purchases: Purchases were made evenly throughout the year, at prices prevailing at the beginning of each year. The supplier changes his prices on January 1 of each year. The following purchases were made:

	During	
	1988	1987
1987 = 24,000 at $500 =		$12,000,000
1988 = 20,000 at $650 =	$13,000,000	

7. Cost of Goods Sold: For reasons of simplicity the value of goods sold in the current replacement cost financial statements is based on the replacement value at the end of the year.
8. Other Expenses: These relate to monetary items and accrue evenly during the year.
9. Dividends: Dividends are declared and paid at the end of each year.

(continued)

Additional Information

GNE implicit price index   180 January 1, 1987
                                 190 December 31, 1987
                                 210 December 31, 1988

Factors (rounded) $\dfrac{210}{190} = 1.11$ $\dfrac{210}{200} = 1.05$

$$\dfrac{210}{180} = 1.17 \quad \dfrac{190}{180} = 1.06$$

Habitant Inc.

Habitant Inc. is a federally incorporated entity engaged in the merchandising business. Its retail department stores sell an extensive range of products. Habitant has never issued shares to the public or obtained debt financing through a public offering. The company's long-term debt was equal to approximately 26 percent of its total assets at January 31, 1988.

At January 31, 1988, the head office was located in Toronto and there were 93 stores in Ontario, Quebec, the Atlantic provinces and the four Western provinces. The Habitant stores were either operated by the company or franchised to dealers. Recent expansion had been by way of franchises, and as of January 31, 1988, 31 of the Habitant stores were franchised.

The terms of a typical franchise agreement are summarized in Exhibit 1.

Habitant has asked you, their new chief accountant, to examine the issue of when they should recognize the revenue associated with their franchise agreements. Your report is to be used for discussion at the next board of directors meeting, and should analyse the issues with reference to the *CICA Guideline,* "Franchise Fee Revenue." (Exhibit 2.) It *must* discuss the concepts underlying revenue recognition behind the guideline, and provide recommendations.

Required

Prepare the report.

EXHIBIT 1   Terms of Franchise Agreement

1. The initial fee ranges from $70,000–$150,000, depending on the location. Twenty percent of this is to be paid in cash on signing the contract. The remainder consists of noninterest-bearing notes, due in equal installments over four years, with the first payment due 12 months after the franchise is opened.

2. Habitant is entitled to an additional 2¾ percent of gross revenue of the franchisee, for advertising, product development, and so on.

3. The franchisee buys most of its inventory from Habitant. Habitant does not wholesale goods to any other "outside" retail outlets. Corporate head office feels that they sell to their franchisees at prices that are about 5 percent lower than they (the franchisees) could otherwise get. This is due to the bulk buying power of Habitant. An average franchise buys $250,000 of merchandise from Habitant in a year.

4. The initial franchise fee paid is refunded (except for a $5,000 flat fee) by Habitant Inc., if, for some reason, the deal "goes sour" and the franchisee does not open a Habitant outlet.

5. The franchise agreement commits Habitant to do the following for the franchisee:
   a. Assist in location choice.
   b. Help negotiate lease.
   c. Provide building plans and specifications.
   d. Help choose a contractor.
   e. Arrange financing of the building.
   f. Provide and finance store fixtures.
   g. Supervise construction.
   h. Provide assistance for the start-up period.
   i. Set up accounting records.
   j. Provide expert advice over the first five years in merchandise control, training, and promotion.
   These services mentioned in item (j) would cost the franchisee on average $8,000–$9,000 in total if they were done on a fee-for-service basis.

6. Store fixtures are sold to franchisees on a delayed payment scheme. They are paid for over six years, and Habitant keeps title to the fixtures until the last payment is made, at which time they belong to the franchisee.

7. All franchisees would be able to borrow at 10 percent from chartered banks. To date, there have been no defaults on notes payable from franchisees.

EXHIBIT 2   Accounting Guideline, Franchise Fee Revenue, *CICA Handbook[1]*

Introduction

1. This Accounting Guideline provides guidance on the recognition and disclosure of franchise fee revenue.[2]

2. A franchise is a contractual privilege, often exclusive, granted by one party (the franchisor) to another (the franchisee) permitting the sale of a product, use of a trade name or rendering of a service in a single outlet at a specified location (individual franchise) or in a number of outlets within a specified territory (area franchise). The rights and responsibilities of each party are usually set out in a franchise agreement which normally outlines specific marketing practices to be followed, specifies the contribution of each party to the operation of the business, and sets forth certain operating procedures.

3. Most franchise agreements require the franchisee to pay an initial franchise fee as consideration for establishing the franchise relationship and for initial services provided by the franchisor. The initial services may include assistance in site selection; in obtaining facilities and related financing, architectural and engineering services; in advertising; in personnel training; in administration and record-keeping; and in quality control programmes. Occasionally, the initial fee includes consideration for tangible assets, such as initially required equipment or inventory. These items, however, are usually the subject of separate consideration.

4. Continuing franchise fees represent the consideration for the continuing rights granted by the franchise agreement and for general or specific services to be provided by the franchisor during the life of the franchise.

Revenue Recognition

Initial Franchise Fees

5. Revenue from initial franchise fees relating to the sale of an individual franchise or an area franchise would ordinarily be recognized, with an appropriate provision for estimated uncollectible amounts, when all material conditions relating to the sale have been substantially performed by the franchisor. Substantial performance is considered to have occurred when:
   a. The franchisor has performed substantially all of the initial services required by the franchise agreement or volunteered by the franchisor as a result of normal business practice.
   b. The franchisor has no remaining obligation or intent—by agreement, industry practice or legislation—to refund amounts received or forgive unpaid amounts owing.
   c. There are no other material unfulfilled conditions affecting completion of the sale.
   In practice, these conditions will not normally be met before the franchisee commences operations.

*   *   *   *   *

EXHIBIT 2 *(continued)*

---

7. Franchise agreements may be structured so that the consideration received by the franchisor for establishing the franchise relationship and for providing initial services includes notes receivable. If the notes receivable bear an interest rate below the market interest rate at the date of sale, discounting may be considered as an aid in their valuation and hence in the determination of the amount of franchise fee revenue to be recognized. If the notes are receivable over an extended period of time and there is no reasonable basis for estimating collectibility of the notes, revenue would be recognized using either the installment or cost recovery method.[3]

8. When an initial franchise fee includes consideration for tangible assets, such as initially required equipment and inventory, it would be appropriate to recognize the fair value of the tangible assets as revenue when title to them has passed. The balance of the fee, relating to services, would be recognized as revenue when the conditions in paragraph 5 have been met.

9. Sometimes, the initial franchise fee is large but continuing franchise fees are small in relation to future services. When it is probable that continuing fees will not cover the costs of the franchisor's continuing services and provide a reasonable profit on those continuing services, it would be appropriate for a portion of the initial franchise fee to be deferred and amortized over the life of the franchise. The amount deferred should be sufficient to cover estimated costs in excess of continuing franchise fees and provide a reasonable profit on continuing services.

*   *   *   *   *

Continuing Franchise Fees

12. Continuing franchise fees would be recognized as revenue in the period in which the services are rendered.

Agency Sales

13. A franchisor may engage in transactions in which the franchisor is, in substance, an agent for the franchisee by placing orders for inventory, supplies and equipment which are then sold to the franchisee at no profit. Such transactions would be accounted for as receivables and payables and not as revenues and expenses in the financial statements of the franchisor.

Franchising Costs

14. Costs directly related to the sale of a franchise for which revenue has not been recognized would be deferred until the related revenue is recognized. The amount of costs deferred would not exceed expected revenue in excess of estimated additional related costs. Indirect costs of a regular and recurring

---

EXHIBIT 2 *(concluded)*

---

nature that are incurred regardless of the level of franchise sales would be expensed as incurred.

*   *   *   *   *

Disclosure

17. The notes to the financial statements would disclose the method of accounting for revenue from franchise fees.

18. Initial franchise fees would be segregated from continuing franchise fees. If it is probable that revenue from initial franchise fees will decline in the future because sales of franchises predictably reach a saturation point, it may be appropriate to disclose this fact in the financial statements.

19. Revenue and costs related to franchisor-owned outlets would be distinguished from revenue and costs related to franchised outlets. The number of franchises sold and acquired during the period, and the number of franchisor-owned and franchised outlets in operation at the end of the period would also be disclosed.

20. The following disclosures would also be appropriate:

    a. The amount of revenue deferred and related deferred costs; and
    b. The particulars of any significant commitments and obligations resulting from franchise agreements (see *Contractual Obligations,* Section 3280).

---

[1] Reprinted, with permission, from the *CICA Handbook,* Canadian Institute of Chartered Accountants, Toronto, Canada.

[2] *Revenue,* Section 3400, issued in September 1986, sets out the general principles governing recognition and disclosure of revenue.

[3] Under the installment method, the gross profit related to the sale is recognized proportionately with actual cash collections of the notes receivable. Under the cost recovery method, equal amounts of revenue and expense are recognized as cash collections are made until all costs have been recovered, thus postponing any recognition of gross profit until that time.

Case 32

Hartford Mills Corporation

Recently, as the auditor for Hartford Mills Corporation, you sat in on a board meeting where the presentation of the current year financial statements was being discussed. Jim MacInnes, the president, started the discussion about the income statement (Exhibit 1). "Well, gentlemen, we sure haven't met our net income target this year. Net income of $60,000 is well below our budget figure of $100,000."

Frank Harvey, the corporate secretary, added "That's certainly true. I notice one of the items on the income statement is an $80,000 gain from settlement of litigation. If it weren't for that, we'd have done much worse."

Jim replied, "If you remember, we sued one of our suppliers when material they shipped turned out to be defective. That was back in 1984, but you know how slow the courts are. At least they came through in a year when we needed it!"

Another board member spoke up, "What about this extraordinary item? It says 'Loss on the bankruptcy of a major customer—net of applicable income tax of $40,000.'"

"Yes, that's the result of the Hardley Company bankruptcy. When they went into receivership, they owed us a lot of money. We've classified the loss as extraordinary because we feel it's a nonrecurring item in the evaluation of our business. After all, major customers don't go bankrupt every day!"

Frank added, "We got a good price for that piece of land, though."

"Indeed!" smiled Jim. "When we bought that piece of land we never had any intention of reselling it. It was to be used for our factory expansion program. But an offer of $220,000 on land that cost $70,000 seemed too good a deal to pass up!"

"Where's that gain?" someone asked. "I don't see it here anywhere."

"Oh," replied Jim. "It's part of 'investment revenue' on the income statement. The land was a long-term investment, so it seemed logical to put the gain there."

"Well, I guess that about covers it, unless our auditor here has anything to say. And listen, if you do, I'd like to see how any change you suggest would affect this statement."

Required

Assume the role of the auditor. Identify the financial accounting issues raised by the above discussion. Provide an analysis of each issue, concluding with your recommendations. If your recommendations differ from the current presentation, redraft the statement(s).

EXHIBIT 1

HARTFORD MILLS CORPORATION
Income Statement and Statement of Retained Earnings
For Year Ended December 31, 1988

Sales	$5,440,000
Cost of goods sold	2,920,000
Gross margin	2,520,000
Selling expenses	600,000
General and administration expenses	1,960,000
Other income:	
Gain on settlement of litigation	80,000
Investment income	160,000
Net expenses	$2,320,000
Income before income tax and extraordinary items	200,000
Provision for income tax	100,000
Income before extraordinary items	100,000
Extraordinary loss on bankruptcy of a major customer (Net of applicable income tax of $40,000)	40,000
Net income	$ 60,000
Retained earnings, January 1	325,000
Retained earnings, December 31	$ 385,000

Helena Cosmetics Corporation

In the early 1970s Helena Cosmetics Corp. (HCC) had acquired some land in Rockville intending eventually to build a warehouse on it. Over the years, however, the company's distribution had changed, and by 1988 management concluded that a warehouse would never be needed at Rockville. Consequently the company sought to sell the land, for which it had paid $60,000. The best cash offer for the land was $170,000, but since an independent valuer hired by HCC had appraised it in April 1988 at $200,000, management was unwilling to accept the cash offer.

The Rockville land was next to a warehouse owned by the Xenon Chemical Company (XCC), one of HCC's regular suppliers of chemicals used to make cosmetics. This company expressed an interest in buying the property to expand its own facilities. XCC was unwilling to pay cash, but offered instead to exchange 250 tons of Type X chemical, to be delivered at the rate of 50 tons per month for five months starting in October. The going market price for this chemical was $1,000 per ton.

HCC typically used more than 50 tons a month of Type X chemical in the manufacture of their normal product line. Normally, orders were placed for delivery not more than two months in future, unless there were firm contracts from customers that required specific products. HCC had no such contracts in the autumn of 1988. After considerable discussion as to the risk involved in the unusually large commitment for this chemical, HCC management finally decided to accept XCC's offer.

The contract was signed on September 13, 1988, and on that day HCC's accountant made the following journal entry, recording the chemical at its

---

Used with permission from Tim Sutton.

market price and showing the differences between this amount and the book value of the land as profit:

dr.	Inventory due from supplier. $250,000	
cr.	Land	$ 60,000
cr.	Gain on sale of land	190,000

During the last three months of 1988, 150 tons of the chemical were received from XCC as promised, and in aggregate the entries made to record these receipts were as follows:

dr.	Chemical inventory $150,000	
cr.	Inventory due from supplier.	$150,000

When he was examining the accounts of HCC for the year ending December 31, 1988, the company's auditor raised questions about this transaction. He pointed out that the net effect of the above entries was that the entire profit on the transaction was shown in 1988, although only 150 tons of chemical had been delivered, of which 100 tons had actually been used in the manufacture of products (50 tons still being on hand in inventory at December 31). Half of the products manufactured from the chemical by December 31 had been sold by that date, of which only half had actually been paid for by the final customer.

A suggested alternative treatment was to split the profit into two parts. One part, $110,000, was the difference between the book value of the land and the best cash offer; this was to be called *profit on price level changes* and shown in the 1988 income statement. The remainder, $80,000, was to be called "gain on sale of land" and divided two fifths to 1988 and three fifths to 1989, representing the fraction of the total chemical consumed each year. The auditor stated that such a separation was not usually made, but neither was this an ordinary transaction.

HCC management disliked the implication in the above treatment that they had not made the $190,000 profit in 1988, especially since the price of Type X chemical had risen to $1,200 per ton by December 31, 1988.

You have been hired by the management of HCC to examine this issue, and present your analysis and recommendations in a report that can be used by the Audit Committee in discussions with the external auditor.

Required

Carry out the assignment.

ICU Lighting Company

The ICU Lighting Company (ICU) has been a valued audit client of Erin, Dale & Co., Chartered Accountants, for many years. The principal challenge with this client, over the years, has been one of trying to keep up with the firm's very bright and aggressive VP of finance, Ian M. Beaming.

ICU is a fairly closely held Canadian public company that manufactures various types of light bulbs with its major seller, in recent years, being long life fluorescent tubes. Sales are made directly to larger commercial consumers; however, the bulk of ICU's product is sold to retail firms that market the bulbs to various types of consumers, often using high-pressure, telephone-selling techniques including offers of promotional gifts as incentives to buy. Generally, the competition in the light bulb manufacturing industry is fierce as a result of the similarity of the various bulb products on the market. However, as a result of the fact that ICU has invested heavily in research and development and quality control over the years, Beaming feels that their product is the best available on the market. Many retailers seem to agree and have been willing to pay the premium price that ICU charges for their product. Ian Beaming has always advocated that although ICU is a manufacturer, its success or failure hinges on their ability to inform the market of the quality of their product. Sales volume, rather than production volume, is what he sees as the best indicator of the firm's well-being. ICU's sales force has done well over the past few years, with sales growing rapidly and profitability approaching almost embarrassing levels at times.

Careful planning has always been stressed at ICU and, consequently, inventory levels have been consistently kept to a minimum. More recently, they have come to the conclusion that sales orders are being lost as a result of slow shipment and, consequently, inventory levels are being raised. The capital intensive nature of the production has resulted, traditionally, in total production costs that include a significant amount of

Adapted, with permission from Mike Longworth.

factory overhead costs. As it happens, the increasing degree of mechanization over the years has been a sensitive issue with the national union of which ICU's production workers are members. At ICU they have always followed a policy of including a pro rata share of fixed factory overhead (plant and equipment depreciation, superintendents' and foremen's salaries and office expenses, maintenance staff wages and supplies and product development costs) in its product cost. This full or absorption costing procedure has never really been discussed before with the auditors; however, this year Ian Beaming has decided that he would like to exclude the fixed portion of factory overhead from product cost treating it as a period cost.

As partner in charge of the ICU audit, you have dealt with Ian Beaming before and realize that he delights in outsmarting the auditors and, perhaps, at times, the statement readers as well. Beaming feels that this direct or variable method of product costing makes sense from the point of view of accounting logic and, also, very much so from a practical point of view. ICU is facing various situations currently, including shareholder demands for increasing dividend payout, labour demands for a fair share of what they see as excessive profits, and retail distributors' concerns over the validity of the premium they are paying for ICU bulbs. Not only are inventory levels rising as a percentage of total production volume but, also, ICU is likely to embark on a major plant expansion and modernization within the next couple of years. As Beaming sees it, the lower levels of plant utilization in the years that follow this expansion and the increased degree of capital intensity will tend to accentuate the downward pressure that direct costing will have on profitability. It was obvious at your recent meeting with Beaming that he had, as usual, done his homework. He first addressed the practical advantages of variable costing as he saw them and then proceeded to give you the following list of points in support of his position:

1. The *CICA Handbook* (Section 3030.06) requires that for work-in-progress and finished goods inventories, cost should include the applicable share of overhead expenses properly chargeable to production but does not specifically define overhead expense as necessarily including the fixed portion of factory overhead.
2. Examples of variable costing, in one form or another, can certainly be found in Canada; for example, Crown Zellerback Canada Limited, T.G. Bright & Co. Limited, Kaiser Resources Ltd., and Daisyfresh Creations Inc. These companies cited are involved in various industries, so one should not see variable costing as an industry peculiarity.
3. Although produced some time ago, a still applicable CICA Accounting Research Study, *Overheads as an Element of Inventory Costs,* includes the following comments concerning the various relevant Canadian, U.S. and U.K. pronouncements:

It is obvious that these pronouncements appear to allow such wide latitude in the determination of the manufacturing overhead to be included for purposes of inventory costing that they do little to promote a uniform accounting treatment for commercial enterprises generally or even among companies in the same industry.

4. When it comes to the accounting logic involved there are two questions to be answered. The first, which pertains to income measurement, is whether fixed factory overhead costs are a period cost or a product cost. There are certain costs which, by their nature, expire with the passage of time, regardless of production activity. They are incurred for the benefit of operations during a given period of time. The benefit is unchanged by the actual level of operations, if any, during that period, and it expires at the end of the period in any event. Surely this description applies to fixed factory overhead costs, and given that they have expired, they should be expensed as a period cost. Also, with respect to income measurement, variable costing achieves an appropriate matching of costs with related revenues. Profits do not accrue on a unit basis, and no income is realized in a period until the fixed costs (including factory overheads) incurred in that period are recovered. If it is accepted that no income is realized until factory overhead costs of the period are recovered, then a relationship does exist between the revenues of the period and the current factory overhead costs and, therefore, the charging of such costs to revenue on a time basis would achieve a matching of costs and related revenues.

   The second relevant question concerns asset measurement with a choice being required between a "cost obviation concept" and a "revenue production concept" of service potential. Assets (at least those that are nonmonetary) by definition are seen as bundles of service potential from which the company will reap some future economic benefit. Assets have service potential to the extent that they avert the necessity for incurring costs in the future. The production of goods for inventory in one period enables ICU to realize some revenue in a subsequent period without reincurring the variable costs of producing that inventory, but the availability of inventory completed in one period does not forestall the incurrence of, or in effect obviate, any fixed costs in a subsequent period. Hence, variable costs are relevant to future periods, but fixed costs are not. This cost obviation approach to asset valuation is consistent with direct costing, which calls for fixed overheads to be treated as period costs. Aside from the income and asset measurement consideration, there is the concern that, especially in this business, profit is only realized through sales. Therefore, accounting rules should be designed so that income reported in the financial statements will also fluctuate in step with sales and only with sales. Under absorption costing, profits reported are influenced not only by the level of sales but also by the level of production. It is hard to accept the fact that for a period with a given level of sales a company can reflect more profit simply by producing more goods, regardless of the fact that they would have produced the goods next period and not adversely have affected sales in any way.

   Finally, from a theoretical point of view, there are serious weaknesses in any arbitrary allocation—for example, one which involves the spreading to each product those costs which are really common to several manufactured products. One of the benefits of expensing research and most of development costs was that some of the incorrigible, arbitrary allocations were being removed from the determination of income. Does using variable costing not tend to do the same thing?

5. ICU's financial statements must be useful to external readers. The variable costing income statement shows directly relationships between costs and volume and makes net income a function of sales volume to the exclusion of production volume. This type of information has been considered essential by management for years and, therefore, should assist our shareholders and other statement readers as well. These readers are part of the efficient market and are, therefore, quite capable of comprehending the significant relationships within the statement.

   Additional disclosure could be given in the notes to the statements concerning the nature of fixed overhead costs expensed in the period and, surely, this plus the more meaningful gross profit figure in the income statement (that is indicative of the trading profit contribution available to meet all other expenses) would be more useful to the readers either in their attempts to predict future performance (and resultant cash flows) or to assess the quality of management's stewardship over the firm's assets.

6. The current cost rules seem to require, in effect, the inclusion of all costs of production (variable and fixed) in inventory valuation by calling for the use of current replacement cost. However, ICU is not so large that we need to present such supplementary current cost information and we do not intend to do so. Besides, the current cost proposed recommendations are not really relevant to the resolution of an accounting issue such as this under the traditional historic cost model.

   You have been inundated, to say the least, by the reasons which I. M. Beaming has gathered to make his case for variable costing. He seems to have covered off most of the areas that should concern you; that is, as dictated by pronouncements and practice, theoretical considerations and relevance to objectives of financial reporting. He has, in fact, tended to play down ICU's immediate objectives in suppressing income to some degree. He has not asked you to bend the rules so that his firm might prosper but, rather, has asked you to accept the change to variable costing because it is in fact a sound, accepted method of product costing.

Required

As the partner in charge of the ICU audit, respond to Ian Beaming's presentation.

Independent Grape Growers (IGG)

Independent Grape Growers (IGG) is a partnership of 125 grape growers in Canada. The partnership was formed in January 1988. In February 1988, the partnership signed a 10-year building lease, bought equipment and supplies, and hired its first employees. Your employer, CA, was auditor for its first fiscal period ended June 30, 1988. There were no sales or sales-related expenses in this period. No depreciation was recorded because, according to management, the assets had not been used for productive purposes. No significant accounting policies had been adopted for the 1988 fiscal period.

Your employer, CA, has been reappointed auditor the year ended June 30, 1989. He has also been engaged to help select suitable financial accounting policies.

CA has asked you to prepare a preliminary report on accounting policies which identifies the major issues, evaluates alternatives, and presents your recommendations. CA will use this report in his discussions with the management and owners of IGG.

In August 1989, you visited IGG's offices and obtained the information in Exhibit 1.

Required

Prepare the report requested by CA.

Adapted, with permission from the *Uniform Final Examination Report,* 1983. © The Canadian Institute of Chartered Accountants, Toronto.

Changes to the original question and/or suggested approach to answering are the sole responsibility of the authors and have not been reviewed or endorsed by the CICA.

EXHIBIT 1 Information on IGG

1. The partners deliver their grapes to IGG where they are graded. Based on the grading, the decision is made as to which grapes will be sold fresh and which will be processed into grape juice, frozen concentrated juice, grape jelly, wine, or other products. IGG sells the fresh grapes to other wineries and to grocery chains. The harvest and fresh grape sales occur in late summer but IGG sells its processed items throughout the year. IGG carries large inventories and has made no decisions on cost flow assumptions or the elements of inventory cost.

2. Partners are credited with 80 percent of the market value of their harvest when they deliver it to IGG. Actual cash disbursement of this amount is to be made in installments of one third each on the following dates: December 31, March 31, and June 30.

    The partners are to receive a cash payment on September 30 for their share of IGG's income for the previous fiscal year. For purposes of the computation of this payment, IGG's partners want to use the annual financial statement income figure. However, they would like accounting policies that give consideration to the cyclical nature of their activities and cash flows as well as those of IGG. They do not want to make any withdrawals that will reduce the capital that is needed to maintain the business.

3. Partnership units can be sold only with the approval of the other partners. The value of partnership units is determined based on the June 30 financial statement results. New partners are admitted on this date.

4. Managers are entitled to bonuses totaling 15 percent of the operating income of the partnership. Bonuses are allocated to individual managers through a point system based on their past experience and performance.

5. IGG borrows funds when inventories and receivables are high, during the autumn and winter period. The bank requires audited annual financial statements. IGG's loan was at its highest level of $12.5 million in early January 1989. The current interest rate is 13 percent per annum. The loan is secured by inventories, receivables, and the guarantees of the partners.

6. IGG operates from a building that houses the facilities for processing, warehousing, wine storage, and administration.

7. IGG's wines will be aged for no more than two years before sale to government liquor stores. Specialized processing equipment is used in winemaking.

8. A portion of sales of nonwine products is made on long-term contracts to grocery chains. For these contracts, cash is usually not received until 120 days after delivery. Other customers pay in cash or within 30 days. IGG's managers project a steady increase in the number of noncontract customers over the next five years.

9. The market for jams and jellies was weak at June 30, 1989. Customers were offering to buy at $4 per kilogram, but IGG would not sell below its estimated cost of $6 per kilogram. In August 1989, the offering price had dropped to $3.50 per kilogram.

EXHIBIT 1   *(concluded)*

---

10. Extracts from the unaudited financial statements of IGG at June 30, 1989, are as follows:

A. Packaging material, jars, boxes and similar
   products on hand . . . . $ 186,230

B. Inventories:
   Wine (1,500,000 bottle equivalent) $2,000,000
   Jams and jellies (100,000 kg)   600,000
   Raisins (800,000 kg)   1,120,000
   Pie fillings (200,000 kg)   410,000
   Juice (800,000 l)   400,000
   Sugar (100,000 kg)   70,000

C. Prepaid lease . . . . $ 10,000

D. Unearned revenue. Deposit on sale of 150,000 kg of
   raisins at $1.00 per kilogram, to be delivered in
   November 1989 . . . . $ 25,000

E. Bonus payable to managers . . . . $ 210,000

F. Balance due to partners for grape harvest $7,462,000

G. Interest and storage charges related to wine inventory
   currently on hand . . . . $ 317,600

Case 36

INCO/CWWE

One of your business associates has recently become interested in investing in common stocks of Canadian companies. In the process of learning more about the sophisticated analysis of financial data, your associate has come across supplemental information on the effects of changing prices in some of the annual reports that she is reviewing. While some of the companies attempt to explain the meaning of the supplemental data, the explanations frequently are not very clear and the data are presented in a variety of formats.

Your associate has come to you with two extracts from the changing prices information of Inco Limited (Exhibit 1) and Canadian Worldwide Energy Limited (Exhibit 2). She would like you to explain some aspects of the information to her. First, she would like to know how it can happen that Inco had a loss of $70 million in 1985 under current cost reporting while the historical cost earnings amounted to a profit of $52 million. She finds this difference in results quite surprising in view of the very low rate of inflation that prevailed in 1985. Second, she is quite surprised that Canadian Worldwide Energy Limited's 1985 net earnings are significantly greater under current cost ($5,053,000) than under historical cost ($3,531,000). Third, she would like to know what the financing adjustments are. And fourth, she would like to understand the meaning of operating capacity capital maintenance and whether either or both companies have been able to maintain their operating capacity in 1985 from the viewpoint of the common shareholders.

Required

Write a letter to your associate in which you explain the issues that she has raised.

_____

Institute of Chartered Accountants of Ontario, adapted.

EXHIBIT 1

INCO LIMITED AND SUBSIDIARIES
Statement of Operations Adjusted for Changing Prices
Year Ended December 31
(in millions)

As reported in the primary statements (historical/nominal dollars)			Adjusted for specific price changes (current cost—average 1985 dollars)	
1985	1984		1985	1984
$1,525	$1,516	Net sales and other income	$1,525	$1,570
1,205	1,317	Cost of sales and operating expenses	1,322	1,443
90	101	Selling, general and administrative expenses*	93	107
22	22	Research and development*	23	25
17	16	Exploration*	18	19
102	122	Interest	102	126
(13)	(7)	Currency translation adjustments	(13)	(7)
$1,423	$1,571		$1,545	$1,713
$ 102	$ (55)	Earnings (loss) before income and mining taxes	$ (20)	$ (143)
50	22	Income and mining taxes	50	22
$ 52	$ (77)	Net earnings (loss)	$ (70)	$ (165)
$143	$140	* Includes depreciation and depletion, which totaled	$279	$288

Financing adjustments based on:
Changes in current cost of inventories and property and
  equipment . . . . $ 44 $ (52)
Current cost adjustment to income . . . . $ 41 $ 25

Gain from decline in purchasing power of net amounts owed $ 53 $ 61

Increase (decrease) in specific prices (current cost) of inventories and property, plant and equipment held
during the year† . . . . $ 121 $ (140)
Effect of change in general price level 154   175
Excess of change in general price level over specific prices $ 33 $ 315

† At December 31, 1985, current cost of inventories was $770 million (1984—$763 million in December 1985 dollars) and property, plant, and equipment net of accumulated depreciation was $3,371 million (1984—$3,558 million in December 1985 dollars). Net assets (common shareholders' equity) on a current cost basis was $2,521 million at year-end 1985 (1984—$2,525 million in December 1985 dollars).

EXHIBIT 2

CANADIAN WORLDWIDE ENERGY LIMITED
Consolidated Statement of Earnings
(on an operating capability concept)
(in thousands)

	Historical Cost	Current Cost (year-end 1985)	
	1985	1985	1984
Sales	$ 42,958	$ 43,757	$ 41,123
Oil and gas operating costs	10,495	10,690	10,590
Gas purchases	2,469	2,515	2,844
Depreciation, depletion and amortization .	13,200	15,538	13,491
General and administration	4,614	4,700	4,982
Interest	5,849	5,958	6,277
	$ 36,627	$ 39,401	$ 38,184
Earnings before taxes and other items . .	6,331	4,356	2,939
Deferred income taxes	2,800	2,800	1,715
Net earnings before financing adjustment .	3,531	1,556	1,224
Financing adjustment		3,497	1,433
Net earnings	$ 3,531	$ 5,053	$ 2,657
Selected consolidated assets:			
Inventories	$ 1,057	$ 1,057	$ 601
Property, plant and equipment—net . .	108,085	129,791	100,536
Net assets (shareholders' equity)	42,891	64,597	45,373
Other information:			
Increase in current cost amounts of property, plant and equipment attributed to:			
Industry price changes		6,832	2,790
General inflation		5,958	3,784
General purchasing power gain on net monetary liabilities		2,402	1,730
Financing adjustments:			
a. Based on the change in current cost of property, plant and equipment		3,497	1,433
b. Based on current cost adjustments for depreciation and depletion		1,197	1,168

J.J. Ltd.

J.J. Ltd. was incorporated in January 1990 by John Jamieson and Allan MacKenzie, computer science graduates who had met while working in the New Product Division at IBM. J.J.'s initial financing included a low-interest loan from Jamieson's wife, Margaret, of $80,000. In addition, each of the two partners purchased one share for $10,000 per share, and the Royal Bank extended the company a working capital loan of $10,000 (a total of $110,000).

Jamieson and MacKenzie had left IBM after 10 years' employment there for several reasons. One of them was the desire to enjoy the challenge of running their own business, but more important was their wish to complete a project on which both had worked at IBM. This project had been dropped from further development by the computer giant.

The product, Inter Act, was a program which people with little computer training could use to write their own programs—it was a question and answer format which converted nontechnical responses into computer code, thereby eliminating the need to hire a programmer.

Because John and Allan had worked on Inter Act for so many years there was very little development work left to do. The partners felt that IBM had tried to produce a product for sophisticated business and scientific usage when in reality potential purchasers would come from smaller firms which could not afford to support a computer department. By October 1990 five contracts had been signed between J.J. Ltd. and purchasers to buy Inter Act early in 1991 for $6,000 each; the contracts would be void if Inter Act was not delivered by March 31, 1991.

During 1990 J.J. Ltd. incurred the following costs:

Salaries for John and Allan, $2,000 per month each, starting May 1	$32,000
Promotional literature and mailing costs	2,000
Attendance at computer shows in Toronto, Montreal and Vancouver (registration fees, hotels, meals, travel)	5,000

Temporary office help, miscellaneous (telephone, etc.) . . . . $ 3,750
Interest   900
Rental of premises   24,000
Rental of computer equipment   15,000
                                                                  $82,650

From January to September, John and Allan had worked on developing Inter Act. The proportion of time spent on various stages was as follows:

Product design 15%
Detail program design . . . 20%
Coding and testing 50%

The remaining time was spent at conferences and making contacts with potential customers; J.J. Ltd. now has a mailing list of over 400 firms which have indicated interest in Inter Act.

In December 1990 John met with Katherine Dickson, CA, to obtain some assistance in preparing J.J.'s 1990 financial statements. During the conversation John said,

> Our company has had no operations this year so I'm just preparing a balance sheet. What I want to discuss with you is Al's and my salaries. As you know, we lived on our savings for the first four months, then started paying ourselves below-market incomes. We feel that a more accurate monthly salary would have been $5,000 each (I expect this to increase substantially in 1991 as we sell Inter Act). As a result, I'm going to include $120,000 ($5,000 × 2 people × 12 months) in the balance sheet amount for "Unamortized Computer Software Costs" and add the difference to capital. I'll show the software development as a long-term asset; we're going to need an increase in our working capital loan next year, and I want the bank to see that we intend to be around for a long time!

Required

Present your recommendations for fair presentation of J.J. Ltd.'s position and results during its first year. Suggest any accounting policies that you feel J.J. Ltd. may wish to adopt.

Case 38

Jaded Jeans Limited

Jaded Jeans Limited operates a nationwide chain of clothing stores which cater to young men and women. Jaded Jeans has been trying to obtain space in a new downtown shopping development which is extremely popular with young people. The management of Jaded Jeans feels that it is important for Jaded Jeans to have a presence in this development, even if the cost of obtaining a sublease offsets the potential profits for this location.

Recently, Jaded Jeans was able to negotiate a sublease with Pencil & Paper Ltd. (PP), an office supply firm which leased a 2,000 square foot store in the development. To induce PP to sublet, Jaded Jeans agreed to pay $500,000 to PP immediately. Jaded Jeans is to make the lease payments directly to the mall owner. None of the $500,000 paid to PP will go to the mall owner; the half million dollars will be retained by PP.

Jaded Jeans accounted for the $500,000 payment by charging it directly to expense for the current period. CA, the auditor of Jaded Jeans, objected to Jaded Jeans's treatment of the item and insisted that the payment be capitalized and allocated to the remaining five years of the sublease, preferably by the declining-balance method. CA argued that treating the payment as a current expense would result in mismatching revenue and expense.

The vice president, finance (VP), has countered by arguing that although Jaded Jeans made the payment in expectation of large future revenues and profits from the new location, there was no way that the profits could reliably be predicted (if indeed, they materialized at all). The VP felt that just as the *CICA Handbook,* Section 3450 prescribes that research

Adapted, with permission from the *Uniform Final Examination Handbook,* 1978. © The Canadian Institute of Chartered Accountants.

Changes to the original question and/or suggested approaches to answering are the sole responsibility of the authors and have not been reviewed or endorsed by the CICA.

costs should be charged to expense due to the uncertainty of future benefits, so should Jaded Jeans's payment be charged to expense. The VP also stated that this payment could be written off immediately for income tax purposes and wondered why he could not do the same for accounting purposes.

In addition, the VP cited arguments from accounting literature that financial accounting allocations are inherently arbitrary. Since allocations are arbitrary, he argued, they must therefore be useless at best and misleading at worst.

The VP indicated that he had just finished cleaning up his balance sheet last year by writing off the balance of intangibles and he was not anxious to introduce a major amount again. He indicated that bankers and financial analysts "discount" intangibles anyway.

Finally, the VP pointed out that although CA argued about the importance of matching as an accounting principle, he could not even find it in the topical index of the *CICA Handbook*.

Required

Discuss the arguments presented and state your conclusions.

Case 39

Kerr Addison Mines Limited

North American mining companies have enormous flexibility in deciding how to account for their reserves. The profession has had to balance the need for relevant information on reserves with lack of reliability in estimating reserves.

Accounting for reserves is important for a number of reasons. Proven reserves are frequently the basis for negotiating sales of properties and companies, for arranging financing, for assessing equity securities, and for evaluating managerial and corporate performance.

The "value" of mineral reserves in excess of capitalized exploration and development costs is an "off-balance-sheet" asset; however, reserve estimates impact net income. Depletion of deferred exploration and development costs is calculated by units of production. Thus the reserve calculations are also vital in writing off capitalized costs and in establishing limits on the extent of capitalization. These calculations are complicated by the fact that reserve estimates are constantly being revised.

Estimating mineral reserves and classifying them according to their likelihood of recoverability is a job that requires the training of a mining engineer or geologist. The quality of the estimate depends on such factors as changes in technology, and market conditions affecting either production costs or selling prices (which are volatile). The estimate must also take into consideration likely future changes in recovery rates, dilution rates, and inefficiencies during extraction, processing, and transportation of the metals. Opinions among geologists and engineers will inevitably vary.

In Canada reference to the measurement and disclosure of mining company reserves is found in Section 4510, "Reporting the Effects of Changing Prices." The recommendations state:

Mining

.56 Supplementary information about the effects of changing prices for enterprises that have interests in mineral reserves, other than oil and gas, should include, except in the situation outlined in paragraph 4510.67, the following additional information:

a. Quantities of mineral reserves as at the beginning and the end of the period or as at disclosed dates as close to the beginning and the end of the period as is practicable. Mineral reserves should be computed on a proved basis, or a proved and probable basis, consistent with the basis used for cost amortization purposes.

b. Quantities expressed in physical units or in percentages of reserves, of each significant mineral product contained in the reserves included under subparagraph (a).

c. Changes in the quantities of mineral reserves during the reporting period, separately disclosing changes attributable to each of the following factors:

  i. Revisions of previous estimates.
  ii. Discoveries.
  iii. Purchases of reserves in place.
  iv. Sales of reserves in place.
  v. Reserves used in production.

d. Quantities of each significant mineral product produced during the period.

e. The amount of each of the following types of costs for the current period, whether such costs are capitalized or charged to expense at the time incurred:

  i. Cost of acquiring mineral rights.
  ii. Exploration costs.

.57 When important economic factors or significant uncertainties affect particular components of an enterprise's mineral reserves, it is desirable that management provide an explanation of those factors. Many such factors can arise as a result of the geographic location of the reserves and therefore an analysis of the reserve quantities by location or geographic area may provide an improved understanding of the nature of reserves and changes in reserves.

.58 In respect of the requirements for disclosure of reserve quantities, as set out in paragraph 4510.56, the following definitions apply:

Proved mineral reserves are the estimated quantities of commercially recoverable reserves that, on the basis of geological, geophysical, and engineering data, can be demonstrated with a reasonably high degree of certainty to be recoverable in the future from known mineral deposits by either primary or improved recovery methods.

Probable mineral reserves are the estimated quantities of commercially recoverable reserves that are less well defined than proved reserves and that may be estimated or indicated to exist on the basis of geological, geophysical, and engineering data.

*   *   *   *   *

.67 The reserve quantity and cost information required by paragraphs 4510.56, .59 and .65 need not be disclosed in those rare circumstances when, in the opinion of management, such disclosures would be harmful to the enterprise.

Kerr Addison Mines Limited is a Canadian mining company whose predecessor company was founded over 50 years ago. The initial mine has produced more than 10 million ounces of gold. During its history, the company has owned and operated mines in Canada, the United States, and Ireland and has also diversified into the oil and gas business. At December 31, 1986, Kerr Addison reported total assets of $518,128,000, of which $196,717,000 was property, plant, and equipment ($68,242,000 related to gas and oil properties). Revenue (value of production) for 1986 was $59,259,000 and profit from operations was $1,049,000. Revenue includes the value of production of concentrates, bullion, and metals awaiting settlement, in transit and on hand at estimated net realizable value.

Kerr Addison's 1986 "Report on Mining Operations," which followed the Director's Report in the company's annual report is presented below.

The Kerr Addison Mine

The Kerr Addison gold mine at Virginiatown, Ontario, produced 366,930 tons of ore during 1986, averaging 1,005 tons per day at a recovered grade of 0.118 ounces of gold per ton. Production amounted to 43,415 ounces of gold and 2,100 ounces of silver having a realized value of $21.3 million or $58.15 per ton milled, an increase of 3.9 percent over the previous year. Overall recovery of gold was 97.15 percent. The average price received per ounce of gold sold during the year was Can. $486 compared to $429 in 1985. Improved revenue in 1986 was due entirely to the higher gold prices.

During 1986, 1,939 feet of drifting and raising were completed, 16 percent less than last year. Underground diamond drilling amounted to 9,202 feet comprising 92 hole completions.

Mining operations were carried on in 9 ore zones on 17 levels between the 1,000 and 4,200 foot horizons. A total of 42 stopes were worked during the year. The internal No. 4 shaft provided 8.6 percent of the total ore mined. The tonnage broken by mining method during 1986 was 9 percent square set, 66 percent cut and fill, 22 percent shrinkage and blasthole with the balance of 3 percent coming from development. The carbonate ore zones provided 37 percent of the tonnage mined at a grade of 0.060 ounces of gold per ton with the flow ore zones providing 32 percent at a grade of 0.150 ounces per ton. The balance came from the graphitic ore zone with a grade of 0.166 ounces per ton. The broken ore reserve at year end was 109,814 tons. Backfill placed underground amounted to 177,500 tons containing 2,771 tons of cement.

Total operating costs per ton of ore milled increased by 9.7 percent from 1985 due in part to the lower tonnage of ore mined and treated. Costs per ounce of gold produced increased by 17.3 percent mainly as a result of the lower grade of ore mined. Labour and material costs increased by 2.9 percent and 9.2 percent, respectively, during 1986.

At the end of 1986 the mineable ore reserves with dilution were as follows:

	Tons	Ounces per ton
Proven	692,684	0.108
Probable . . .	263,031	0.145
Total	955,715	0.119

After the milling of 366,930 tons in 1986, total reserves increased by 152,825 tons over those reported at the end of 1985. The substantial tonnage of new ore found during 1986 is mainly in the low-grade carbonate zones resulting in a slightly lower overall ore reserve grade.

*   *   *   *   *

From the start of production in May of 1938 to December 31, 1986, the Kerr Addison mines have milled 37,888,051 tons of ore at a recovered grade of 0.270 ounces of gold per ton producing 10,217,993 ounces of gold and 562,869 ounces of silver.

Corporation Falconbridge Copper

Corporation Falconbridge Copper is a diversified precious and base metal producer comprising four mining divisions in Quebec and Ontario which, during 1986, had three producing operations, Lac Shortt, Lac Dufault and Opemiska and two mines, Ansil and Winston Lake, in the exploration and development stages.

Lac Shortt Division

The Lac Shortt gold mine, in which Corporation Falconbridge Copper holds 94.2 percent interest, is located in Gand Township some 115 kilometres by road west of Chapais, Quebec. During 1986, it treated an average of 1,095 tonnes of ore per day for a total of 399,647 tonnes grading 5.32 grams of gold per tonne, a tonnage increase of 25 percent over that of 1985. The cost per ounce of gold produced was Can. $293 compared to Can. $326 in 1985. The operation contributed $30.9 million to C.F.C.'s total net revenue.

Underground exploration drilling totaled 13,438 metres, a threefold increase over that drilled in 1985. Delineation drilling amounted to 20,420 metres, about the same as in 1985. Underground production development was 4,728 metres of drifting and raising, with an additional 571 metres of exploration drifting being completed.

Two specific underground exploration programs were initiated in 1986. An explorations drift was started on the 250 level to test a gold bearing structure approximately 1,000 metres west of the mine workings, and a crosscut was commenced north into the hanging wall on the 500 level to test extension of the main orebody below the 500 level. It is hoped that both programs, which are expected to be completed during the third quarter of 1987, will add materially to the ore reserve picture.

Diluted ore reserves in all classifications at December 31, 1986 were estimated at 1,552,000 tonnes having a grade of 4.90 grams of gold per tonne. New reserves of 112,000 tonnes grading 4.22 grams per tonne were insufficient to replace the 399,647 tonnes milled during the year.

*   *   *   *   *

Opemiska Division

The Opemiska Division located at Chapais, Quebec, consists of three underground mines, the Springer, Cooke, and Perry. Production during 1986 totaled 507,732 tons grading 1.22 percent and 0.087 ounces gold per ton with Springer contributing 46 percent, Cooke 38 percent, and Perry 16 percent. Metal production amounted to 12 million pounds of copper, 39,586 ounces of gold, and 112,825 ounces of silver having a net revenue of $25.5 million. Owing to diminishing reserves this performance represents a 25 percent reduction from the previous year. A further reduction of 12 percent is forecasted for 1987. A strike at Noranda's Horne smelter forced the division to stockpile its copper concentrate production at the mine site from November 1986 through February 1987.

Underground exploration and ore definition diamond drilling totaled 233,467 feet, a 20 percent reduction from 1985. Exploration development advance totaled 34,364 feet compared to 35,666 feet in 1985.

At December 31, 1986, the diluted, proven and probable reserves were estimated at 731,000 tons grading 1.52 percent copper and 0.084 ounces of gold per ton, about the same as at the end of 1985. The reserves at the Springer and Cooke mines remain essentially unchanged from 1985 at 740,000 tons grading 1.5 percent copper and 0.086 ounces of gold per ton. New proven and probable reserves delineated in 1986 totaled 419,000 tons grading 1.5 percent copper and 0.08 ounces of gold per ton. . . .

*   *   *   *   *

Lac Dufault Division

The Corbet mine of the Lac Dufault Division, located 15 kilometres north of Noranda, Quebec terminated operations in September of 1986 following exhaustion of reserves. By year-end the mine had been decommissioned and sealed. Production for the year, which was treated in the Norbec mill, amounted to 381,504 tons grading 2.57 percent copper and 1.37 percent zinc producing 19 million pounds of copper, 7 million pounds of zinc, 7,363 ounces of gold and 131,861 ounces of silver. Net revenue amounted to $15.2 million.

Corporation Falconbridge Copper has a nonparticipating 30 percent interest in the Mobrun deposit, operated by Audrey Resources Inc. The deposit is located approximately 18 kilometres north of the Norbec mill in which 86,689 tons of Mobrun ore were treated during the fourth quarter of 1986 as an extensive test to establish metallurgical grades and recoveries. Audrey will provide the necessary funds to develop and exploit the Mobrun deposit and Corporation Falconbridge Copper will make the Norbec mill available for a specific period of time to treat Mobrun ore on a custom basis.

*   *   *   *   *

. . . Underground exploration of the Ansil Deposit of the Lac Dufault Division, located 5 kilometres west of the Norbec mill, continued during the year. The production shaft reached the initial planned depth of 1,400 metres below surface, where it has been stopped temporarily in order to delineate the ore body by diamond drilling from three levels. The ventilation shaft was collared and had reached a depth of 200 metres by year-end. It is expected that the Ansil mine will be in production at 1,400 tonnes per day early in 1989. Expenditures to year-end have amounted to $12 million, net of grants received. Planned expenditures on the project for 1987 are $20 million.

Drill indicated reserves with dilution are estimated to be 2,100,000 tonnes grading 7.0 percent copper, 0.5 percent zinc, 24.0 grams silver per tonne, and 1.7 grams of gold per tonne.

Winston Lake Division

The Winston Lake Division is developing a high-grade zinc copper deposit approximately 27 kilometres north of Schreiber, Ontario. Following a decision in November 1985 to put the project on hold pending a better zinc price and market, the decision was made in July 1986 to bring the property into production. By year-end the mine access road had been upgraded, the water storage dam constructed, plant design was 35 percent complete, the service complex building had been closed in, and a start was made on the erection of the concentrator structural steel. The underground development was also fully under way. An application for environmental permitting was submitted and a public hearing was held in February 1987, following which approval was given to commence the clearing of the tailings disposal area.

Total cost to bring the mine into production of 1,000 tonnes per day during the first quarter of 1988 is estimated at $72 million of which $27 million has been spent to year-end. Expenditures during 1986 amounted to $13 million.

Probable and possible ore reserves with dilution are estimated at 3,100,000 tonnes with a grade of 15.9 percent zinc, 1.0 percent copper, 30.3 grams of silver per tonne, and 1.0 grams of gold per tonne.

Exploration—Kerr Addison

In 1986, the minerals explorations budget for Kerr Addison Mines Limited was raised to $7.0 million to cover expanded drilling activities in Quebec and to a lesser extent in Ontario. Actual expenditures were increased by a further $4.0 million as a result of the application of outside funds to Quebec/Ontario projects. More than 140,000 feet of diamond drilling on 22 projects was performed in Ontario and Quebec as a result of outside funding. A large zone of gold mineralization was discovered by drilling in Dasserat Township. Several scattered gold intersections were found in Montgolfier Township and in the Frotet area of Quebec by drill testing of geophysical targets. The objectives in these areas are to extend the known mineralization by drilling and to direct the search toward mineable ore bodies in the areas of gold mineralization. It is encouraging to have obtained several gold intersections of up to 0.15 ounces per ton over 10 feet during the first large reconnaissance drilling program.

In British Columbia 17,950 feet of diamond drilling was completed on 4 project areas. Drilling on the Abo property in southern British Columbia has outlined a gold rich system of quartz veins on a steep mountain slope. It is expected that further testing of this zone will be carried out in 1987 with outside funds and will include driving a short adit, cross cutting, raising and underground diamond drilling. The property has the potential of a modest tonnage producer.

In Quebec, 6,600 feet of overburden drilling on 2 properties was completed while in Nevada 4,190 feet of reverse circulation drilling was performed on 3 projects. In all areas a total of 3,700 miles of airborne and ground geophysics was completed, and several hundred property submissions were examined or evaluated during the year.

Exploration—Corporation Falconbridge Copper

Corporation Falconbridge Copper pursued an active surface exploration program in 1986. A total of $8.3 million was spent distributed as follows:

Location	Expenditure	Percent
Quebec	$3,718	44
Ontario	2,257	28
British Columbia	1,497	18
United States	250	3
Toronto Office	550	7
Total	$8,272	100

An additional $6.0 million was spent on underground exploration, entirely in Quebec at Opemiska, Lac Shortt, and the Callahan property.

Exploration expenditures in 1986 were directed approximately 55 percent to polymetallic massive sulphide deposits and 45 percent to gold. Surface diamond drilling totaled 65,087 metres in 237 holes at a direct contract cost that accounted for 57 percent of the total surface exploration expenditure.

Surface drilling in the immediate area of the Lac Shortt mine located three new zones of gold mineralization, two of which are currently being explored underground by drifting and follow up diamond drilling. A third zone of gold mineralization has been confirmed 600 metres northeast of the shaft.

Diamond drilling on the Delbridge Kerraldo property near Noranda, Quebec, funded by Syngold Exploration Inc. on an earn-in arrangement, has outlined a narrow but apparently continuous mineralized quartz vein structure interpreted to be an extension of the formerly productive Donalda No. 1 gold vein. Mineral potential of the zone is presently estimated at 450,000 tonnes grading 9.3 grams gold per tonne. Fill-in drilling to confirm continuity and grade as well as drill testing of other targets on the property is planned for 1987.

Drifting and underground bulk sampling at the Callahan property located 15 kilometres west of Val d'Or and in which Corporation Falconbridge Copper holds a 49 percent interest was completed during the year. The gold mineralized zone proved to be erratic and discontinuous. Work was suspended and the workings allowed to flood.

Drilling and trenching on the property optioned from Rea Gold in the Adams-Barriere region of British Columbia outlined a complex sulphide deposit with potential for 670,000 tonnes grading 0.95 percent copper, 2.43 percent lead, 2.08 percent zinc, 717.5 grams silver per tonne, and 1.23 grams gold per tonne. Additional drilling is planned in 1987 to test the strike and dip potential of the mineralized horizon.

Required

Evaluate the 1986 disclosure by Kerr Addison Mines Limited of its reserves. Suggest other information which would be useful to an investor in predicting the company's future results.

Case 40

Kett Brothers

It is a sunny day in April 1991, and you have just sat down to work when the phone rings. George Gainsborough, one of your original clients and the president of Kett Brothers, is calling for some advice. He is not happy with the earnings per share reported by Kett in 1990 and has two ideas on how to improve the figures in 1990 and in the future.

One of George's ideas is to change Kett's depreciation policy from declining balance to straight line on some of the company's fixed assets. Last year Kett had some major acquisitions which were unlike the fixed assets previously owned by the company, and George feels that adopting the same depreciation policy for the new assets as has been used for all other fixed assets was a mistake.

George's other idea is to defer the purchase of a building which had been planned for 1991. He feels that the additional depreciation expense will further impair the 1991 earnings per share reported, and he would like to have at least 1990 and 1991 showing improved results before increasing the expenses.

You had completed the audit of Kett Brothers' 1990 financial statements at the end of February this year. On checking them you note that they showed net income before extraordinary items of $34,000 and net income of $29,800. Kett's share capital at January 1, 1990 had consisted of

1. 6,000 Class A common shares.
2. 1,000 Class B noncumulative convertible shares with an annual dividend of $1.00 which had most recently been declared and paid in December 1989. One Class B share was convertible into two class A shares.
3. 500 Class C cumulative preference shares paying a fixed dividend of $4.00 per annum.
4. 1,000 Class D noncumulative preference shares with a fixed dividend of $2.25 per annum; this dividend was declared in 1990.

5. 100 options giving the holder the right to purchase any time during the next two years one Class A share for one option and $350 cash.

Kett's tax rate is 45 percent, and the company expects to earn 12 percent before tax on its assets.

No options were exercised in 1990. However, the following events took place during the year for Class A shares:

March 1	Sold for cash	600
July 1	Issued for converted Class B shares	2,000
Sept. 1	Purchased and canceled.	300
Dec. 1	Issued in return for equipment.	3,000

The fixed assets George referred to during the telephone call had cost $50,000. They had a useful life of 10 years and no salvage value. In 1990 Kett Brothers had depreciated these assets at a rate of 20 percent declining balance, which was the rate allowed by Revenue Canada.

Required

What earnings per share figures were reported on Kett Brothers' 1990 financial statements (ignore 1989 comparative figures). What earnings per share figures will be reported this year for the 1990 comparative figures if the company changes its depreciation policy for the new fixed assets?

Advise George Gainsborough on the wisdom of changing the depreciation policy. Also advise him about the deferral of the building purchase.

Case 41

LAC Minerals Ltd.

LAC Minerals Ltd. is a Canadian company engaged in gold mining and oil and gas exploration. The current company ("LAC") was created by an amalgamation in 1985 of Lac Minerals Ltd., Lake Short Mines Limited, Wright-Hargreaves Mines Limited, Little Long Lac Gold Mines Limited, and two wholly owned subsidiaries of these companies.

In 1986 the company held five producing gold mines and mills in Ontario and Quebec, and a limestone quarry, in addition to oil and gas and mineral interests in Canada, the United States, and Australia.

In May 1981, representatives from Lac Minerals Ltd. and another mining company, International Corona Resources Ltd., were engaged in negotiations toward a joint venture operation to develop an area adjacent to Corona land holdings in Hemlo, Ontario. The area had been staked in 1945 by Dr. Jack K. Williams, a physician who spent several summers making claims and prospecting in the Hemlo area. Reports about the area's gold potential were written between 1945 and 1947 by Trevor Page, a geologist. After Dr. Williams's death in 1953 his family continued to pay the taxes necessary to maintain the claims.

During the 1981 Lac/Corona discussions the Lac representatives were able to examine maps, drill core, and cross sections of drilling that Corona had done. There was also publicly available documentation about drilling in the area and on Corona's property which Lac was able to use in its assessment of the area's worth.

In July 1981, Lac representatives approached Dr. Williams's widow and acquired the claims for Lac. A feasibility study on the development of the Hemlo project was carried out in 1983, and on December 6, 1985 Ontario Premier David Peterson and LAC President Peter Allen poured the first gold bar at a ceremony held at the Page-Williams Mine. Extracts from LAC's financial statements before and after the opening of the Page-Williams Mine are presented in Exhibit 1.

In October 1981 International Corona Resources Ltd. launched a law-suit against Lac Minerals Ltd. charging breach of a confidential relation-ship in LAC's acquisition of the Williams claims. Reference to the lawsuit first appeared in Lac's 1983 statements as a note "Commitments and Contingencies" (Exhibit 2).

On March 7, 1986 Mr. Justice Richard E. Holland of the Supreme Court of Ontario ruled that Lac had breached a fiduciary duty it owed to Corona and had used confidential information acquired from Corona. Ownership of the Page-Williams mine was awarded to Corona, upon payment to LAC of $153,978,000 plus interest from the date of judgement to the date of payment to compensate LAC for amounts spent to develop the site. LAC immediately appealed the judgement.

LAC's 1985 audit report was dated March 11, 1986 with regard to the reporting of the trial. In addition, the audit report included "Comments on Differences in Canadian-United States Reporting Standards" (LAC shares trade on the New York Stock Exchange as well as in Paris, Brus-sels, and Antwerp) in accordance with the requirements of a CICA *Audit-ing Guideline*. The "Comments" indicated that if the audit report had been prepared according to U.S. reporting standards the opinion would have been qualified as being subject to the outcome of significant uncer-tainties described in Note 14(c). The "Comments" explained that Cana-dian reporting standards do not include such a qualification when the uncertainty is adequately disclosed in the financial statements. The 1986 statements contained a similar audit report and note disclosure. In addi-tion, the 1986 results were reported on two bases—including and exclud-ing the Page-Williams Mine.

On October 2, 1987 the Ontario Court of Appeal upheld the 1986 Su-preme Court decision.

Toronto Stock Exchange share prices of LAC and Corona before and after the 1987 ruling are presented in Exhibit 3.

Required

Evaluate LAC Minerals Ltd.'s disclosure of International Corona Re-sources Ltd.'s lawsuit from 1983 to 1986 inclusive.

EXHIBIT 1   Extracts from Annual Reports (in thousands)

	1986	1985	1984	1983	1982
Mining interests	$388,532	$327,821	$164,753	$ 94,047	$ 68,588
Oil and gas interests.	27,046	31,264	35,370	37,380	35,033
Total assets	597,229	463,759	397,751	221,368	122,261
Hemlo component of mining interests	233,485	194,077	75,464	14,314	512

EXHIBIT 1 *(concluded)*

	1986	1985	1984	1983	1982
Revenue	229,657	142,363	169,673	157,232	130,398
Hemlo component of revenue	112,121				
Net income before extraordinary items . . .	19,118	6,128	39,307	27,969	21,928
Hemlo component of net income before					
extraordinary items	12,558				
Ounces of gold produced, total	478,394	265,925	299,571	257,064	201,181
Ounces of gold produced from the					
Page-Williams Mine	204,034	1,900			

EXHIBIT 2 Commitments and Contingencies Notes

1983

9(a). In October of 1981 International Corona Resources (Corona) commenced an action against, among others, a predecessor of the Company in which it now claims general damages of $500,000,000 for breach of a confidential relationship which precluded the acquisition of certain patented mining claims in the Hemlo area of Ontario, a declaration that the Company's interests in the subject mining claims are held in trust for Corona and an order directing their transfer to Corona, an injunction to prevent the Company from dealing with the claims, and an accounting for profits from the claims. Based on evidence provided by the Company and subject to any evidence revealed by further examinations for discovery that must be conducted, counsel for the Company is of the opinion that Corona should not succeed in its claim.

1984

11(a). In October of 1981 International Corona Resources Limited (Corona) commenced an action against, among others, a predecessor of the Company in which it now claims general damages of $3 billion for breach of a confidential relationship which precluded the acquisition of certain patented mining claims in the Hemlo area of Ontario, a declaration that the Company's interests in the subject mining claims are held in trust for Corona and an order directing their transfer to Corona, an injunction to prevent the Company from dealing with the claims, and an accounting for profits from the claims. Based on evidence provided by the Company and subject to any evidence revealed by further examinations for discovery that must be conducted, counsel for the Company is of the opinion that Corona should not succeed in its claim.

EXHIBIT 2 *(continued)*

1985

14(c). Judgment was rendered by the Supreme Court of Ontario on Friday, March 7, 1986 in the action against LAC by International Corona Resources Ltd. ("Corona") with respect to certain patented mining claims in the Hemlo area of Ontario owned by LAC, now the location of the Page-Williams Mine.

The Court held that in acquiring the claims on which the mine is now located, LAC had breached a fiduciary duty it owed to Corona and had used confidential information it had acquired from Corona.

The Court ordered that the Page-Williams Mine be transferred by LAC to Corona upon payment by Corona to LAC of $153,978,000 plus interest on such amount from the date of the judgment until payment, together with all sums, other than royalties, paid by LAC to the vendor of the property. The Court also gave judgment in favour of Corona for the amount of profits, if any, obtained by LAC from the operation of the Page-Williams Mine from the date on which the production of gold commenced, and its cost of the action.

LAC has reviewed the judgment and completely disagrees with the findings and considers them to be contrary to the evidence at trial. It therefore has filed an appeal of the judgment to the Ontario Court of Appeal.

It is believed that the appeal could be heard as early as September 1986.

Any adjustments arising from the resolution of this matter will be recorded in the year the case is finally determined.

1986

14(d). Judgment was rendered by the Supreme Court of Ontario on March 7, 1986, in the action brought against LAC by International Corona Resources Ltd. ("Corona") with respect to 11 patented mining claims in the Hemlo area of Ontario owned by LAC, now the location of the Page-Williams Mine.

The Court held that in acquiring the 11 patented claims LAC had breached a fiduciary duty it owed to Corona and had used confidential information it had acquired from Corona.

The Court ordered that the Page-Williams property be transferred by LAC to Corona upon payment by Corona to LAC of $153,978,000 plus interest on such amount from the date of the judgment until payment, together with all sums, other than royalties, paid by LAC to the vendor of the property.

The Court also gave judgment in favour of Corona for the amount of profits, if any, obtained by LAC from the operation of the Page-Williams property from the date on which the production of gold commenced, and its cost of the action. LAC reviewed the judgment and completely disagreed with the findings and considered them to be contrary to law and the evidence at trial. It therefore filed an appeal of the judgment to the Ontario

---

EXHIBIT 2   (*concluded*)

Court of Appeal. The appeal was heard during November 1986; the decision of the Court of Appeal has not yet been published.

Any adjustments arising from the resolution of this matter will be recorded in the year the case is finally determined.

EXHIBIT 3   Selected Share Prices, Toronto Stock Exchange

	High	*Low*	*Close*
LAC Minerals Ltd.:			
53 weeks ended September 25, 1987	18.50	7.87	18.25
October 2, 1987			18.00
October 5, 1987			15.12
53 weeks ended October 9, 1987 . .	20.00	7.87	16.25
International Corona Resources Ltd.:			
October 2, 1987			47.50
October 5, 1987			79.00

Case 42

Lakeside Church

Lakeside Church was founded in Brandon, Manitoba, in 1908 by several of the town's wealthy families. The initial membership was 200; it grew over the decades to a high in the early 1960s of over 1,500 but since then has fallen to 1988's level of 1,000. In Lakeside's early years the members shared the premises of a neighbouring church; in 1911 a spectacular building on two acres of land in what became downtown Brandon was constructed after several years of fund-raising. The design of the church included 10 magnificent stained glass windows, a chapel, a small kitchen and auditorium to provide for meetings and wedding receptions, and office space for the ministerial and support staff. In 1958 an addition was built which contained a larger kitchen and auditorium. The church's property included one manse until 1950 when a second house was purchased to accommodate an additional full-time ministerial appointment.

From the time the church was founded, members received an audited set of financial statements prior to the Annual General Meeting. The statements showed not only a balance sheet and statement of revenue and expense but also details of changes in each of the church's funds during the preceding year. The statements were prepared on a cash basis. The audit was awarded to a new firm about every 10 years, and the statements had been audited by all sizes of firms during the church's history.

In 1988 the recommendations of the *CICA Handbook* were extended to include nonprofit organizations. The introduction to the *Handbook* was amended, and Section 4230, ''Non-Profit Organizations—Specific Items,'' was added. The new section is effective for fiscal years commencing January 1, 1989, with retroactive application. Unlike the Exposure Draft, Section 4230 did not include a recommendation with regard to the accounting measurement of fixed assets, pending further study. The new section recommended that fixed assets be disclosed in accordance with Section 3060, ''Fixed Assets.'' Section 3060 recommends that unless special circumstances exist, such as a reorganization, fixed assets should be accounted for on the basis of their historical cost. Disclosure should include the basis of valuation, depreciation expense, and accumulated depreciation.

Required

Write a report to the Congregational Board of Lakeside Church evaluating the church's fixed asset accounting and disclosure compliance with the new *Handbook* section. What would the impact be on Lakeside's statements if the measurement recommendations in Section 3060 were ultimately applied to nonprofit organizations? Would Lakeside's statements be more or less informative using Section 3060 recommendations?

LAKESIDE CHURCH
Extracts from the Financial Statements
For the Year Ended December 31

	1988	*1987*
Assets:		
Church capital fund:		
Church buildings	$10,392,000	$10,467,000
Furniture, fixtures, and equipment	1,187,000	1,209,000
Total assets	$11,579,000	$11,676,000
Liabilities and Capital:		
Church capital fund:		
Replacement cost of fixed assets	$11,579,000	$11,676,000
Church capital fund, statement of revenue and expense		
Revenue:		
Interest	$ 90,683	$ 95,443
Dividends	20,810	19,235
Gain on sale of investments	7,612	2,871
Total	$ 119,105	$ 117,549
Expense:		
Allocation to the Trustee's Fund	$ 49,500	$ 161,540
Miscellaneous expense	4,950	6,226
	$ 54,450	$ 167,766
Excess of revenue over expense for the year. .	$ 64,655	$ (50,217)
Treasurer's general fund, statement of revenue and expense		
Revenue (details omitted)	$ 463,920	$ 426,910

(continued)

	1988	1987
Expense:		
Worship	$ 35,517	$ 30,833
Pastoral care	7,046	6,843
Education	4,514	4,344
Communications	33,108	31,086
Occupancy cost.	107,726	107,188
Salaries, honoraria, and benefits	197,656	199,598
Administration	25,853	26,931
Total expenses	$ 411,420	$ 406,823
Excess of revenue over expense	$ 52,500	$ 20,087

SIGNIFICANT ACCOUNTING POLICIES

Fixed Assets

Buildings, furniture, fixtures, and equipment are carried at replacement value as determined for insurance purposes.

Fixed assets do not include any amount in respect of land.

Depreciation is not provided on church buildings, furniture, fixtures, and equipment.

Longhouse (Canada) Ltd.

GAAP

Longhouse (Canada) Ltd. is a public company which was founded in 1930. The company is a publisher of textbooks for elementary, secondary, and university-level courses. In addition to its own titles (175 new titles were published in 1987 alone) the company imports texts from affiliated companies located all over the world. The majority of the imported texts come from the U.S. parent company which owns 70 percent of Longhouse's outstanding common shares. Approximately 55 percent of Longhouse's revenues come from titles manufactured and published in Canada.

The major ordering activity at all levels of educational institutions occurs between June and September with mid-August to mid-September being especially heavy months, often with rush orders. Activity at the Boards of Education across the country is slow during the summer, and it is frequently several months into the school year before Longhouse receives even a partial payment for books shipped. In addition, universities do not receive their major cash inflows until the fall so payment to Longhouse from this source is also delayed.

Competition in the industry is intense. All levels of educational institutions are experiencing declining enrollments. Provincial governments annually cut back the allocation of funds from the purchase of educational material. As well, students and instructors are resisting purchasing imported texts. The currency differences on these books can result in prices on an imported text being 20 to 40 percent higher than on a Canadian text. Instructors are switching to Canadian texts wherever possible, and students are buying secondhand copies or illegally photocopying expensive books. Fortunately for the industry, major curriculum revisions are being implemented in most provinces. In addition, due to lower annual sales, authors are producing revised editions of their books more frequently, sometimes as often as every two years.

Obsolete
Inventory

To encourage bookstore managers and purchasing agents to use any influence they might have in textbook selection Longhouse has adopted a generous policy for payment and returns. No payment is due on any shipment until 60 days after receipt. At that point, only texts which have been sold by the bookstore or distributed to students (as is the case with most secondary and elementary schoolbooks) must be paid for. All remaining copies may be returned at any time at the bookstore's or board's expense. If storage for texts before they are sold or distributed is scarce, Longhouse will keep the order in its warehouse and ship quantities as requested. Payment terms are identical on all orders, whether shipped when the order is received or stored by Longhouse for later delivery. Longhouse has designed an easy-to-use form for its customers to report sales and distributions.

In accordance with its parent company's policies, Longhouse recognizes revenues as soon as books are invoiced if shipment is immediate or as soon as an order is received for books Longhouse will store. If books are returned or if the entire order is not subsequently shipped a reduction in sales is recognized.

Extracts from Longhouse (Canada) Ltd.'s December 31, 1990 financial statements are included as Exhibit 1.

Required

Evaluate Longhouse (Canada) Ltd.'s revenue recognition policies. Discuss other problems the company is facing and their impact on the financial statements.

EXHIBIT 1

LONGHOUSE (CANADA) LTD.
Extracts from the Financial Statements
As of December 31, 1990

	1990	1989
Bank term deposits and Treasury bills	$ 2,488,431	$ 3,937,930
Accounts receivable	8,665,335	8,414,657
Amounts due from affiliated companies	711,245	278,636
Inventories and prepublication costs	13,614,630	14,125,710
Total current assets	$25,479,641	$26,756,933
Net property, plant, and equipment	$ 4,700,579	$ 4,435,326
Contracts, copyrights, trademarks, agency rights and goodwill	$ 540,000	$ 540,000
Total assets	$30,720,220	$31,732,259

EXHIBIT 1   (*concluded*)

	1990	1989
Sales, less returns	$31,138,990	$31,516,958
Net income	$ 2,179,928	$ 3,265,711
✗ Earnings per share	$ 1.09	$ 1.64

Schedule of Sales (less returns) by Quarter

January 1–March 31, 1990 . . .	$ 4,425,000
April 1–June 30	7,881,092
July 1–September 30	12,209,000
October 1–December 31	6,623,898
	$31,138,990

Note to Financial Statements

Note 1: Summary of Significant Accounting Policies

Inventories and prepublication costs: Inventories are stated at the lower of cost (generally on the first-in, first-out basis) and net realizable value. These inventories include certain prepublication costs, principally outside preparation and plate costs, which are amortized from the year of copyright over their estimated useful lives using the following rates and methods:

Serialized educational publications—straight-line, not exceeding five years
Nonserialized educational publications—four years (20%, 30%, 30%, 20%)
General books—over the life of the first printing

Lynx Inc.

In late May 1987 Jim Sullivan, the partner responsible for the Lynx audit, was pondering a situation which had arisen with regard to his client's financial statement for the year ended March 31. On December 31, 1986, Lynx had entered into a six-month speculative futures contract to purchase 1.5 million German marks on June 30, 1987. The rate to sell on December 31 was $0.6939; the rate to buy in the contract was $0.7122.

The value of the mark had been rising steadily for over a year, and Lynx's vice president, finance, William Poston, felt that a profit could be made on the transaction. Lynx is a major Canadian corporation with shares traded on the Montreal and New York Stock Exchanges. The company manufactures and retails high-quality office and household furniture. Lynx has a strong earnings history and has expanded rapidly; the share price has risen from $3 on the date of issue to the current level of $52.

Bill Poston had phoned Jim Sullivan earlier that day to confirm that the statements would be finalized by the end of the week, to remind Jim (politely) that this was the latest the audit had ever extended and to discuss the German futures contract, among other items.

The rate to sell German marks on March 31 was $0.7199. If the contract had matured that day, Lynx could have sold the currency for a profit of $11,550. Poston felt that Lynx should be able to accrue this gain on the 1987 financial statements. The rate after year-end had continued its climb (April—$0.7283; day of phone call—$0.7502), providing further proof in Poston's mind of the value of the contract at year-end.

Required

Draft Jim Sullivan's response to William Poston.

M.T. Mines Limited

M.T. Mines Limited is a federally incorporated Canadian-controlled mining company whose shares are traded on the Vancouver Stock Exchange. The company operates various mines in Canada and is in its 10th year of operation. Profits have been erratic due to world economic conditions. The company has reported losses for the last three years, but hopes to break even in the current fiscal year.

M.T. has been very concerned about the fluctuating world prices of zinc, which it mines in an operation in northern Alberta. In order to minimize the risk and ensure a buyer for its output, it sold zinc under three-month contracts for the first time this year. M.T. and the buyer would sign the contract, which established the selling price and payment terms, and delivery would be fixed at three months in the future. The board has been encouraged by the results of these contracts, which have resulted, during this year, in a $412,000 "contract gain"; that is, sales by three-month contracts netted $412,000 more than the going market price of zinc on the day of delivery.

M.T. is left with two problems concerning these contracts. First, how should the $412,000 be reflected in the financial statements? Adjusting gross profit (the sales figure would be left at the higher contract figure, and this would have the effect of increasing gross profit) or separate recognition (showing the $412,000 as "other revenue") have been proposed. Second, one contract will be outstanding at the year-end and M.T. must decide on an accounting policy for this position. It is an advantageous contract, and inventory levels at year-end will be sufficient to meet the contract, although delivery is not scheduled until six weeks later.

Production has just commenced in one of M.T.'s mines, located in northern Ontario. Common with industry practice, all preopening costs

Society of Management Accountants, adapted.

have been charged to a Deferred Development Costs account on the balance sheet. These costs will be amortized as production occurs. Deferred Development Costs for this project are $4.2 million. Included in these costs are $250,000 of interest paid on loans directly relating to the project, and $470,000 paid under operating leases for equipment used prior to commencing production.

Much to the board's dismay, the initial production results indicate much lower reserves than originally estimated. Indeed, if these results are accurate, the mine would not be a viable operation. However, engineering reports indicate the presence of further geological formations that could contain significant ore bodies.

Reports from another of M.T.'s mines, the Neushaft, located in northern Manitoba, indicate that the quantity of ore reserves is considerably lower than the geologist's reports had originally predicted. In fact, the scheduled closing time, which was to have been 13 years from the beginning of this year, has now been revised to 5 years. Because of the nature of mining operations, the physical assets cannot be transferred to other locations. One proposal currently put forward is to write the assets down from a net book value (at the beginning of the year) of $4.550 million to $1.750 million. Company officials are unsure how a write-down would be reflected in the financial statements. The president favours the write-down of these assets with the adjustment being made directly to retained earnings.

Required

M.T. is preparing for its annual audit, and decisions have to be made on a number of accounting issues. The board of directors reviewed these issues with the controller, Rocki Rhodes, and she has been asked to prepare a report addressing the accounting issues. Her report is to present possible alternatives and her recommendations with reasons to support each recommendation.

Assume the role of Rocki Rhodes and write the report requested by the board of directors.

Case 46

MacDonald Limited

MacDonald Ltd. (ML) is controlled by the Harnish family, and has been in operation for seven years, manufacturing and selling blank tapes for use in VCRs. Presently, the Harnish family owns 70 percent of the shares, with the remaining 30 percent owned by a wealthy entrepreneur, David MacIntosh. The shareholders judge the success of the company on its cash flow available for salary and dividend distribution. Harold Harnish, the largest shareholder, is ML's president. The tapes have been well received in the marketplace due to their quality, price, and shrewd marketing. To handle the large U.S. market, ML has just set up a subsidiary in the United States called MacDonald U.S. Ltd. (MUSL). While Canadian operations have been quite successful, MUSL is not expected to be profitable for two to three years due to fierce competition in their chosen market.

Bill Countway, an assistant to the controller, noted the following:

1. Tape packaging material is purchased from Packing Unlimited, a company in which Harold Harnish has a 40 percent interest. Packaging material costs amount to 6 percent of the cost of production.
2. ML provides data processing services to MUSL. Further, the controller, Dave Corkum, goes to Buffalo, New York, once a week to review the accounting records. MUSL is not charged for these services. Dave explained to Bill that there is no point in doing so because MUSL is expected to be in a tax-loss situation for several years.
3. MUSL purchases all its tapes from ML. It also sells cassette tapes (35 percent of its sales) but it buys these from a Japanese supplier. Customs duty and excise tax is assessed by U.S. customs on all merchandise MUSL buys.

Atlantic Provinces Association of Chartered Accountants, adapted.

4. Of MUSL's sales, 50 percent are to one department store chain. MUSL's management are confident about increasing sales to the chain at a pace faster than sales to other retail outlets.
5. MUSL has borrowed U.S. $500,000 from a U.S. bank. The loan has a 10-year term. ML has guaranteed the loan for its subsidiary.

The company controller has asked Bill to consider the foreign currency translation policy that should be adopted to account for the U.S. subsidiary. The trial balance for the subsidiary is given in Exhibit 1. Regardless of your conclusion he has asked you to translate the trial balance into Canadian dollars using both the temporal method and the current rate method, explaining the likely impact of the differences.

Required

Assume the role of Bill Countway and respond to the requests of the controller.

EXHIBIT 1

MACDONALD UNITED STATES LIMITED
Trial Balance
December 31, 1989
(U.S. dollars)

	Dr	Cr
Cash.	$ 40,000	
Accounts receivable.	329,000	
Allowance for doubtful accounts		$ 10,000
Inventory (closing)	200,000	
Plant and equipment.	539,000	
Accumulated depreciation		18,000
Accounts payable.		410,000
Long-term debt.		500,000
Common stock		300,000
Retained earnings.		—
Sales		1,040,000
Cost of goods sold	860,000	
Expenses.	310,000	
	$2,278,000	$2,278,000

Other Information

1. The subsidiary commenced business on July 1, 1989, at which time its only assets were an inventory of $100,000; cash of $200,000; and the common stock investment of the parent for $300,000.

EXHIBIT 1   *(concluded)*

---

2. Fixed assets and the 10-year term loan were acquired on July 15, 1989.
3. Purchases, sales, and other expenses were incurred evenly over the third and fourth quarters. Closing Inventory related primarily to fourth quarter purchases.
4. $300,000 of MUSL's accounts payable are to ML. ML has recorded these at $370,000.
5. Selected Exchange Rates:

	$1 U.S. =
July 1, 1989	$1.43 Cdn.
July 15, 1989	$1.41 Cdn.
December 31, 1989	$1.33 Cdn.
3rd quarter average, 1989 . . .	$1.39 Cdn.
4th quarter average, 1989 . . .	$1.35 Cdn.

Case 47 *Revenue Recognition*

Maple Farm

_____

Jason Thomas, the owner of Maple Farm, has recently asked you to reconsider one of the bases on which you prepare his annual financial statements. You have always valued his herd at purchase price, recognizing revenue when the cattle were sold. However, Jason is approaching retirement and will be putting his operation up for sale within the next five years as he has no heirs. He wishes to show the most favourable history possible to prospective buyers.

Maple Farm is a feedlot operation located in southwestern Ontario. A feedlot farm is one which buys cattle from beef cow farms and fattens them for slaughter. The operation may also use part of the herd for breeding, then fatten their own calves, but the primary source of revenue is the sale of younger animals (heifers and steers) which bring higher prices than those which have been bred and are therefore older (cows and bulls). Cattle are purchased from the beef cow farms when they are 6 to 12 months old and are sold for slaughter at between 18 and 24 months. Occasionally a heifer will have been used to produce one calf before sale.

Several events in the past few years have changed the competition in the livestock industry. In 1984 Alberta experienced its worst drought in 50 years, resulting in a sell-off of cows because of a lack of feed for the winter months. The Alberta beef cows were purchased by feeder operations in provinces where government subsidies designed to protect producers from unfavourable market conditions have actually stimulated entry into the feeding business. In spite of this activity, overcapacity exists in slaughter houses. (Cow slaughter in western Canada fell 22.1 percent between 1984 and 1986.) In addition, consumers have become more aware of the risk of high-fat diets, particularly with the publication of studies linking these diets with the incidence of cancer and heart disease. In 1985 the beef industry began an information campaign to address some of the concerns and misconceptions about beef consumption.

Thomas's draft balance sheet and income statement are attached (Exhibit 1). He has requested that the increase in the value of his herd be recognized as the cattle are fattened, rather than having to wait until the stockyard sales. Thomas points out that all cattle are sold. The only variance may be the price per pound, which is dependent on the age and grade of the animal and market conditions. The market is guaranteed, as provinces with government subsidies will buy Ontario cattle if the Ontario price weakens. In addition, falling herd sizes will assist in price maintenance.

Required

Describe how a change in the timing of revenue recognition would affect Thomas's statements. Present your recommendation.

EXHIBIT 1

MAPLE FARM
Balance Sheet (Draft)
December 31, 1986

Assets

Current assets:

Cash	$ 5,781
Accounts receivable	7,357
Market livestock	186,722
Home-grown crops	53,315
Purchased feed and supplies	7,256

Intermediate assets:

Field machinery	110,880
Barn equipment	9,011

Long-term assets:

Land	226,555
Farm buildings	105,653
Total farm assets	$712,530

Liabilities

Accounts payable	$ 6,736
Other current debt	126,495
Intermediate debt	35,147
Long-term debt	84,198
Total farm liabilities	$252,576
Equity in farm business	$459,954

EXHIBIT 1   *(continued)*

MAPLE FARM
Selected Statistics for Year Ended December 31, 1986

Average selling price per head.	$942
Average selling weight per head	1,133 lb.
Average buying price per head	$642
Average buying weight per head	681 lb.
Average rate of gain per day	1.87 lb.
Death loss.	5 head

MAPLE FARM
Income Statement (Draft)
Year Ended December 31, 1986

Revenue:	
Cattle	$390,264
Crop sales	47,468
Total cash revenue	$437,732
Change in receivables	1,298
Inventory change:	
Home-grown crops	(7,027)
Supplies and purchased feed	2,535
Market livestock	(5,643)
Total farm revenue	$428,895
Expenses:	
Livestock expenses:	
Purchased livestock	247,291
Purchased feed	27,861
Veterinary and medicine	2,537
Marketing and trucking	4,770
Stable supplies	2,231
Crop expenses:	
Seed and plants	6,999
Fertilizer and pesticides	18,995
Crop insurance	243
Crop drying.	348
Allocated expenses:	
Hired labour	12,251
Gas, oil, and fuel	9,964
Repairs.	14,226
Hydro, telephone	2,091
Taxes, insurance	6,845
Car and house expenses	1,551

EXHIBIT 1   (*concluded*)

Interest (term)	$ 10,092
Interest (operating)	12,882
Total cash expenses	$381,177
Change in current payables	nil
Depreciation	18,673
Total farm expenses	$399,850
Net farm income	$ 29,045

Case 48

McBeans Ltd.

McBeans Ltd. was incorporated in Canada in 1978. It was a private company closely held by the Burton family. The company owned fast-food outlets; the main dish on the menu was chili. Customers could order hot, medium, or lightly spiced servings so that all members of a family could enjoy the meal. Sales increased rapidly, and by the end of 1979 the company had over a dozen outlets and was taking steps to expand across the country. All outlets were company owned and the board of directors felt that McBeans would benefit from having the majority of the subsequent outlets operated as franchises; this would take the day-to-day, on-site operating pressures off Head Office and help develop a team of highly motivated managers, while promoting a consistent image for the company and the product. It would also allow for expansion without having to issue shares to the public. During the next four years almost all the McBeans opened were franchises. The units were primarily located along major roads and highways, rather than in shopping centres; customers could park on the unit's property and eat in the restaurant or use the take-out service. With the increase in meals eaten away from home and the tasty, reasonably priced product, the large, bright McBeans sign became well known along Canadian roads.

In July 1990 Catherine Anderson, the manager in charge of the McBeans audit, was called to a meeting at the Winnipeg Head Office to discuss the upcoming 1990 audit, some possible changes in the financial statements, and preparation of a prospectus for a public share offering. The following is an excerpt from the remarks made at the meeting by Bob Stewart, McBeans V.P. finance:

> Catherine, there's an accounting treatment required by Section 3450 that has been applied to our results more strictly than I believe was the *Handbook*'s intention. I'm referring to the section on research and development, of course. Certain of our costs are being defined as research and are being expensed immediately, while others are treated as development and aren't expensed until the new menu item is introduced in the outlets.

Our development process actually begins much earlier than the point at which we're accumulating costs which can be deferred. You and the members of the audit team have all been on a tour of our test kitchen here at Head Office so you've seen the type of activities which go on. Our staff tries various levels and types of preservatives in the chili to ensure that each batch will taste freshly cooked. They also experiment with different spices to produce a varied menu. They test the flavour and consistency effect of cooling the mix and reheating it, and they also blend various ratios of the meat, beans, peppers, tomatoes, and spices to minimize cooking time for the product. Of course we also do menu planning here so that all ages of customers can eat a balanced, nutritious meal at any McBeans. When we've decided on a particular blend of ingredients we hold dinners for our staff and invited guests to get their reaction to the item.

We've had to expense the costs of all the test kitchen activities as they were incurred, and this seems unreasonable. Every product on the McBeans menu has been developed incorporating the knowledge from our kitchen's activities. This is where we devise a satisfactory ratio of ingredients for an item which will be introduced to our outlets, and you insist that we immediately expense all the costs associated with that item. Catherine, all test batches are *development*! Every one brings us closer to the final product which will appear on our menu, even if we subsequently decide that the particular item isn't going to be adopted (remember when we were working on new desserts and we invented Pink Punk ice cream with the cookie shaped like a razor blade sticking out of it? The Board of Directors didn't think that fit our family image so we modified the recipe slightly and produced our highly successful Strawberry Cloud dish). You won't let us start deferring costs until we begin modifying our production line for a new item. Our selling price doesn't just cover the costs incurred when production begins; we have months of prior expenses to recover in that price.

What I'd like to do is to treat all the test kitchen expenses as development. I'd be happy to include in the notes a breakdown between expenditures on the test kitchen and the products in production. Readers know that a careful study of the notes is essential to understanding a company's performance, and they can calculate the effect on the statements of other treatments.

Required

Assume the role of Catherine Anderson and respond to Bob Stewart's suggestions.

McGraw Corporation

McGraw Corporation is a medium-sized, privately held Canadian corporation which operates stores across Canada selling a wide variety of home gym equipment. The company was founded in the mid-1970s by a group of businesspeople who were convinced that there was an opportunity for a company which catered to the physical fitness boom. After a slow start, McGraw prospered and, in 1987, it owned more than 50 stores.

The company's 1987 fiscal year has just ended and you, as assistant controller, have been involved in preparing draft financial statements. The executive committee, consisting of the company president, four vice presidents, and the controller, spent all Monday morning reviewing the 1987 draft financial statements.

Following the meeting, Joe Wilson, the controller, called you into his office to brief you on the proceedings. After thanking you for your work on the financial statements, and passing along the general comments of the executive committee, he outlined a number of issues he wished you to investigate.

The committee discussed changes in accounting policy and practice which it was considering for this year. An inventory accounting error was also discussed. The committee wished to have an explanation of how each item should be reflected in the financial statements and of each item's dollar impact on net income for 1987. The notes that Mr. Wilson took during the meeting are shown in Exhibit 1.

Also, the committee spent time discussing existing accounting policies and some alternatives which might be adopted in the future. Several committee members were confused about the pros and cons of the alternatives and the effects they would have on the firm's operating results and financial position. Mr. Wilson's notes on the discussion are in Exhibit 2.

Society of Management Accountants, adapted.

To satisfy investors and creditors, management would like to present a steady growth in accounting income. A significant portion of the company's financing is obtained through bank loans, and the bank loan agreements require audited financial statements.

Mr. Wilson has asked you to prepare a report, complete with your recommendations, to be circulated to the members of the executive committee.

Required

Write the report requested by Mr. Wilson.

EXHIBIT 1 Notes from Financial Statements Review Meeting, Proposed Changes for 1987

---

1. Change in depreciation method:
   - Was straight-line, $400,000 per year.
   - Proposed change to declining balance, $600,000 for 1987 year.
   - Uncertain as to whether information is available to restate specific prior years.

2. Leasehold improvements:
   - Leasehold improvements of $450,000 made in fiscal 1984, useful life estimated at 10 years.
   - "Improvements" now obsolete, major renovations planned for early next month. Useful life should have been four years.
   - President suggests writing undepreciated balance off to retained earnings as cost should have been matched to revenues in prior periods. If not, president favours extraordinary item treatment.

3. Inventory error:
   - Error in determination of the closing inventory, fiscal 1985, discovered last week.
   - Inventory as reported approximately $200,000 understated.

4. Note: Tax rate is 45 percent.

EXHIBIT 2 Notes from Financial Statement Review Meeting, Proposed Policies for Future Implementation

---

1. Inventory:
   - Proposed change is from FIFO to LIFO inventory valuation.
   - LIFO closing inventory value about $500,000 lower than FIFO for 1987.
   - LIFO opening inventory about $700,000 lower than FIFO for 1987.
   - Other Canadian companies generally use FIFO.

EXHIBIT 2 *(concluded)*

---

2. Doubtful Accounts:
   - Existing policy is to age receivables and estimate uncollectible portion based on past experience.
   - Proposed change is direct write-off of accounts as soon as they are deemed uncollectible.
   - Tighter credit policy to be instituted for fiscal 1988.
   - Vice-president, administration, expects improved collections.

3. Bond Interest:
   - 25-year, $10 million debenture issued in fiscal 1987, at 1 percent discount amortized on a straight-line basis.
   - Proposal is to use the effective interest method.

4. Warranty Expense:
   - Results from two-year product guarantee on electronic exercise bicycles being offered in fiscal 1987 for the first time.
   - Current method is to write off expenses as incurred.
   - Proposed change is to estimate and accrue cost.

Megadata Ltd.

Megadata Ltd. is a Canadian public corporation with head office in Montreal and branch operations located all over the world. The company is a developer of computer software and provides custom software and predesigned packages to its customers. The related services include scientific and engineering applications, business data processing, education (computer-based training and education is provided through a network of vocational schools established by Megadata), consulting, health care, and small business services. Customers can share the resources of large-scale computer systems or integrate on-site mini- and microcomputing capabilities with proprietary or licenced software and custom-designed data bases. Megadata also offers specialized information services in audience measurement, sports and entertainment ticketing, and a variety of finance and securities industry applications.

The Megadata group includes the operating company and a number of subsidiaries, two of which are Megadata Credit Company Ltd. and Megadata International Banking Corporation (both are wholly owned). Megadata Credit Company Ltd. is engaged in casualty, business credit, and life insurance. The operations of Megadata International Banking Corporation include leasing and consumer and business financing services.

In 1987 Megadata began reporting the activities of Megadata Credit Company Ltd. on a consolidated basis. Previously the equity method of accounting was used. In a related change, the balance sheet classification of assets and liabilities as current or noncurrent was eliminated because of the significance of nonclassified financial accounts. In its 1987 annual report management noted that

> The consolidation method is intended to provide shareholders a more appropriate and complete view of Megadata than did the previous method. The change is due to an evolutionary process of increasing similarities in the businesses of Megadata Ltd. and Megadata Credit Company Ltd., particularly as to small businesses services.

Operations of Megadata Ltd. and Megadata Credit Company Ltd. are now principally reported as Information Services/Products and Financial Services, respectively. The computer-related small business services (revenues of approximately $10,000,000 in 1987) of Megadata Credit are, however, reported with Information Services/Products.

In 1988 Megadata Ltd.'s management decided to also consolidate the results of Megadata International Banking Corporation. The Accounting Policies note mentioned that the statements included the accounts of Megadata Credit and that the accounts of most of the international subsidiaries were included as of November 30 to facilitate timely reporting. A separate note, entitled "Changes in Basis of Consolidation and Accounting Principle" stated that

Effective January 1, 1988 Megadata Ltd. has changed its method of accounting for its investment in Megadata International Banking Corporation from the equity method to consolidation. Management believes that consolidation is preferable because it provides a more comprehensive view of the company's financial position and results of operations since the lending and funding activities of Megadata International are very similar to other financial services businesses of Megadata Ltd. Prior years' financial statements have been restated; however, the change had no effect on net earnings or shareholders' equity.

Required

Assess (individually) the impact that consolidation of Megadata International Banking Corporation and Megadata Credit Company Ltd. had on the results of Megadata Ltd. Is consolidation of these results more or less informative than the previous presentation?

MEGADATA LTD.
Consolidated Balance Sheet
December 31, 1988
(in thousands)

	Restated for Policy Change	Previous Policy
Assets		
Cash	$ 8,910	$ 10,390
Information Services/Products:		
Trade and other receivables	52,380	52,380
Inventories	66,760	66,760
Leased and data centre equipment	40,160	40,160
Property, plant, and equipment	30,290	30,290

(continued)

	Restated for Policy Change	*Previous Policy*
Financial Services:		
Finance receivables	$375,740	$339,470
Marketable securities	97,850	93,240
Property, plant, and equipment	3,580	3,580
Other assets	47,470	54,920
Total assets	$723,140	$691,190

Liabilities

Accounts payable and accrued liabilities	$ 78,160	$ 77,180
Debt obligations	401,800	370,710
Deferred income taxes	12,930	13,050
Minority interests in consolidated subsidiaries . . .	4,370	4,370
Other liabilities	53,380	53,380
Total liabilities	$550,640	$518,690

Shareholders' Equity

4½% cumulative preferred stock, $100 par, authorized 37,114 shares, issued 11,492 shares	$ 1,150	$ 1,150
Common stock, $0.50 par, authorized 10,000,000 shares, issued 3,752,063 shares	1,880	1,880
Additional paid-in capital	48,000	48,000
Retained earnings	123,590	123,590
Other items decreasing shareholders' equity	(2,120)	(2,120)
Total shareholders' equity	$172,500	$172,500
Total liabilities and shareholders' equity	$723,140	$691,190

MEGADATA LTD.
Consolidated Income Statement
Year Ended December 31, 1988
(in thousands)

	Restated for Policy Change	*Previous Policy*
Revenues:		
Information services/products:		
Net sales	$169,890	$169,890
Services	123,900	123,900
Rentals	36,320	36,320
Total	$330,110	$330,110

(continued)

	Restated for Policy Change	Previous Policy
Financial services:		
Interest and discounts.	$ 66,900	$ 62,230
Insurance premiums	26,830	26,830
Investment and other income	10,190	10,030
Total	$103,920	$ 99,090
Total revenues	$434,030	$429,200
Expenses:		
Information services/products:		
Cost of sales	$118,860	$118,860
Cost of services	72,420	72,420
Cost of rentals	12,740	12,740
Selling, general, administrative.	69,300	69,300
Technical expenses	32,590	32,590
Interest expense	10,040	10,040
Total	$315,950	$315,950
Financial services:		
Interest expense	$ 35,860	$ 32,340
Operating expenses	32,920	32,660
Provision for credit losses	5,430	5,350
Insurance losses and reserves	20,940	20,940
Total	$ 95,150	$ 91,290
Total expenses	$411,100	$407,240
Earnings before income taxes and other items:		
Information services/products	$ 14,160	$ 14,160
Financial services	8,770	7,800
Total	$ 22,930	$ 21,960
Provision for income taxes	$ 6,760	$ 6,310
Earnings before other items	$ 16,170	$ 15,650
Minority interests and equity in operations of affiliates	(660)	(140)
Net earnings	$ 15,510	$ 15,510
Earnings per share	$ 4.11	$ 4.11

MEGADATA LTD.
Supplemental Information Treating
Megadata Credit Company Ltd.
as a Non-Consolidated Subsidiary
(in thousands)

Condensed balance sheet information (December 31, 1988):

Current assets.	$125,910
Investment in Megadata Credit Company Ltd.	80,850
Leased and data centre equipment	40,010
Property, plant, and equipment	28,750
Other assets	17,670
Total assets.	$293,190

Liabilities and shareholders' equity:

Current liabilities	$ 74,000
Long-term obligations, less current portions	13,180
Amounts due Megadata Credit Company Ltd.	
less current portions.	22,340
Deferred income taxes.	1,850
Other noncurrent liabilities.	5,000
Minority interests in consolidated subsidiaries	4,320
Shareholders' equity.	172,500
Total liabilities and shareholders' equity	$293,190

Condensed earnings information (year ended December 31, 1988):

Revenue	$318,260
Expenses.	301,770
Earnings before income taxes.	$ 16,490
Provision for income taxes	4,650
Minority interests and equity in operations of affiliates	(890)
Net earnings excluding Megadata Credit	$ 10,950
Net earnings of Megadata Credit (equity method)	4,560
Net earnings	$ 15,510
Earnings per share.	$4.11

Case 51

Midnight Express Ltd.

Midnight Express Ltd. is a trucking company, and an audit client of the CA firm where you are employed. The company is privately owned, and has an audit primarily to satisfy the chartered bank that provides long-term, fixed rate financing for its truck fleet and short-term demand loans to finance working capital requirements at various peak seasons.

Doug McKenzie, the controller, is a competent professional who believes in giving the auditors "a hard time." One of his recurring themes is accounting rules that Midnight must follow to get an unqualified audit report, that McKenzie does not agree with or does not think meaningful.

Two weeks before this year's audit field work was to begin, Mr. McKenzie sent a letter to the partner-in-charge of the audit, outlining his objections to comprehensive tax allocation and deferred taxes (see Exhibit 1). The partner has asked you to prepare some notes outlining McKenzie's objections and opposing arguments, for him to refer to in his upcoming discussion with Mr. McKenzie.

Required

Respond to the request of the partner.

EXHIBIT 1   Letter to Partner

MIDNIGHT EXPRESS LTD.

January 14, 1990

Mr. Bob McGraw, Partner,
Audit & Co.,
100 Main Street,
Anytown, British Columbia.

Dear Bob,

I wish to take this opportunity to lay out my objections to the accounting rules that require Midnight Express Ltd. to set up deferred taxes each year. If possible, I would like to eliminate this accounting policy for the 1989 year just ended.

First of all, the way our truck fleet has been growing, and is expected to grow over the foreseeable future, timing differences caused by the depreciation versus CCA problem will never reverse. If they never reverse, why should we set them up?

Even if we held our truck fleet at a constant size, the increase in truck prices would also guarantee that timing differences would not go down. This year we're replacing trucks that originally cost $27,000 with those costing $47,000. Some of this price differential is caused by a decision to upgrade the fleet, but the result is the same.

Secondly, our legal liability is only to pay the taxes payable on the tax form. Why set up this "thing" called deferred taxes when we don't owe it to anyone? After all, it's taxable income that incurs tax, not accounting income.

Finally, my bank manager, who is the major reason we have an audit and conform to all these rules, seems to be more interested in "cash from operations" than anything else. All he seems to be concerned about is that we can make our loan payments, and his calculations always seem to involve "adding back" things like deferred taxes. Why don't we produce statements that are tailored to his needs?

I look forward to seeing you and your staff in a couple of weeks when we will have the opportunity to discuss these issues further.

Yours truly,

Doug McKenzie

Mills' Audio Limited

Mills' Audio Limited was a small but aggressive company that began by manufacturing hearing aids, but has since expanded into the production of speakers for car stereos. It was controlled by the company president and founder, Mr. T. Mills, who owned 63 percent of the company's shares. The remaining shares were owned by five individuals who all served on the company's Board of Directors.

At a recent meeting, the Board had discussed possible ways to continue expansion, including going public. The Board, therefore, asked Mr. Mills to meet with Jim Acta, the company controller, to discuss the preparation of the 1985 financial statements. Future expansion plans will depend on the profitability of the company in 1985, and the Board needs an estimate of the pretax income as quickly as possible. In addition, the directors want to be advised of any accounting issues that may affect the estimated income and thereby influence the expansion plans.

Immediately after the meeting with the president, Jim Acta sat down with his assistant, Art Simpson, to discuss the financial statements for the year just ended. Art presented Jim with a first draft of the balance sheet and income statement for the year ended December 31, 1985 (Exhibit 1).

The following conversation ensued:

Jim:

I see you have made all of the usual adjusting entries. What problem areas did you run into this year?

Art:

First, our January 2, 1985 purchase of 30 percent of Lanibald Limited has yielded the results we expected. This year our purchases from Lanibald totaled $421,000 and inventory of their product at year-end totaled $50,000. They deliver twice as fast as last year, but sell to us on the same terms as anyone else. They work on a 25 percent markup over cost.

Institute of Chartered Accountants of Ontario, adapted.

When we purchased the shares, I recorded it as a $300,000 investment. There had been five shareholders, each owning 20 percent of the common shares. We bought an equal amount from each one, so that each now owns 14 percent. We paid each shareholder $15,000 cash and gave each a $45,000 note, noninterest bearing, due January 1, 1990 even though we would have borrowed at 12 percent from the bank. The promissory notes payable on our balance sheet are still recorded as $225,000. The details on acquisition book values and fair market values are here [Exhibit 2].

The Lanibald accountant says their consolidated net income for 1985 is $123,000. No dividends were declared and no common shares were issued during 1985. Our share has not been recorded on our draft statements although it would be nice if we could justify increasing our income by including our share of Lanibald's income.

Jim:

I can see why Lanibald is a problem area. What's next?

Art:

We entered into an equipment lease agreement on July 1, 1985. The $70,000 annual payment was paid on that date. I expensed one half of it, and set up the remainder as a prepaid on the draft statements. Here is a summary of the details [Exhibit 3].

Jim:

We will have to examine that in greater detail. What is number three on your list of problem areas?

Art:

The employees are very happy about the new pension plan introduced at the end of 1985. Each year of employment provides 2 percent of the employee's final year salary. It is a noncontributory plan; the average employee age is 36.

The actuary used the accrued benefit valuation method to project the present value of past service pension costs. We paid the trustee $96,000, which will provide for the past service obligation over the 15 years allowed by law. The current service costs were an additional $100,000. I recorded both of these amounts as pension expense. It's too bad the law required a 15-year maximum period for funding. If we were allowed to fund over 20 years, our payments would have dropped to $84,000.

Required

Assume that you are Jim Acta. Prepare a report to the president which addresses the concerns of the board of directors. The report should identify the relevant reporting issues and present recommendations that are appropriate for the company's reporting situation. Clearly indicate the impact that your recommendations will have on the company's financial statements and the notes thereto. You need not prepare revised statements.

EXHIBIT 1

MILLS' AUDIO LIMITED
Balance Sheet (first draft)
As at December 31, 1985

Assets

Cash	$ 17,000
Accounts receivable.	1,034,000
Inventory	1,320,000
Prepaid expenses	81,000
	2,452,000
Land	284,000
Building	493,000
Equipment	2,060,000
Accumulated depreciation	(1,039,000)
	1,798,000
Investment in Lanibald Limited	300,000
Total assets	$ 4,550,000

Liabilities and Equity

Bank loan	$ 190,000
Accounts payable.	980,000
Accrued expenses and liabilities	240,000
	1,410,000
Promissory notes payable	225,000
Bonds payable	1,320,000
Term bank loan.	420,000
	1,965,000
Capital stock	360,000
Retained earnings.	815,000
Total liabilities and equity	$ 4,550,000
Revenue	$11,372,000
Cost of goods sold	9,458,000
Gross profit	1,914,000
Expenses:	
Administrative and selling	$ 910,000
Interest	268,000
Pension	196,000
Other	192,000
Total	$ 1,566,000
Income before income taxes	$ 348,000

EXHIBIT 2

LANIBALD LIMITED
Condensed Balance Sheet
At December 31, 1984

	Book Value	Fair Value
Current assets	$ 540,000	$555,000
Land	120,000	184,000
Plant (net).	180,000	220,000
Equipment (net)	345,000	345,000
Goodwill	10,000	?
Total	$1,195,000	
Current liabilities . . .	$ 370,000	$370,000
Long-term debt	365,000	345,000
Common stock	125,000	—
Retained earnings . . .	335,000	—
Total	$1,195,000	

1. All of the differences between fair value and book value of current assets relate to inventory.
2. The plant has a remaining useful life of 20 years.
3. The goodwill arose 10 years ago when Lanibald Limited purchased 100 percent of Mimdar Inc. The goodwill is being amortized over a 30-year period on a straight-line basis.
4. The long-term debt matures on December 31, 1989.

EXHIBIT 3 Memorandum

To: Jim Acta
From: Art Simpson
Re: Equipment Lease

The details of the lease are as follows:

Effective date:	July 1, 1985
Term:	10 years
Payments:	$70,000 annual payments beginning July 1, 1985
Disposition at the end of the lease:	Two options available at that date:
	Option A: pay $20,000 to acquire title to the equipment
	Option B: return equipment and pay $20,000; lessor will refund proceeds when he sells equipment

We could have purchased the equipment in July 1985 for:

Sales price:	$450,000
Salvage value:	$30,000 at the end of 10 years; 0 at the end of its 12-year estimated useful life
Bank interest rate:	12%

Miller Manufacturing Limited

Miller Manufacturing is a small private company in the plastic molding business. The market is very competitive for these products, but Miller has a good reputation for quality products delivered on time.

Your firm, Audit & Co., has been appointed auditors of Miller for the 1988 fiscal year-end. Miller's bankers, who provide an operating line of credit secured by inventory and receivables, and long-term financing secured by fixed assets, have requested an audit. Previously, Miller had your firm review the statements and attach "Accountant's Comments." Audit & Co. has also prepared tax returns.

You are part of the audit team, and have been assigned to the Fixed Assets section. Analysis of the various accounts has been provided to you (see Exhibits 1 and 2). The senior in charge of the audit has asked you to examine the accounts, comment on the acceptability of Miller's policies, and prepare any journal entries necessary.

Required

Respond to the requests of the audit senior.

EXHIBIT 1   Miller Manufacturing Limited—Fixed Asset Accounts

Land

Balance, January 1, 1988	$400,000
Adjustment, November 22, 1988 . . .	320,000
Balance, December 31, 1988	$720,000

The "Adjustment" recorded increases land to its fair market value ($720,000) per appraiser's reports. The credit was made to "Unusual item—gain on land value increase," an income statement item.

Buildings

Balance, January 1, 1988.	$329,000
Additions during year:	
New roof, June 24, 1988	20,000
Paint and general repairs, July 19, 1988 . . .	17,000
Balance, December 31, 1988	$366,000

Automotive Equipment

Balance, January 1, 1988.	$41,900
Balance, December 31, 1988 . . .	$41,900

Note: During 1988, John Miller, the major shareholder, gave the company a 1983 Chevy Van, which his children had used but no longer wanted. No entry was made to record this asset, as it was acquired at no cost to the company. It was worth $5,000.

Manufacturing Equipment

Balance, January 1, 1988.	$129,400
Additions during the year:	
Injection molder, March 31, 1988	12,000
Packaging equipment, December 31, 1988 . . .	6,000
Balance, December 31, 1988	$147,400

The injection molder was bought used, at a bankruptcy sale. Miller estimated it was really worth $17,000, but they got a bargain. It cost $2,000 to transport and install the machine. This was expensed.

Packaging equipment had an invoice price of $15,000. Miller got a $9,000 government grant, under an upgrading program, to partially offset the purchase price.

EXHIBIT 2   Miller Manufacturing Limited—Depreciation

Depreciation is recorded at rates sufficient to amortize the cost of fixed assets over their useful life.

   Buildings—4 percent, straight-line
   Automotive—20 percent, straight-line
   Equipment—15 percent, straight-line

A full year's depreciation is charged in the year of acquisition unless the item was not used in the year of acquisition, in which case no depreciation is charged.

   Depreciation expense, buildings. $13,040

Note: An existing storage building, original cost, $40,000, was not used in 1988, so no depreciation was charged (matching).

   Depreciation expense, automotive equipment. . . . . $ 8,380

   Depreciation expense, manufacturing equipment . . . $22,110

Case 54

Molson

The Molson Companies Limited (Molson) is a diversified Canadian public corporation with operations in brewing, industrial and institutional cleaning and sanitation, and retail merchandising. The company is comprised of three principal operating companies: Molson Breweries of Canada Limited, Diversey Corporation, and Beaver Lumber Company Limited. Molson has more than 11,000 employees across Canada and abroad. The company was founded in 1786 and is now in its third century of business in Canada.

Selected data from the company's March 31, 1987 annual report (in thousands) is presented below:

Intangible assets	$ 67,780
Fixed assets	448,312
Total assets	1,236,840
Sales and other revenues	2,250,364
Depreciation and amortization	54,902
Depreciation	51,234
Net earnings	52,320

Notes to the Financial Statements

Note 1: Accounting Policies

Intangible Assets

Intangible assets include principally goodwill and hockey franchises. Goodwill is amortized on a straight-line basis over periods not exceeding 40 years. Hockey franchises are not amortized as the corporation believes there has been no decrease in their value.

Note 2: Business Acquisitions

Effective July 1, 1986, the corporation acquired for cash all the outstanding shares of Crown Stores Limited, a chain of stores servicing the lumber, building materials, and related hardgoods markets in Saskatchewan, Alberta, and British Columbia.

The corporation also acquired, effective December 1, 1986, for a combination of cash and capital stock, all the outstanding shares of Lighting Unlimited Corporation Limited, a specialty retailer of light fixtures for residential and commercial use.

The foregoing acquisitions are accounted for by the purchase method. Their results of operations are included in the accounts from the effective dates of acquisition. Details of the acquisitions are as follows:

Net assets, at fair value:	
Working capital	$13,731
Fixed assets	4,799
Other assets	146
Goodwill	10,271
	$28,947
Consideration given:	
Cash	$28,252
Capital stock	695
	$28,947

Required

Evaluate Molson's accounting policy for the valuation of intangible assets. Include in your discussion a general description of the accounting issues relating to intangibles.

Case 55

Monthly Magazine Limited

Monthly Magazine Limited (MML) has recently been incorporated under the Canada Business Corporations Act. At present, MML is owned by a small group of investors, but their plans include eventual sale of common stock to the public.

They have prepared an operating cash flow forecast for the first five years of operations. These show an excess of cash disbursements for publication costs over cash receipts for the first three years. In the fourth year, cash receipts and cash disbursements for publication costs are expected to be equal. In year 5 it is expected that cash receipts will exceed cash disbursements.

MML already has agreements with a major supermarket chain and with several magazine distributors, who have agreed to display or distribute the magazine for 24 months, as a minimum, and 10 years, as a maximum. Selling price is to be 95 cents of which 43 cents goes to the supermarket chain and distributor. Both the supermarket chain and the distributor are allowed to return 20 percent of the quantities ordered each month, if the magazines do not sell.

The major costs of a new magazine fall into three categories: (1) initial costs: market surveys, design costs, salaries prior to publication of the first issue, and similar items; (2) publication costs: printing, salaries, and similar cash costs of operating an office; and (3) expenditures for fixed assets, leasehold improvements, and similar long-lived assets.

Adapted, with permission from the *Uniform Final Examination Handbook,* 1977. © The Canadian Institute of Chartered Accountants, Toronto.

Changes to the original question and/or suggested approach to answering are the sole responsibility of the authors and have not been reviewed or endorsed by the CICA.

The president of MML has told you, the controller, that he wishes to use the following accounting principles and policies for external reporting purposes:

1. Initial costs are to be capitalized and, commencing in year 5, amortized over five years.
2. Publication costs in excess of revenue in the first three years are to be capitalized and amortized in equal portions in years 5 and 6.
3. Long-lived assets are to be capitalized. Depreciation and amortization will commence in year 5.
4. Revenue from sales of magazines is to be recognized when sales are made to the supermarket chain or distributor.
5. An allowance for magazine returns is to be established initially at a rate of 10 percent of quantities published. (Quantities published will increase month by month if the magazine is successful.) This return rate will be adjusted every six months based on experience.
6. Advertising revenue is to be recognized during the month in which the ads are published in the magazine. Advertisers generally sign contracts for multi-issue, multi-month advertising space.

The president has asked you to advise on the acceptability of these principles and policies now so that all monthly, quarterly, and annual financial statements can be prepared on this basis. Since MML wishes to go public eventually, the president is not anxious to change accounting principles and policies.

Required

Write a letter to the president outlining your recommendations with respect to the accounting principles which MML should adopt. Explain your reasoning thoroughly.

Case 56

Moonbeam Mining Ltd.

Moonbeam Mining Limited (MML) is a federally incorporated company with shares traded on Canadian stock exchanges. The company has a number of public issues of bonds outstanding, and bond covenants contain restrictions regarding the ratio of consolidated debt to shareholders' equity. In addition, top executives of MML receive bonuses based upon net income measured in accordance with generally accepted accounting principles (GAAP).

MML operates several silver mines in Canada. In 1980, 3.6 million ounces of silver were produced at the mines. Independent mining engineers have estimated that as of January 1, 1981, the company's proven and probable silver reserves are about 24.3 million recoverable ounces.

In April 1981, MML issued to the public $25 million of 8.50 percent silver-indexed bonds due April 15, 1996. The bonds were issued at par. Each $1,000 face value bond is payable at maturity in $1,000 cash or 50 ounces of silver at the holders' option. The bonds are secured by an agreement entitling the Trustee to receive, upon default, and on behalf of the bondholders, 3.7 percent of the annual mining production of MML, limited to not more than an aggregate of 50 ounces of silver per outstanding bond.

The transaction may be viewed as an issuance of convertible debt. Debt securities are often issued with a conversion feature which permits the holder to convert a bond into a predetermined number of shares of common stock, whereas MML bonds permit the holders to convert a bond into a predetermined number of ounces of silver. This call option on silver allowed MML to issue the bonds initially at a substantially higher price than it could have obtained for a bond with an 8.50 percent interest rate

Reprinted with permission from the *Uniform Final Examination Report* (1981). © The Canadian Institute of Chartered Accountants, Toronto.

but without the call option on silver. Major considerations in deciding how MML should account for the proceeds from the issuance of the convertible debt are:

1. The valuation of the liability at the date of issuance and subsequently;
2. The measurement of interest expense in each period the debt is outstanding; and
3. The treatment of the bond retirement at maturity.

One possibility for accounting for the bonds at issuance, though not one proposed by management, is to view the convertible debt as possessing the characteristics of both a debt and a call option on silver. Consistent with this view, a portion of the proceeds could be allocated to the call option and credited to a separate account. The amount so allocated would be a measure of the excess of the fair value of the bond liability expected at maturity over its par value. The remainder of the proceeds would be allocated to the debt. To reflect the bond liability at its par value, the recording of a bond discount would be required. The amount assigned to the call options could be measured as the excess of the amount received for the bonds over the estimated price that could have been obtained for similar bonds without the call option on silver since estimation can be made with reasonable accuracy. The amount recorded in the deferred credit account would be included in the liabilities of the company's balance sheet. The following entry reflects this interpretation (all amounts are hypothetical):

Cash	1,000	
Discount on silver-indexed bond	300	
Silver-indexed bond payable		1,000
Deferred credit—call option on silver		300

    To record the issuance of one silver-indexed bond.

Consistent with this method, the bond discount would be amortized to interest expense in each year the debt is outstanding. The deferred credit would be adjusted upward or downward each year to reflect changes in the fair value of the call option on silver because of changes in the market price of silver. Any such adjustment would be charged or credited to interest expense in each year.

The entry at maturity, assuming the market price of silver is $40 per ounce, at that time, is as follows (all amounts are hypothetical):

Silver-indexed bond payable	1,000	
Deferred credit—call option on silver	1,000	
Revenue from the sale of silver		2,000

    To record the delivery of 50 ounces of silver to the Trustee to satisfy the debt obligation on one silver-indexed bond.

Alternatively, the management of MML has proposed another method to record the silver-indexed bond in a manner consistent with a "debt only" view of the transaction. The bonds would be recorded at their face value. Interest expense reported in each period would reflect the coupon rate of interest. If bondholders elect to take silver as payment at maturity, management proposes to record the delivery to the Trustee as a sale of silver at $20 per ounce.

This method would result in the following journal entry at maturity (all amounts are hypothetical):

Silver-indexed bond payable.	1,000	
Revenue from the sale of silver		1,000

To record the delivery of 50 ounces of silver to the Trustee to satisfy the debt obligation on one silver-indexed bond.

Under management's proposed method, MML would realize, at maturity, a loss or profit from the delivery of silver depending on whether or not the cost of producing silver exceeds $20 per ounce at maturity. If the market price of silver at maturity falls below $20 per ounce, bondholders will take cash rather than silver to satisfy the debt obligation, so that all of the company's silver production would be sold in the normal course of operation.

The silver-indexed bonds of MML reflect an unusual and unique response to inflation; namely, providing bondholders with a hedge against inflation. As inflation continues at or near double-digit rates, we are likely to see an increased number of debt obligations similar to that of MML which are convertible into various commodities such as silver, gold or oil, all of which give the bondholder the opportunity to share in the appreciation of nonmonetary assets over long periods of time. These types of complicated option contracts are likely to put considerable pressure and strain on transaction or exchange-based accounting, since such transactions or exchanges may effectively be held open for many years.

Required

a. Discuss the advantages and disadvantages of the silver-indexed bonds with respect to the financial management of the issuing company.
b. Provide a critical evaluation of both the accounting treatment proposed by management and the alternative accounting treatment illustrated in the question for the silver-indexed bonds. Conclude by stating which treatment you consider as most appropriate and why.

NSTR

Nova Scotia Timber Resources Ltd. (NSTR) is a privately held company incorporated under the companies legislation of Nova Scotia. It is owned by a family syndicate based in Bonn, West Germany. The syndicate has been actively involved in acquiring timberland in the Province of Nova Scotia for the past five years. Early in 1989, the decision was made to roll the assets into a corporation, and harvest timber for the first time. Previously, land acquired had been left idle.

While a primary purpose of the land acquisition was to gain profit from the timber resources, the syndicate's long-term goals included profits on the land itself. Germany, with its high-density population, uses any recreational land to the utmost. Nova Scotia properties, including ocean access to unpolluted water, represent attractive acquisition targets.

The syndicate has retained finance contracts on the properties in their personal names—the land, not the debt, has been transferred to NSTR, although the land is often collateral for the debt securities. In addition, though, the owners provided personal guarantees on an operating line of credit for NSTR of up to $4 million with the Royal Bank of Canada. The loan is also secured by a floating charge on inventory and receivables.

NSTR, in its first year of production, leased a building (for 10 years) which housed sawmill operations, administrative offices, and a warehouse. It also acquired about $400,000 of processing equipment, trucks, tools, and other necessary assets.

As trees are harvested, the decision must be made whether to sell the logs to other sawmills or users of timber, or process the logs in NSTR's own facilities. The quality of logs varies. A five-year contract was signed with a plant in Nova Scotia that used low-quality logs to produce chipboard and paneling. The price agreed on was "fair market value," deter-

Atlantic Provinces Association of Chartered Accountants, adapted.

mined monthly, and minimum delivery quantities were established on a monthly basis.

Higher quality logs, processed internally, become lumber of various dimensions, sold to both building supply companies and independent contractors in the Maritimes and in the Quebec and Ontario markets. Transportation costs made it difficult to compete strongly in the Quebec and Ontario markets. Terms have usually been cash payment within 60 days of delivery.

Prices of these finished products are a function of supply and demand at the date of sale. Inventory is stored in NSTR's warehouses, incurring interest and storage costs, if the current market price is deemed unacceptably low by management. They refused to accept prices below cost, and lumber prices had been quite volatile in 1989. For example, one of the by-products associated with the sawmill process, wood chips, can be sold in retail stores (bagged), sold to industrial concerns for fuel, or sold as an input to chipboard plants. Management has decided that the prices offered for the last two uses do not cover costs and are carrying wood chips in inventory.

Management has the responsibility for making these decisions; they also make decisions concerning how much lumber to harvest in any one year, based on their market predictions.

The syndicate has set a policy of reforestation of harvested land, consistent with their long-term goals of land appreciation. The costs to fulfill this policy, while not large in 1989, are expected to be material in future years.

The company's first year-end has just passed. The syndicate has not indicated how net income is to be computed, nor has the Canadian management spent much time considering financial accounting policies. There has been some indication that the syndicate wishes to be able to draw funds, in the form of dividends, to meet debt service charges and principal repayment. In addition, some consideration had been given to awarding senior management some bonus on net income, although details for this have yet to be worked out. In addition, they have not established a uniform internal information system that will provide needed information to management.

Required

Assume the role of an accounting adviser to the company, and explain the financial accounting policies and principles the company should adopt. Outline an acceptable information system, and deal with any other issues you find important.

Case 58

National Design Productions Ltd.

You have just returned from a meeting with a client who is considering an opportunity to invest in nonvoting shares of National Design Productions Ltd. (NDP). Your client was very enthusiastic about the company, pointing out the company's high return on assets, low long-term debt : equity ratio and high operating margin on production activities. Your client is also impressed with NDP's large positive cash flow from operations.

NDP is offering to sell 100 shares of nonvoting common shares to private investors for $10,000 per share. The nonvoting shares would receive the same dividends as the voting shares. Before investing in a few of these shares, however, your client wants to have your advice as to the apparent advisability of the investment. The client has given you the financial statements of NDP and some additional background information upon which to base your opinion.

National Design Productions is a private Ontario corporation that was founded in 1968 by Cy Gilbert. Cy was a fashion consultant who was often called upon to help stage fashion shows and other promotional events in the fashion industry. Cy began to videotape the shows and promotions to use as sales tools to show other prospective clients the type of work that he could do and then realized that videotape could in itself be a useful promotional tool. He therefore established National Design Productions as a video production company, initially dedicated to fashion productions.

Before long, NDP had built a solid reputation for video productions, and the rapidly growing company began producing videos for other commercial and promotional ventures outside of the fashion industry. Within

Institute of Chartered Accountants of Ontario, adapted.

20 years, the company had grown to encompass video productions of many types and had become a vertically integrated video company with owned and franchised operations across Canada.

NDP's core business is still the production of videos, but the scope of the business has increased dramatically. About 60 percent of the production volume is for videos made under contract for commercial users. About two thirds of that volume is done under retainer, wherein the customer signs an annual contract to pay a flat amount per month plus the cost of any videos produced. The flat fee is therefore NDP's profit, and NDP gets to keep that amount whether the customer wants a dozen productions or none during the year. Of course, the size of each customer's fee is set in relation to the past and expected volume of production for that customer.

NDP recognizes the full amount of the retainer as revenue when the retainer contract is signed. The customer makes 12 equal monthly payments throughout the contract year. NDP began the retainer programme in 1986 and has been placing increasing emphasis on retainer contracts. Retainer contract signing was particularly heavy in the last quarter of 1987; those contracts run into the third and fourth quarter of 1988.

The remaining one third of the commercial production volume is performed under individual cost-plus-fixed-fee contracts.

The other 40 percent of the video production volume consists of independent productions of adult videos undertaken by NDP. These videos are exhibited commercially in Quebec and British Columbia, with a specially edited version exhibited in Ontario. The videos are also rented and sold at retail by the exhibitors as well as by other video outlets across the country. The exhibitors are unrelated to NDP but pay a percentage of their gross receipts to NDP as a rental fee.

The costs of producing these adult videos are capitalized and amortized. The amortization period is four years on a modified straight-line basis of 15 percent, 30 percent, 30 percent, and 25 percent per year consecutively.

The video stores that rent and sell the adult videos are of three types. The first type is independent dealers who buy the videos (with the right to return up to 30 percent of unsold and unopened videos) and rent or sell them.

The second type is the remnants of a chain of video outlets called White Heat Videos that operates mainly in British Columbia. This chain had been an independent company, but 100 of its stores were purchased by NDP in 1985. NDP has been following a policy of reselling these stores as independent units tied to a franchise agreement. The franchise name (and the new name under which former White Heat stores operate) is White Knight Video.

The third type is stores that are franchised by White Knight. Most of the franchisees are in Quebec and have been opened during the past two years (i.e., since NDP acquired White Heat). Twenty-two franchises have been sold during the past two years, and NDP management expects that franchise sales will decline in future years. The franchise fee is recognized as revenue when the franchisee is substantially open for business. The franchisee pays most of the price of the franchise over a period not to exceed three years after opening.

NDP also has a leasing subsidiary, Video Equipment Leasing Limited (VEL). VEL was founded by NDP to acquire the equipment and other fixed assets needed by NDP and to lease it to NDP. VEL also leases to other, smaller production companies, but NDP accounts for about 85 percent of VEL's leasing volume. NDP management felt that it was easier to pass the rental costs of equipment on to the customers than it was to pass on depreciation allocations. NDP guarantees the secondary debt of VEL by which the equipment was financed.

Required

Submit a report to your client in which you discuss the advisability of investing in nonvoting shares of NDP. Support your recommendations with specific numerical analyses that are relevant to the prospective investment decision. Ignore income tax considerations.

Auditor's Report

To the shareholders of
National Design Productions Ltd.:

We have examined the consolidated balance sheet of National Design Productions Ltd. as at December 31, 1987 and the consolidated statements of income and of changes in financial position for the year then ended. Our examination was made in accordance with generally accepted auditing standards, and accordingly included such tests and other procedures as we considered necessary in the circumstances.

In our opinion, these consolidated financial statements present fairly the financial position of National Design Productions Ltd. as at December 31, 1987 and the results of its operations and the changes in its financial position for the year then ended in accordance with generally accepted accounting principles applied on a basis consistent with that of the preceding year.

(signed)

Leban and Wolfe, Chartered Accountants
February 14, 1988

NATIONAL DESIGN PRODUCTIONS LTD.
Consolidated Balance Sheet
December 31

	1987	1986
Assets		
Current assets:		
Cash and deposits.	$ 256,000	$ 419,000
Accounts receivable (Note 2).	2,289,000	1,068,000
Inventories:		
NDP.	233,000	187,000
Stores	100,000	628,000
Total current assets	$2,878,000	$2,302,000
Furniture and fixtures—stores	1,401,000	4,916,000
Accumulated depreciation	649,000	2,371,000
	752,000	2,545,000
Other assets:		
Notes receivable—franchisees (Note 3)	805,000	400,000
Investments in unconsolidated subsidiaries		
(Note 6)	254,000	264,000
Deferred production costs (Note 1)	2,429,000	1,688,000
Total assets	$7,118,000	$7,199,000
Liabilities and Shareholders' Equity		
Current liabilities:		
Bank operating loan (Note 7).	$1,100,000	$ 500,000
Current portion of term loan (Note 7)	—	306,000
Accounts payable: NDP	462,000	277,000
Stores	201,000	635,000
Income taxes and accrued expenses.	119,000	87,000
Total current liabilities.	$1,882,000	$1,805,000
Long-term debt:		
Term loan payable (Note 7)	1,519,000	2,994,000
Deferred income taxes (Note 8).	1,392,000	383,000
Shareholders's equity:		
Common shares (Note 9).	500,000	500,000
Retained earnings.	1,825,000	1,517,000
Total shareholders' equity	$2,325,000	$2,017,000
Total Liabilities and Equity	$7,118,000	$7,199,000

NATIONAL DESIGN PRODUCTIONS LTD.
Consolidated Statement of Income and Retained Earnings
Year Ended December 31

	1987	1986
Revenue from production activities:		
Contract production revenue	$3,219,000	$1,797,000
Video sales and rental	1,327,000	1,113,000
Less: allowance for returns	(116,000)	(97,000)
	4,430,000	2,813,000
Other revenue:		
Franchise fees (Note 5)	1,080,000	840,000
Equity in earnings of unconsolidated subsidiary (Note 6)	44,000	41,000
Total revenue from continuing operations	5,554,000	3,694,000
Net revenue from store operations:		
Store revenue (Note 4)	1,396,000	4,710,000
Store operating expenses	1,384,000	4,569,000
	12,000	141,000
Gains on sale of stores	572,000	73,000
Revenue from operations being discontinued	584,000	214,000
Total revenue	6,138,000	3,908,000
Expenses:		
Contract production costs	1,514,000	1,344,000
Amortization of production costs (Note 1)	599,000	432,000
General selling and administration	862,000	738,000
Interest expense	369,000	276,000
Income tax expense (Note 8)	1,286,000	514,000
Total expenses	4,630,000	3,304,000
Net income	1,508,000	604,000
Balance of retained earnings, January 1	1,517,000	1,413,000
Dividends on common shares	(1,200,000)	(500,000)
Retained earnings, December 31	$1,825,000	$1,517,000

NATIONAL DESIGN PRODUCTIONS LTD.
Consolidated Statement of Changes in Financial Position
Year Ended December 31

	1987	1986
Operations:		
Net income	$1,508,000	$ 604,000
Amortization of production costs	599,000	432,000
Deferred income taxes	1,009,000	319,000
Excess of dividends over equity earnings in subsidiary	10,000	—
Gains on disposal of stores	(572,000)	(73,000)
Net changes in receivables, inventories and payables	(1,361,000)	(637,000)
Cash provided by operations	1,193,000	645,000
Financing activities:		
. Repayment of term loan	(1,781,000)	(226,000)
Dividends declared and paid	(1,200,000)	(500,000)
Cash provided (used) in financing activities	(2,981,000)	(726,000)
Investing activities:		
Investment in video production.	(1,340,000)	(513,000)
Proceeds from sale of stores	2,365,000	360,000
Cash provided (used) in investing activities	1,025,000	(153,000)
Increase (decrease) in cash	$ (763,000)	$(234,000)

Notes to Financial Statements, Year Ended December 31, 1987

1. Accounting Policies

Consolidation: All subsidiaries are consolidated with the accounts of National Design Productions Ltd. except for wholly owned Video Equipment Leasing Ltd. (VEL). As a leasing company, VEL has a financial structure which is significantly different than that of the other operations in the consolidated group and therefore is reported on the equity basis for better understanding. Condensed financial statements of VEL are reported in Note 6.

Revenue: (a) Revenue from video sales is recognized when the videotapes are shipped to the dealers. Rental revenue is recognized monthly as the rental receipts are reported by the dealers to NDP. *(b)* Revenue on cost-plus contracts is recognized as the contracts proceed, using the percentage of cost completion basis. Retainers are recognized when the contract is signed. *(c)* Franchise fees are recognized when all substantive effort has been performed by NDP and the franchisee has begun operations.

(continued)

Production Costs: The costs of producing videos for sale and rental are capitalized and amortized to income on a straight-line basis over four years at rates of 15 percent, 30 percent, 30 percent, and 25 percent per year consecutively.

Income Taxes: NDP uses the full allocation basis of reporting income taxes, whereby the future or past income tax effect of revenues and expenses is reported in the income statement in the period in which the related items of revenue and expense are themselves recognized in income.

Furniture and Fixtures: The store furniture and fixtures are reported at cost less accumulated depreciation. Depreciation is straight line at a rate of 8 percent per year.

2. Accounts Receivable

	1987	1986
Dealers	$ 443,000	$ 325,000
Production contracts	431,000	407,000
Retainers	1,101,000	213,000
Franchise fees	510,000	263,000
	$2,485,000	$1,208,000
Allowance for returns	(116,000)	(97,000)
Allowance for doubtful accounts	(80,000)	(43,000)
Net accounts receivable	$2,289,000	$1,068,000

3. Notes Receivable—Franchisees

The notes receivable from franchisees are due over a period of four years and mature as follows:

	1987	1986
Due in 1988	$345,000	$260,000
Due in 1989	260,000	140,000
Due in 1990	200,000	—
	$805,000	$400,000

4. White Heat Stores

In 1985, NDP acquired a group of 16 retail video stores operating under the name of White Heat Video. NDP has undertaken a program of selling these stores on an individual basis to be operated by the purchasers as White Knight franchises (Note 5). Twelve of the stores have been sold, 3 in 1986 and 9 in 1987. The remaining four stores are expected to be sold in 1988. The assets, liabilities, revenues, and expenses relating to these stores are segregated in these financial statements.

(continued)

5. Franchises

NDP has established the name of White Knight Video Stores as a trademarked name and sells this name as part of a franchise operation. Fourteen such franchises were sold in 1987 (1986: 8). The former White Heat Video stores are operated as franchises by the purchasers under the White Knight name.

6. Video Equipment Leasing Ltd.

Video Equipment Leasing Ltd. (VEL) is a wholly owned subsidiary of National Design Productions. VEL is engaged in the acquisition and lease of video production equipment and furniture and fixtures. NDP is the primary lessee, accounting for 85 percent of VEL asset leases. NDP's investment in VEL has been reported on the equity basis, whereby the earnings of VEL are reported in the NDP income statement. The condensed balance sheet and statement of income for VEL for 1987 are shown below:

VIDEO EQUIPMENT LEASING LTD.
Balance Sheet
December 31

	1987	1986
Assets available for lease:		
Video production equipment	$4,215,000	$3,765,000
Furniture and fixtures	972,000	1,012,000
Less: accumulated depreciation	(1,383,000)	(1,023,000)
Total assets	$3,804,000	$3,754,000
Long-term debt:		
Debentures payable	$3,209,000	$3,176,000
Deferred income taxes	341,000	314,000
Shareholders' equity:		
Common shares	200,000	200,000
Retained earnings	54,000	64,000
Total shareholders' equity	254,000	264,000
Total liabilities and equity	$3,804,000	$3,754,000

VIDEO EQUIPMENT LEASING LTD.
Statement of Income
Year Ended December 31

	1987	1986
Rental revenue	$1,191,000	$1,161,000
Expenses:		
Depreciation expense	498,000	465,000
Interest expense	397,000	373,000

(continued)

	1987	1986
Losses on asset disposal	$ 215,000	$ 247,000
Income taxes (deferred)	37,000	35,000
	1,147,000	1,120,000
Net income.	$ 44,000	$ 41,000

7. Bank Loans Payable

National Design Productions Ltd. carries an operating line of credit with the CIBC which is limited to 60 percent of billed accounts receivable, excluding franchise fees. The operating loan is payable on demand and bears interest at the rate of 2 percent above the prime rate, as established on the 15th of each month.

As part of the acquisition of White Heat Video Stores in 1986 (Note 4), NDP arranged a seven-year term loan with the CIBC. This loan is payable in blended payments of not less than $434,000 per year for seven years. As the result of the disposition of most of the stores, loan repayment is well ahead of schedule and thus there is no current portion due at the end of 1987.

NDP is the unconditional guarantor of the debentures issued by Video Equipment Leasing Ltd.

All of the aforementioned liabilities are secured by a first fixed and floating charge against the assets of National Design Productions Ltd. and its subsidiaries, including Video Equipment Leasing Ltd. Accounts receivable are specifically assigned as security for the operating loan.

8. Deferred Income Taxes

Deferred income taxes arise from the fact that income tax expense on certain items of revenue and expense are recognized for income tax purposes in a different year than their recognition in the income statement. The items to which these differences apply are franchise fees and deferred production costs for NDP and CCA/depreciation for VEL.

9. Share Capital

There are 300 common shares issued and outstanding. There is no public market for the shares, and there were no transactions in these shares in 1987 or 1986.

Neuvo Inc.

Neuvo Inc. is incorporated under the Canada Business Corporations Act. Neuvo is a computer software company whose business is the custom design of large-scale software packages for large corporations, provincial governments, and so forth. The company's products are unique and of such a size that copying and unauthorized duplication are not feasible and therefore are not a problem for Neuvo. Neuvo is at the leading edge of software development and while it has a number of competitors, its market position is not threatened.

The company was founded four years ago by Chris Covert and Frances Ferris, two of Canada's most prominent software designers. Two thirds of the shares of the company are owned indirectly by Frances through a personal holding company and the other third is owned directly by Chris. The two founders brought several major clients with them from their previous employers, so that Neuvo had a significant base of customers right from the beginning. The prominence of Chris and Frances enabled them to attract other highly talented analysts and programmers.

In order to give the professional staff a sense of participation in the company, a profit sharing plan was put into effect whereby the staff who participated on a project received bonuses that totaled 20 percent of the gross margin on the project (i.e., of the difference between the total revenue and the direct and directly assignable costs). The bonuses on each project are determined only after the project is completed and is accepted by the customer.

The company has seen its revenues grow dramatically in the three years since its founding, from \$1,695,000 in the first year to \$7,411,000 in the most recent year. These revenues are derived solely from custom software design contracts, and have been reported on a completed contract

Institute of Chartered Accountants of Ontario, adapted.

basis. The contracts have been charged with all direct costs and with all costs that can be directly assigned to the project, such as an internal allocation for computer time and any overhead that can be directly allocated to the projects. All indirect overhead and administrative costs have been charged to the income statement as period costs. Using these accounting policies, net income has gone from $11,109 in the first year to $166,046 in the most recent year. Work in process at the end of the past year amounts to $2,776,623.

The company's custom work has resulted in the development of highly sophisticated products, such as a cartography program and a province-wide health care monitoring system. The owners, therefore, have decided to rewrite some of these programs in order to make them generally usable on computer systems other than the one for which they were specifically designed, and to sell them as proprietary products to other large-scale potential customers. For example, the health care system that was designed for one provincial government could be sold to other provinces and perhaps to some states in the United States.

In order to implement this new line of business, Neuvo had to expend considerable time and money to develop the generalized programs. These costs are being classified as "development costs" in Neuvo's accounting records.

In addition to the head office in Ottawa, the company set up five new offices to act as sales offices for the newly developed proprietary products. New offices were established in Toronto, Quebec City, Calgary, Vancouver, and Halifax. In each location, office space was leased, leasehold improvements were carried out, furniture and equipment were purchased and installed, and professional staff were hired. The equipment consisted mainly of powerful minicomputers that were linked to Neuvo's main computer in Ottawa. All of the costs incurred in setting up these offices, including the personnel costs and interest on the bank loan, have tentatively been classified as "start-up costs" in Neuvo's books.

Financing for the custom design work has been provided by the Queens Bank of Canada through an operating line of credit. The line of credit is limited to the sum of 70 percent of Neuvo's billed accounts receivable and 50 percent of contract work in progress (unbilled). The bank has not required audited financial statements from Neuvo. Neuvo has been borrowing against this line of credit to help finance the costs of proprietary product development and of the new offices. The line of credit is almost completely used up, however, and Chris and Frances have undertaken two courses of action to obtain additional funds. One source of financing is a completed sale-and-leaseback arrangement; the other source is a term loan that is currently being negotiated.

The sale-and-leaseback arrangement was for the company's mainframe computer. The computer had been completely written off in the first three years of operation, and the sale therefore generated a gain equal to the proceeds of the sale, almost $1 million. The leaseback arrangement took the form of a one-year lease with six-month renewals at the same monthly payment at the option of Neuvo. The computer was expected to be serviceable for at least three more years (with periodic upgrades to be paid for by Neuvo). Neuvo guaranteed the secondary financing that the lessor had obtained to finance the deal.

The term loan is potentially for a five-year period and is being negotiated with the bank to finance the development costs. Chris has been negotiating with the bank but the bank has not yet given an answer either way. The bank has made it clear, however, that if the loan is granted, there will be explicit maintenance tests (i.e., covenants) included as part of the loan agreement. The maintenance tests would include at least a minimum debt: equity ratio, a limit on dividend payout and owners' salary as a proportion of earnings, and a minimum interest coverage ratio. Failure to meet any of these tests would render both the term loan and the operating loan immediately callable by the bank.

In view of the changing nature of Neuvo's operations and the prospective bank financing, the owners have decided to reconsider the company's financial reporting policies. They have engaged Ned Norem as an expert accounting adviser and are looking forward to Ned's recommendations on accounting policies for the future.

Required

Assume the role of Ned Norem. Prepare a report for Chris Covert and Frances Ferris.

New Horizons Ltd.

New Horizons Ltd. was incorporated in 1987, with common shares owned equally by the three principals. Christine Newell, Nelson Wong, and Reginald Lee. Previously, these three engineers held positions in the research group of a large public plastics company. New Horizons was formed to develop, produce, and sell a process that would render various types of packaging "tamperproof," a booming market in the mid 1980s.

Newell, Wong, and Lee had been working on this concept for their previous employer. However, when the project was shelved, the three decided to go ahead with it on their own. They agreed to pay a royalty of 5 percent of sales in exchange for the use of research done to date, and left in 1987 with their employer's blessing and promises of their old jobs back if "things did not work out."

The year 1987 was spent developing the product to the point where it was technologically and economically viable. By February 1988, New Horizons' operations were well under way. A coordinated marketing effort and careful recruitment of sales representatives, as well as a little help from their previous employer, resulted in good manufacturer acceptance of the line. New Horizons dealt mostly with small manufacturers.

Since every application was unique, the machinery and process was custom tailored to each manufacturer's needs. This turned out to be easier than anticipated, although New Horizons had to provide engineering support for the first month or two of production to iron out any problems that developed.

From the beginning, the firm's accounting and related clerical activities were supervised by Dave Madden, a recent B. Comm. graduate with a background in accounting. Initially, attention was directed towards controlling cash, establishing cost records, and implementing a cost control system. Orders from customers were accepted after reference to a credit-rating publication.

It is now the end of 1988, and various accounting policies have to be established before the 1988 statements can be prepared. The principals wish to pick policies they will not have to later change, especially if they are successful in their ultimate goal of taking the company public.

They have asked Dave Madden to evaluate the alternatives for recording bad debt expense: direct write-off, setting up a percentage of sales, or aging the receivables and attempting some provision based on percentages or specific identification.

At present, the principals prefer the direct write-off method. It seems to them to be the only one based on objective, real events. They point out that there is no history to base a percentage on for either percentage of sales or an aging method. Specific identification makes them uncomfortable, as they point out that if a particular firm were not creditworthy, they never should have accepted the sale.

Required

Adopt the role of Dave Madden and write a brief report evaluating the alternative policies for calculating bad debt expense.

Nile Manufacturing Ltd.

Jaspar Jones is the president of Nile Manufacturing Ltd. (Nile), a small, privately owned company. The company manufactures numerous products. The family that owns the company prefers to remain out of the day-to-day operations because they have complete trust in Jaspar's judgement. In fact, they are so pleased at having Jaspar on the management team that they have instituted a bonus for him based on net income before taxes and extraordinary items. The family elected you as Nile's auditor at a recent board of directors meeting. Their only instruction to you was that they consider everything material. You have done all the audit work for the December 31, 1989 statements and have requested a meeting with Jaspar to discuss the following items:

1. One of Nile's fixed assets is a machine which makes doors. The unique characteristic of these doors is that they are very difficult to open and close due to their weight. The company felt that this would be a safety factor in that it would slow down a burglary. You have noticed that sales of this product have not broken any records. In fact, the only door that Nile has made is still in inventory after two years. The machine was very expensive and cannot be used for any other purpose. You have suggested that the value of both the door and the machine be written off. Jaspar agrees with you—he fully supports a charge against either 1988 net income (since it was known last year that the product would not be successful) or 1989 net income as long as it is disclosed outside operating items. You are willing to consider Jaspar's ideas.

2. On a tip from his broker, Jaspar had Nile purchase 10 common shares of British Enterprises during 1989. (British Enterprises is a major Canadian public company which trades on stock exchanges all over the world.) Jaspar intends that Nile hold these shares for many years, unless some cash is needed to meet the payroll. The shares cost $38 each and were trading for $35 each on December 31, 1989.

During the year, British Enterprises paid a dividend of $2 per share and reported basic earnings per share of $4. Jaspar recorded the following journal entries:

Dr. Cash 20
    Cr. Dividend income   20
  To record receipt of dividend.

Dr. Investment in British Enterprises 40
    Cr. Income from investment   40
  To record earnings attributable to common shares for 1989.

3. Nile has a product which is both extremely successful and very profitable—a battery-operated swizzle stick. The company can hardly produce this item fast enough. At a New Year's Eve party Jaspar ran into one of Nile's customers who said that he had been meaning to phone the company to order 100,000 of the swizzle sticks. They will be used as gifts to the employees at the customer's annual Valentine's Day party. Jaspar told the customer to phone him personally to arrange a cut price, full refund if not satisfied, deal on the sale. You have noticed a journal entry dated December 31, 1989 recording this sale "in anticipation."

Required

Present your analysis and recommendations for the treatment and disclosure of each of the above items on Nile Manufacturing Ltd.'s December 31, 1989 financial statements.

Case 62

Northern Lights Limited

Northern Lights Ltd. (NLL) is one of the largest federally incorporated companies in Canada. It is involved in transportation, steel, forest products, and other natural resources. It is a major employer in seven provinces.

By the end of 1987, NLL had fallen upon hard times. The steel and forest products industries were in recession, and company earnings were adversely affected. (See Exhibit 1.) NLL's cash flow situation was dismal, as they had invested heavily in fixed assets beginning in 1985. The majority of these expenditures had been financed by debt. In 1986 alone, NLL doubled its level of long-term borrowings and more than tripled its short-term borrowings. The effect of this was to increase the debt : equity ratio from close to 3 : 1 in 1984 to 5.7 to 1 shortly before the 1987 year-end.

A significant portion of NLL's debt was U.S. denominated, raised privately in the United States in the early 1980s. One of the covenants associated with this debt was that the debt : equity ratio could not exceed 5.5 to 1. Since the interest rate on the debt was favourable to NLL, and less attractive to the lenders in 1987, there was little question but that violation of this covenant, putting NLL into technical default, would trigger calling the debt. There was some considerable doubt about whether NLL would be successful in negotiating another loan deal to replace this one as the company's cash flow problems were growing serious and were well known. It became clear that new financing would only be available at high interest rates.

Budgets for 1988 indicated a projected loss of $600 million. This would further erode the equity base and exacerbate the cash flow problem. Concern was widely expressed over the company's short-term viability, and the spectre of widespread layoffs was raised. The government came under pressure to lend some aid.

Under the free trade deal with the United States the Canadian government was not permitted to give a direct operating subsidy to NLL.[1] Since NLL sold many of its products in the United States such a subsidy would be viewed as giving NLL, in competition with unsubsidized U.S. firms, an unfair advantage. Instead, the government extended a $600 million loan to NLL. This loan was made to NLL on December 28, 1987, three days before the close of the 1987 fiscal year. No funds were actually transferred between the government and NLL; the transaction was more in the nature of a guaranteed line of credit, that would allow NLL to draw upon the government as it needed funds.

The loan was repayable only when NLL wished to pay dividends to its common shareholders. That is, there were no fixed principal repayments required. Repayment had to be "substantially" complete, or a payment scheme approved between NLL and the government, before any dividends could be declared on common stock. In spite of this indefinite term, the company and the government clearly envisioned reasonably prompt repayment of the loan. Neither side viewed the company's cash flow problems as anything other than temporary as the resource and transportation industries were strong and expected to expand through the next decade. The financial community agreed with this assessment. Thus, the capital the government extended was clearly viewed as a temporary loan and not permanent equity.

While the $600 million would solve NLL's cash flow problems over the next year or so, it did not address the difficulty over the bond covenant specifying an acceptable debt : equity ratio. Under *CICA Handbook* rules on accounting for government assistance (see Exhibit 3) the loan was to be recorded as just that: a loan. This would worsen the debt : equity ratio, not improve it.

The *CICA Handbook* is considered to be the source of accounting principles which federally incorporated companies must use to prepare their annual financial statements. The requirement for financial statements is found in Section 149 of the Canada Business Corporations Act. The *Handbook* is endorsed in the Regulations (see Exhibit 2). However, Regulations can be changed by a simple resolution of the federal cabinet and no piece of formal legislation is required.

The board of directors of NLL has approached the government to request an amendment, through an Order-in-Council, to Regulation 44 of the CBCA. They have requested that Regulation 44 endorse the *CICA Handbook,* except for their specific loan, which would be a revenue item. That is, they wished to debit a receivable from the federal government and credit Revenue for $600 million in 1987. Repayment would be an

---

[1] Take this as a given. Regardless of one's views on free trade, it makes this situation much more interesting.

expense of the period when the loan was paid off. NLL has pointed out, quite correctly, that such an amendment is fully within the power of the government.

NLL, being such a large company and a major employer, has significant political influence. Obviously, they had enough power to obtain the loan. They argue that if the situation is serious enough to warrant a loan, then an accounting rule, which after all costs nothing, and which is necessary to avert their potential crisis, is relatively minor. They argue that Canada's interests (hopefully a major concern of the political system) would be well served by such a one-time exception. They also point out that this loan, regardless of how classified, will not violate the free trade agreement.

You are a staff member, working for one of the cabinet ministers who is being intensively lobbied to support this recommendation for a change in Regulation 44. He has asked you to prepare a report, outlining the pros and cons of the government taking such an action.

Required

Prepare the report.

EXHIBIT 1 Operating Statistics (in millions)

	Net Income (Loss)	Capital Expenditures
1980	$ 92	$107
1981	44	124
1982	32	126
1983	176	118
1984	486	120
1985	238	288
1986	(155)	531
1987 (unaudited)	(448)	477

EXHIBIT 2 Extracts from the Canada Business Corporations Act and Regulations, 1975

Canada Business Corporations Act

Financial Disclosure

149. (1) Annual financial statements.—Subject to section 150, the directors of a corporation shall place before the shareholders at every annual meeting
   (a) comparative financial statements as prescribed relating separately to
      (i) the period that began on the date the corporation came into existence and ended not more than six months before the annual

---

EXHIBIT 2   (*concluded*)

---

       meeting or, if the corporation has completed a financial year, the period that began immediately after the end of the last completed financial year and ended not more than six months before the annual meeting, and
    (ii) the immediately preceding financial year;
  (b) the report of the auditor, if any; and
  (c) any further information respecting the financial position of the corporation and the results of its operations required by the articles, the by-laws or any unanimous shareholder agreement.

* * * * *

163. (1) Examination.—An auditor of a corporation shall make the examination that is in his opinion necessary to enable him to report in the prescribed manner on the financial statements required by this Act to be placed before the shareholders, except such financial statements or part thereof that relate to the period referred to in subparagraph 149(1)(a)(ii).

Canada Business Corporations Act Regulations

Part V—Financial Disclosure

General

44. The financial statements referred to in section 149 of the Act and the auditor's report referred to in section 163 of the Act shall, except as otherwise provided by this Part, be prepared in accordance with the recommendations of the Canadian Institute of Chartered Accountants set out in the *CICA Handbook.*

EXHIBIT 3   Excerpts from Section 3800, Government Assistance,
                   CICA Handbook[2]

.01 Various levels of government in Canada have adopted assistance programmes designed to influence the amount and direction of business activity. The number, variety and extent of these programmes have resulted in a need for guidance as to how such government assistance should be accounted for by the recipient.

.02 Experience has shown that programmes adopted by governments to influence business activity are continually changing. Accordingly, this Section deals with broad categories of government assistance rather than specific programmes.

---

[2] Reprinted with permission from the *CICA Handbook,* Canadian Institute of Chartered Accountants, Toronto, Canada.

EXHIBIT 3 *(continued)*

Application

.03 In this Section, the term "government assistance" refers to governmental actions that provide specific assistance to an individual enterprise in order to influence business decisions on matters such as investment, hiring, plant location, etc. Loans having normal commercial characteristics from governments and their agencies are not considered to be "government assistance" for the purposes of this Section. Accelerated tax write-offs or tax rate reductions that are available to businesses generally or to broad sectors of business, such as small businesses or manufacturing and processing businesses, are also not covered. Guidance as to the accounting treatment of the effects of such measures is given in CORPORATE INCOME TAXES, Section 3470 and CORPORATE INCOME TAXES—ADDITIONAL AREAS, Section 3471.

.04 Although Accounting Recommendations in the *Handbook* are intended to apply to profit-oriented enterprises (see INTRODUCTION TO ACCOUNTING RECOMMENDATIONS), some of the Recommendations in this Section may be appropriate for non-profit organizations. Care should be exercised, however, in extending the Recommendations in this Section to non-profit organizations since the nature of the relationship between governments and non-profit organizations often differs from that between governments and profit-oriented enterprises.

Approach to Accounting for Government Assistance

.05 Two broad approaches, the capital approach and the income approach, have been suggested to deal with the question of accounting for government assistance.

.06 The capital approach requires that government assistance be treated as a capital transaction and credited to contributed surplus.

.07 Those favouring the capital approach argue that:
(a) government assistance is a "financing" device since it reduces the amount of capital required through loans and issuance of share capital to finance certain expenditures; it does not reduce the assets employed in the business;
(b) government assistance programmes are selective and reflect government policies which will change from time to time. Therefore, it is inappropriate to reflect the government assistance in income during a period of time when the relevant policies may have changed;
(c) government assistance is not earned but is a gratuitous payment.

.08 The income approach requires that government assistance be credited to income in the following ways, depending upon its nature:
(a) direct increases in revenues, or reduction in expenses;
(b) reduced depreciation and amortization charges based on reduced asset costs;
(c) amortization of deferred credits.

EXHIBIT 3   (*continued*)

.09 Those favouring the income approach argue that:
  (a) receipt of government assistance confers a benefit on a business and its owners, whether or not such assistance was anticipated. Benefits received by a business, other than transactions with its shareholders, should be reflected in income over an appropriate period of time;
  (b) reported results should reflect the benefits of government assistance received which generally offset costs incurred, recognize efforts expended or compensate for restraints imposed by the conditions of the assistance;
  (c) the income statement should reflect the results of operations after taking into account all factors which bear on the profitability of the enterprise. Government assistance is one such factor;
  (d) government assistance is not a gratuitous payment in the absolute sense. There are usually conditions attaching to its receipt and, therefore, it must be "earned" by complying with those conditions.

.10 Although government assistance may well have "financing" characteristics, its receipt nevertheless confers a benefit on an enterprise which should be reflected in income sooner or later. The Committee has concluded that arguments in favour of the income approach are more persuasive. Therefore, the Recommendations in this Section provide that government assistance will, in current or future accounting periods, affect income.

Economic Substance

.11 An enterprise should examine the economic circumstances surrounding its entitlement to government assistance in order to determine the appropriate accounting treatment, including the timing of the recognition of the benefits.

.12 In many cases, the accounting treatment for government assistance will be readily apparent as, for example, assistance towards current expenses. However, the appropriate accounting for some forms of government assistance is not readily apparent. For example, government assistance may be provided because of factors such as high labour costs, excessive start-up costs or high transportation costs but the amount of the assistance may be calculated by reference to fixed asset expenditures. In these circumstances, the assistance should be related to the period(s) in which such expenses are incurred. On the other hand, assistance may be logically related to fixed assets even though it may not be calculated by reference to them.

.13 In some cases, the receipt of government assistance relates to a combination of items, for example fixed asset acquisitions and high labour costs. In such cases, the components would be accounted for according to their nature, in accordance with the appropriate Recommendations in this Section.

.14 *Government assistance should be analyzed and the resulting components accounted for in accordance with the appropriate Recommendations in this Section.*   [SEPT. 1975]

.15 The fact that an enterprise may elect to apply the amount of government assistance against its income tax liability does not change the economic sub-

---

EXHIBIT 3   *(continued)*

---

stance of the assistance. The method of payment chosen does not affect the accounting for the benefits obtained under a particular government assistance programme.

.16 Assistance may be received from a government which holds an equity position in an enterprise. Where the assistance is provided by the government by virtue of its position as a shareholder, it would be credited to contributed surplus (see SURPLUS, Section 3250 and CAPITAL TRANSACTIONS, Section 3610). In contrast, where assistance is unrelated to the government's position as a shareholder, it would be accounted for in accordance with the Recommendations in this Section.

General Disclosure

.17 Since government assistance accounted for in accordance with this Section affects the profitability of an enterprise, appropriate disclosure is necessary to assist in evaluating the impact of government assistance on the results of operations of the enterprise.

.18 *The following disclosure of government assistance should be made:*
   (a) with respect to assistance received and receivable in the current period:
      (i) the amount thereof;
      (ii) the amounts credited direct to income, deferred credit or fixed asset;
      (iii) the relevant terms and conditions applicable to the assistance; and
      (iv) the amount of any contingent liability for repayment.
   (b) with respect to assistance received in prior periods for which any contingent liability for repayment exists:
      (i) the amount of the contingent liability; and
      (ii) the relevant terms and conditions applicable to the assistance.

(See also paragraphs 3800.22, 3800.24, 3800.26, 3800.29 and 3800.30 dealing with disclosure of government assistance.)   [SEPT. 1975]

ASSISTANCE RELATED TO NON-CAPITAL ITEMS

Assistance Related to Current Expenses and Revenues

.19 Many government programmes provide for the reimbursement of certain current eligible expenses. Similarly, an enterprise may receive direct payments from the government to supplement selling prices. Since these types of assistance are related to current expenses or revenues, they are logically included in the determination of net income for the period.

.20 *Government assistance towards current expenses or revenues should be included in the determination of net income for the period.*   [SEPT. 1975]

.21 The presentation of government assistance in the income statement will depend on circumstances. The alternatives available are to show expenses net of assistance or to show the assistance as a deduction from aggregate expenses or as revenue.

EXHIBIT 3   *(concluded)*

.22 The extent to which assistance related to current expenses or revenues will continue into the future is an important factor in the evaluation of an enterprise. It is, therefore, desirable that the financial statements disclose the extent to which assistance currently being received is expected to continue in the future.

Assistance Related to Expenses of Future Periods

.23 Some types of government assistance are received or receivable in a period but relate to expenses which will be incurred in future periods. It would not be appropriate to apply all of the assistance to the expenses in the current period if subsequent accounting periods will continue to bear relevant expenses.

.24 *Where government assistance relates to expenses of future accounting periods, the appropriate amounts should be deferred and amortized to income as related expenses are incurred. The amount of government assistance deferred, the period of amortization and the basis of amortization of the deferral should be disclosed.*   [SEPT. 1975]

* * * * *

Case 63

Read

PIP Grants

The National Energy Policy, legislation of the Canadian federal government, established Petroleum Incentive Program (PIP) grants for the oil industry in 1982. These were created to encourage oil and gas exploration in Canada at a time when energy self-sufficiency in the face of high world energy prices was a top priority. PIP grants replaced a system of "super depletion" allowances and investment tax credits for oil exploration. This latter system was phased out.

The CICA rule on such government grants, according to Section 3800 of the *CICA Handbook,* "Accounting for Government Grants," is that grants must be amortized to income over the life of the related exploration assets. If the exploration assets were to be amortized straight line over 10 years, so too should the government grant be amortized. When these rules were developed, there was no particular objection made by the oil industry or the federal government.

The introduction of PIP grants in early 1982 abruptly changed that. Under the 1982 rules for investment tax credits (the old exploration incentives), any tax credits received in the year would be treated as income, or a reduction of expense, in the year. There were no deferrals, and income was boosted. Under the new system, the impact of government assistance was to be shown over a period of years.

The oil companies were very unhappy at this prospect, particularly since their earnings were drastically reduced by other provisions of the National Energy Policy.

The difference to net income would be material. For example, Norcen Energy Resources recorded energy exploration grants in income on the cash flow, or immediate recognition basis, in its 1981 quarterly statements. Its nine-month report, dated September 30, 1981, noted that if the new CICA rule had been used, earnings per share would have been reduced to $1.26 from $1.71, a decrease of more than 25 percent.

The oil companies represent a powerful lobby group in Ottawa. Getting nowhere with the CICA, they approached the federal government to change the accounting rule through the provisions of the Canada Business Corporations Act. The regulations to this Act specify that the generally accepted accounting principles required in the Act are to be those principles prescribed by the *CICA Handbook*. However, the federal government could easily amend the regulations by an Order in Council which would require *CICA Handbook* treatment for everything except PIP grants, which would be recorded on a cash flow basis.

The oil companies used the following arguments to defend their request:

1. Cash flow treatment for PIP grants was consistent with the treatment for investment tax credits, which PIP grants replaced.
2. Deferral would cause a lower net income to be reported by oil companies, which would reduce their attractiveness to investors and thus increase their cost of capital.
3. With a higher cost of capital, fewer exploration programs would be undertaken. This would be contrary to the expressed desire of the federal government, who wished to establish energy self-sufficiency by the 1990s.

The CICA was opposed to such an exception. The research director, R. D. Thomas, pointed out that the only way a company should earn income is to earn revenue on its capital assets. Grants are not income. The basic accounting principle of matching revenues and expenditures period by period requires that the grants be deferred.

A letter, sent by 14 of the major accounting firms, was sent to cabinet ministers, supporting the CICA position.

The Ontario Securities Commission (the OSC), which requires *CICA Handbook* rules for all companies listed on the Toronto Stock Exchange (TSE), indicated that they would not automatically accept a federally legislated exception to those rules. Their position was that they would require a public hearing to determine if such statements were misleading in any way. At the same time, the OSC made it clear that they supported the accounting profession and its independence. They strongly objected to government influence or the setting of policies to suit government positions.

Eventually, the federal government decided to leave the accounting rules as they were, and not interfere.

Required

Outline the arguments for and against government intervention in the standard setting process, using the PIP Grant case as an example. What are the benefits of an "accounting theory" in this context?

Case 64

Pension Issues

For organizations with defined benefit pension plans, the actuary's esti-mate of the organization's obligation to accumulate pension benefits is sometimes disclosed. The market value of pension plan assets available to satisfy that obligation may also be disclosed in the notes to financial statements. Within accounting circles, there is considerable debate as to the appropriate disclosure of pension information in an organization's financial statements. Consider, for example, the following conversation, which took place at a social gathering between the chief financial officer (CFO) of a large corporation and a financial analyst (FA) from a brokerage firm:

FA:

I'm sick and tired of having to adjust liabilities on the balance sheet for footnote liabilities such as the pension obligation! The obligation is that of the organization, not the pension fund, and it belongs, along with related plan assets, on the organization's balance sheet.

CFO:

I was under the impression that it was the extent of disclosure, not the form, that mattered to you analysts.

FA:

That's not the point. A balance must be complete to be useful. It seems to me that the pension obligation meets any reasonable definition of a liability, and it belongs on the balance sheet along with other liabilities. Besides, some users might be misled because they expect the balance sheet to contain all liabilities.

Reprinted with permission from the *Uniform Final Examination Report* (1986). © The Canadian Institute of Chartered Accountants, Toronto. This case predates the CICA's revisions to Section 3460 of the *CICA Handbook*.

I also object to the games some organizations play with pension amounts in their income statements. A few years ago, one organization I know took a revaluation gain, amounting to 90 percent of profit for that year, immediately into income.

CFO:

I have some concerns about putting the pension obligation on the balance sheet. For one thing, the pension fund is a separate legal entity. Take my organization for example. We have agreed with our union to work towards a goal of having the plan, which is currently underfunded, fully funded by 1995. Our only obligation is to make contributions to the pension fund as suggested by the actuary in order to achieve our funding objective.

For another thing, I believe that the obligation is too soft a number to warrant balance sheet recognition along with other liabilities. There are many uncertainties related to measurement. For example, consider our plan formula, which provides for an annual postretirement pension benefit of 2 percent of the employee's career average earnings for each year of service, to be paid each year beyond retirement until death. All payments are fully indexed to cost-of-living increases after retirement.

And one more thing. How is our auditor supposed to be able to express an opinion as to whether the obligation on the balance sheet is fairly presented? That means a lot of hours spent with the actuary, hours that our organization will have to pay for! Things are much simpler for the auditor when the obligation appears in a footnote only.

FA:

The need to make estimates about the future is not unique to pensions. I wonder whether the claim about uncertainties related to measurement is just an excuse you executives use to conceal your real concerns.

CFO:

Well, to be honest, our organization does have concerns about the economic consequences resulting from putting the pension obligation and the plan assets on the balance sheet. Our stock price could be adversely affected, not to mention our credit rating, borrowing capacity, and management compensation contracts.

FA:

It seems that the controversy regarding pension accounting continues!

Required

Discuss the issues raised in the above conversation.

Case 65

Plastics Ontario

Plastics Ontario (PO) has recently been incorporated under federal legislation. All the shares are owned by one man, Jimmy Arbuckle. PO will be active in the molded plastics industry, making everything from custom lettered signs to consumer products (e.g., toys) and industrial products (e.g., car dashboards). They will also supply chemicals to other, smaller plastic molding operations.

Arbuckle has 20 years' experience in both production and sales with a large Canadian plastics firm. He took advantage of several recent bankruptcy sales to acquire the manufacturing and molding equipment necessary to start his own firm. He has obtained a 10-year, fixed interest loan from the Federal Business Development Bank, a line of credit from a chartered bank for working capital, and he has invested $200,000 of his own money. Both banks require audited annual financial statements.

The major pieces of equipment acquired cost $350,000. Another $30,000 will be spent transporting them to PO's new, leased facility. Arbuckle estimates another $40,000 will be spent "debugging" the equipment.

Sales are expected to be made on three bases:

1. Custom signs on a prepaid basis. Signs would normally be completed within five business days but could take up to a month for a large order or if volume was high.
2. Direct sales to distributors and manufacturers on terms of 2/10, n/30. Interest on overdue accounts will be 1.4 percent per month. Customers can return defective goods for full credit, and, in common with the industry, goods carry a six-month warranty.
3. Consumer goods to retail outlets on a consignment basis. Arbuckle does not expect to be able to run his molding equipment at full capacity from "outsider" orders for at least two years. Therefore, he plans to design and market a few consumer products—cassette tape holders,

doll houses—to keep his operation busy. Several large retail chains have expressed interest in carrying these items but only on a consignment basis. Arbuckle estimates that it will cost $20,000 to design and develop these items.

Arbuckle hopes to break even in his second year of operation and show a profit in his third year. Losses are anticipated in the first year. He has planned to take an extremely low salary for the first three years until he is satisfied that the company can prove its viability. Arbuckle has established relatively low salary levels for his management team but has promised them all generous bonuses based on net income.

Arbuckle has approached you, CA, to act as a financial adviser. He has requested advice on accounting policies and any other relevant issues.

Required

Adopt the role of adviser to Mr. Arbuckle, and draft a report responding to his request.

Case 66

Printech Ltd.

On August 6, 1985, your accounting firm was engaged by Mark Laban, the president of Printech Ltd., to advise the company on its accounting policies. Forty percent of the company's shares had recently changed hands, and the president felt that it was time to consider the company's external reporting policies.

Printech is one of over 700 printers located in the metropolitan Toronto area, the most highly concentrated group of printers in the country . Over 40 percent of the commercial printing in Canada is done in the Toronto area, and Printech is one of many such companies competing for the local market share.

Printech had annual sales of approximately $6.0 million in 1984, having grown from only $1.5 million in 1975, its first year of operation. The company was founded by Mark Laban and Dan Wolfe, both of whom had worked for another printer. Mark was a master printer and Dan had been a senior salesperson. When they founded Printech, Dan had taken several of his best customers' business with him to the new company. Mark had acquired 60 percent of the founding shares, and Dan had acquired 40 percent. A shareholders' agreement allocated the votes for the board of directors equally to the two founders.

Since Dan and Mark had been owner-managers of Printech, they controlled their own salaries, bonuses, and dividends in accordance with their own income needs, and tax minimization was the dominant financial reporting objective.

The company's initial area of expertise was high-quality, four-colour printing. The first year's production consisted mainly of advertising flyers and brochures, using Printech's four-colour press. Quality colour printing remained as a principal line of business for Printech, comprising about 55

Institute of Chartered Accountants of Ontario, adapted.

percent of the company's current sales volume. However, the capacity of the press was limiting the company's ability to gain business in this area. As well, the profitability of this line of business was being depressed by the necessity to make two press runs if the customer wanted a varnish or coated finish to the product. Competitors were able to offer printing on six-colour presses that could apply varnish or other paper coatings as part of a single run, rather than by using two runs as was necessary on a four-colour press. To protect this line of business, Printech feels that it will be necessary to acquire a new press in the coming year. A new press would cost close to $2 million, and it would be necessary to obtain bank financing in order to pay for the press.

Printech also does substantial business in two other areas. One is the printing of custom stationery and forms for small businesses, especially for professional practices such as lawyers and doctors. The other is the printing of covers for paperback books on heavy stock, usually on a two-colour press.

The custom forms business was an innovation of Dan's. Large forms companies such as Moore seemed not to be serving that market effectively, while other small companies that were serving the market tended not to be able to offer top quality. Professional service firms generally are very sensitive to the image communicated to their clients by their stationery and forms, and Dan was able to provide an effective service combining quality and low price. The quality was made possible by the expertise of Mark and the production staff, while the low price was made possible by printing in large volumes but delivering to the clients in small quantities. The clients contracted to buy a minimum total volume of output over a two-year period without committing themselves to delivery or payment at specified times. Printech would then design the forms or stationery, make the printing plates, and print the entire order. Printech would then store the material for the client until needed. Some clients requested delivery only about once a month, while others might call for delivery two or more times a week. Delivery was always made within 24 hours. The custom forms business had grown from zero to 25 percent of Printech's sales volume in just three years and was expected to increase substantially in the future.

The bulk of the book cover business (about 60 percent) was under contract to a single book printer, Owl & Pen, Inc. (OPI). Press runs for the covers varied from 5,000 to 100,000 copies. For larger runs, it was not unusual for Printech to hold most of the covers for OPI until the contents of the book were reprinted by OPI, a period that could run two years or more. OPI typically paid 50 percent of the contract price at the time of printing and then paid the remainder as the covers were shipped by Printech.

OPI is a Canadian company that is a wholly owned subsidiary of a U.S. broadcasting company that is publicly owned. In June 1985, Dan and

Mark completed a transaction with OPI in which each of the founders transferred 20 percent of the total number of outstanding Printech shares to OPI (a total of 40 percent) in return for treasury shares in OPI's parent company. This deal permitted the two founders to liquidate part of their investment if they so desired without losing control of the company. Dan and Mark still would control Printech jointly, each having 30 percent of the votes. OPI, of course, would have the other 40 percent of the votes.

The deal between OPI and Dan and Mark brought no new financing into the company and therefore would not affect the debt : equity ratio. In keeping with normal practice in the industry, Printech was highly leveraged; the debt : equity ratio was 3 : 1, which was about average. The proposed financing for the new six-colour press would more than double that ratio. Printech's banker had indicated a willingness to finance the new press, but also indicated that he would be required to place a restriction on any new debt thereafter by imposing a limit on Printech's maximum debt : equity ratio.

Now that part of the shares were owned by OPI, the salary arrangements for Dan and Mark were regularized and a formal bonus scheme had been put in place, with the managers' bonuses tied directly to the profitability of the company. An OPI nominee on Printech's board of directors would represent OPI when setting the various components of the managers' compensation.

Required

The engagement partner has asked you to draft a letter to the president of Printech Ltd. to advise him on the changes in Printech's financial reporting objectives which you believe will arise as a result of the changed circumstances described above. He further indicated that the letter should include your recommendation of accounting policies for revenue recognition and related matching of costs which would best meet these revised reporting objectives.

Case 67

Provincial Hydro I

Provincial Hydro (PH) is an electric utility which generates, supplies, and delivers electric power throughout a small Canadian province. It is incorporated as a Crown corporation, which operates as a cooperative partnership with the relevant municipalities and the provincial government. It is a financially self-sustaining company without share capital, regulated by the provincial government. Its primary customers are the municipalities (which serve about 600,000 end users), 40 large industrial companies (direct service), and 100,000 rural retail customers. PH operates various generating stations, including both nuclear and fossil fuel fired plants. As a result, it is very capital intensive. This, in turn, makes PH sensitive to the cost of money.

PH plays a major role in attracting industry to the province by maintaining competitive rates for electricity. It is profoundly affected by various pieces of provincial legislation.

The financial statement results are used to set utility rates, although there are specific rules about which expenses are permissible and at what time. Many accounting policies are chosen based on the rules for rate recovery. Profits of the corporation are to be applied toward the reduction of the cost of power for the municipalities with whom it has a cooperative partnership.

Management and the municipalities are very sensitive to political pressures. PH is in the public spotlight, and financial results and policies can generate considerable publicity.

A major component of the cost of electricity is fuel cost, which includes the following components: fuel (quantity and price), interest on funds tied up in inventory, transportation, overheads, and a provision for future irradiated fuel transportation, storage, and disposal. The last component relates only to nuclear plants (PH has three) and is provided for based on estimates of future disposal costs.

For example, if the estimate of future cost for disposal of 10 years' accumulated irradiated fuel (also known as nuclear waste) was $60 million, the following entry would be made:

Costs	$6,000,000	
Liability for future disposal		$6,000,000
To accrue one tenth of the cost of disposal.		

The problem of disposal has yet to be satisfactorily resolved, however. It seems clear that the solution will involve large elements of fixed cost for even minimum quantities.

There are some that suggest the following alternative treatment for the $60 million estimate:

Costs	$ 6,000,000	
Deferred costs	54,000,000	
Liability for future disposal		$60,000,000
To accrue one tenth of the cost of disposal.		

A third alternative is to treat the cost of future disposal as a contingency: while the probability of payment is known (i.e., definite), the amount is not determinable. Thus, the issue should simply be disclosed in the notes to the financial statements. The proponents of this alternative point out that no technology currently exists to "safely" dispose of the irradiated fuels. Estimates, such as the $60 million, are based on a number of assumptions, some of which have already proven false.

At present, PH follows the first alternative and has done so for four years. None of the cost is included in utility rate formulas.

PH is in the process of reexamining a number of their accounting policies. Accordingly, they have hired you as an external adviser in this area. They have requested that you write a report on this issue, incorporating your recommendations.

Required

Assume the role of external adviser and prepare the report.

Case 68

Provincial Hydro II

Provincial Hydro (PH) is an electric utility which generates, supplies, and delivers electric power throughout a small Canadian province. It is incorporated as a Crown corporation, which operates as a cooperative partnership with the relevant municipalities and the provincial government. It is a financially self-sustaining company without share capital, regulated by the provincial government. Its primary customers are the municipal utilities (which serve about 600,000 end users), 40 large industrial companies (direct service), and 100,000 rural retail customers. PH operates various generating stations, including both nuclear and fossil fuel fired plants. As a result, it is very capital intensive. This in turn makes PH sensitive to the cost of money.

PH plays a major role in attracting industry to the province by maintaining competitive rates for electricity. It is profoundly affected by various pieces of provincial legislation.

The financial statement results are used to set utility rates, although there are specific rules about which expenses are permissible and at what time. Many accounting policies are chosen based on the rules for rate recovery. Profits of the corporation are to be applied toward the reduction of the cost of power for the municipalities with whom it has a cooperative partnership.

Management and the municipalities are very sensitive to political pressures. PH is in the public spotlight, and financial results and policies can generate considerable publicity.

A major component of the cost of electricity is fuel cost, which includes the following components: fuel (quantity and price), interest on funds tied up in inventory, transportation, and overheads.

PH has two mothballed generating stations, which are not producing energy at present but may be used during peak demand periods when needed. The plants, all oil-fired, were mothballed as more efficient generation methods were developed.

PH has chosen to reflect the situation by accelerating the rate of depreciation to "reflect the reduced economic value" of the assets. PH has produced demand forecasts (which are regularly updated) that predict when and how much energy will have to come from the mothballed plants. Based on these probability factors, PH establishes an amortization rate, higher than the original rate, which takes the change of circumstances into account. Depreciation is only charged when the plant is used. Care is taken to avoid premature write-off while the plant may still be useful.

PH uses the CANDU reactor in its nuclear stations. This reactor has relatively low fuel cost but must use "heavy water," H_2O_2 (versus "light water," H_2O, which other reactors use). Heavy water is not consumed in the fissioning process but acts as a moderator of the process. With periodic in-station upgrading to remove impurities, heavy water has an indefinite life.

Heavy water costs, plus interest on inventoried heavy water designated for future use, are capitalized. These capital costs are being written off over 60 years, which is the date PH estimates heavy water will be replaced by new technology. However, the last committed CANDU nuclear unit is due to be retired in 40 years. Management has indicated that nuclear units are regularly upgraded by replacing pressure tubes, which extends their useful life. In addition, the useful life of heavy water does not depend on the life of the station since it can be transferred to another station.

Inventories of fossil fuels are expensed based on an average cost system where the average is calculated monthly on a rolling basis. Average cost was chosen as it seemed the most fair to current and future customers and had a smoothing effect on price fluctuations. Recently, however, with significant declines in fossil fuel prices, there has been considerable public comment as electricity prices did not fall accordingly. Management is beginning to consider the alternatives and their advantages and disadvantages.

Management has reminded you that one-time write-downs are not permissible costs in utility rate-setting formulas, nor is it possible to make retroactive changes to the rate structure.

PH has asked you, an external adviser, to consider accounting issues raised. They have requested a report incorporating your recommendations.

Required

Prepare the report.

Case 69

Provincial Tire Corporation

Provincial Tire Corporation operates a chain of hardware stores across Canada. It is now January 1988, and the controller's department, where you work, is preparing the financial statements for the fiscal year ended December 31, 1987. Draft consolidated financial statements are shown in Exhibit 1.

The controller's office has just learned that one of Provincial Tire's subsidiaries, Black Stores Inc., is going to be sold. The subsidiary has not performed well in recent years. It was learned that the purchase price would be in the vicinity of $10 million, and the deal would close at the end of February 1988.

You have been asked how this state of affairs should be reflected in the 1987 financial statements which, at present, consolidate the results of Black Stores Inc. The information used to consolidate Black Stores Inc. has been provided to you (Exhibit 2).

Required

Respond thoroughly to the request.

EXHIBIT 1

**PROVINCIAL TIRE CORPORATION
AND ITS SUBSIDIARIES**
Consolidated Balance Sheet (Draft)
December 31, 1987
(in thousands)

Assets

Current assets:

Cash and short-term investments	$122,600
Accounts receivable	130,000
Merchandise inventories	300,100
Prepaid expenses	3,500
Total current assets	$556,200
Long-term receivables	17,000
Property and equipment	365,000
Other assets	7,000
Total assets	$945,200

Liabilities and Shareholders' Equity

Current liabilities:

Bank indebtedness	$ 14,000
Accounts payable	190,000
Income taxes payable	13,300
Dividends payable	4,300
Current portion of long-term debt	7,100
Total current liabilities	$228,700
Long-term debt	185,500
Deferred taxes	3,200
Minority interests in subsidiaries	27,200

Shareholders' equity:

Share capital	$232,700
Retained earnings	267,900
Total shareholders' equity	$500,600
Total liabilities and shareholders' equity	$945,200

EXHIBIT 2

BLACK STORES INC.
Balance Sheet
at December 31, 1987
(in thousands)

Assets

Cash and temporary investments.	$ 4,000
Accounts and loans receivable.	22,400
Merchandise inventories	32,700
Prepaid expenses.	1,500
Property and equipment	44,600
Other	200
Total assets	$105,400

Liabilities and Shareholders' Equity

Liabilities	
Bank indebtedness	$ 12,250
Accounts payable	21,000
Long-term debt	42,000
Total liabilities.	$ 75,250
Shareholders' Equity:	
Common stock.	25,000
Retained earnings	5,150
Total shareholders' equity.	$ 30,150
Total liabilities and shareholders' equity	$105,400

Black Stores Inc. was incorporated in 1974 by Provincial Tire Corp., who owned 95 percent of the common stock. They originally invested $23,750,000 in the company.

During 1987, intercompany sales (from Black to Provincial) amounted to $5,000,000. Of this, 10 percent was unsold at year-end. There were $900,000 of similar goods in opening inventory. Normal profit margins were 40 percent.

23

Raymond Ltd.

In January 1991 Douglas Raymond, the founder and president of Raymond Ltd., met with you to discuss an exciting business prospect for his company. Janelle Corporation, a rapidly growing chain of retail outlets carrying men's and women's sportswear, wishes to lease a computer system and equipment from Raymond Ltd. to try out in some of its stores. If the system is successful in helping Janelle keep track of inventory, the company plans to have Raymond Ltd. install systems in the remaining stores and in each new store before its opening. The stores would not only have their own records but would be able to access the inventory records of other outlets when trying to find an outfit for a customer.

Raymond Ltd. buys and leases computer systems and equipment to various types of businesses. Most of the customers are well-established businesses which have decided to replace their current computer facilities with upgraded systems, and are leasing in order to trade up to more advanced technology during the contract period.

Raymond Ltd. deals in both financing and operating leases. When incorporated in 1982 the company concentrated on shorter term operating leases. However, the current focus is on longer term finance leases which minimize residual risk.

You have received the following description of the terms of the lease offered to Janelle:

Cost of the equipment and system	$163,590
Lease payments	$27,500 per year in advance; the payments include $2,500 executory costs
Lease term	10 years
Life of the equipment.	10 years

Raymond will retain title, although there is no expected value remaining at the end of the lease.

Douglas Raymond is excited about this particular customer because of the fast growth of the chain and North America's constantly increasing interest in sports and fitness. After only one year in business, Janelle already has stores in major shopping centres across Canada and is negotiating the purchase of a chain in the United States. Douglas feels that over the next three to five years this could become one of his largest accounts. He is not interested in offering Janelle a shorter lease as he wants Janelle to be committed to Raymond Ltd. for a longer period of time.

During your meeting with Raymond, you mentioned that Janelle had received some attention in the business press in the past few months because of its rapid expansion. Janelle was carrying a heavy debt load. However, all the reports indicated that there was a market for Janelle's service and that, although the company was currently high risk, this could change rapidly as successful operations would return large cash flows.

Required

In your position as Raymond Ltd.'s auditor, present your recommendations to Douglas Raymond on the treatment of a lease to Janelle Corporation. Describe the impact and required disclosure that this lease would have had on Raymond Ltd.'s financial statements if it had been signed on January 1, 1991.

EXHIBIT 1

RAYMOND LTD.
Balance Sheet
December 31

	1990	1989
Assets		
Cash	$ 79,968	$ 9,071
Accounts receivable	132,761	89,927
Net investment in financing transactions:		
Equipment lease receivables.	10,235,824	8,926,047
Estimated residual value	497,200	447,694
Unearned income	(3,325,292)	(3,189,828)
	7,407,732	6,183,913
Allowance for doubtful accounts.	(137,018)	(128,060)
	$ 7,270,714	$ 6,055,853

EXHIBIT 1 (*continued*)

	1990	1989
Equipment on operating leases:		
Cost	$ 1,709,850	$ 3,000,940
Less: accumulated depreciation	(1,072,305)	(2,390,069)
	637,545	610,871
Assets held for sale or lease	42,379	17,209
Fixed and other assets	45,590	33,415
Total assets	$ 8,208,957	$ 6,816,346

Liabilities and Owners' Equity

	1990	1989
Accounts payable	$ 1,415,700	$ 1,575,877
Security deposits	165,106	179,397
Rentals received in advance	15,746	25,910
Bank loans	—	2,736,868
Current portion of long-term debt	508,203	609,424
	2,104,755	5,127,476
Long-term debt	3,916,491	305,877
Owners' equity:		
Capital stock	1,210,119	514,101
Retained earnings	977,592	868,892
	2,187,711	1,382,993
Total liabilities and owners' equity	$ 8,208,957	$ 6,816,346

RAYMOND LTD.
Income Statement
For the Year Ended December 31

	1990	1989
Revenues:		
Finance lease earned income	$ 967,856	$ 506,002
Operating lease rentals	356,817	656,657
Interest and other income	81,197	23,206
	$1,405,870	$1,185,865
Expenses:		
Interest	400,376	73,171
Depreciation	218,742	603,694
Selling, administrative, and other operating expenses	239,380	134,544

EXHIBIT 1   *(concluded)*

	1990	1989
Provision for doubtful accounts.	$ 155,461	$ 31,523
Other direct costs	53,319	44,215
	$1,067,278	$ 887,147
Earnings before income taxes	338,592	298,718
Income taxes:		
Current	23,054	1,400
Deferred	150,046	149,139
	173,100	150,539
Net earnings	$ 165,492	$ 148,179

Robertson Holdings Ltd.

At the end of 1987, Robertson Holdings Ltd. had $11,080,000 invested in Minouge Ltd., a public company. This consisted of:

40,000 common shares, at cost . . .	$ 9,600,000
5,000 preferred shares, at cost . . .	1,480,000
	$11,080,000

On April 1, 1988, Minouge Ltd. declared a stock dividend payable on April 15, 1988, of one preferred share for each five shares held (preferred or common). Robertson received 9,000 preferred shares as its portion of the distribution and immediately sold these shares on the market for $2,340,000, representing average proceeds per share of $260. The directors of Robertson are undecided as to the accounting treatment of this transaction and have asked you for your analysis and advice. The following suggestions have been made:

1. By selling the shares on the market, Robertson has in fact received a cash dividend. Accordingly, the proceeds should be credited to an income account and shown on the 1988 income statement.
2. The proceeds should be credited directly to retained earnings and shown on the 1988 statement of retained earnings. This will avoid the distortion to net income that the first treatment would cause.
3. The proceeds of the shares received by virtue of the common stock holdings should be classified as income. The stock dividend received by virtue of the investment in preferred shares represents a proportion-

Adapted, with permission from the *Uniform Final Examination Report, 1976,* © Canadian Institute of Chartered Accountants, Toronto.

Changes to the original questions and/or suggested approaches to answering are the sole responsibility of the authors and have not been reviewed or endorsed by the CICA.

ate increase in all preferred shareholders' holdings and cannot be classed as income.

4. None of the proceeds should be recorded as income. The proceeds should be credited to the carrying value of the investments.

Required

Prepare the required analysis. This should include comment on each of the alternatives raised, and your recommendations. Prepare a journal entry to record the transaction.

Rossington Sales Limited

Rossington Sales Ltd. is a Canadian-controlled private corporation owned by Phil Symms and his wife, Eliza. Their operation, which was incorporated in 1979, involves importing toys which they then sell to major retailers across Canada. Phil Symms has been very successful at predicting trends in this very seasonal business. That, plus his reputation for reliable delivery, has earned him a solid reputation with his Canadian customers.

In 1989, Symms ordered a shipment of stuffed toys, called Pupplets, from the United States. The order, for U.S. $400,000, was placed on March 1 for delivery on July 31, with payment due September 30.

Normal payment terms are two months from the point of delivery. Also on March 1, Symms entered into a forward exchange contract to hedge the order. The exchange contract ran until the payment date and was for U.S. $400,000. The transaction went as scheduled except it was delivered on June 30 instead of July 31. Symms negotiated with the vendor so that he paid for the goods on September 30, two months after the original agreed-upon delivery date.

Selected Exchange Rates:
(U.S. $1 = Cdn, as follows)

	Spot		Forward
March 1	$1.33	. . .	1.43 (7 month)
June 30	$1.41	. . .	1.45 (3 month)
July 31	$1.43	. . .	1.41 (2 month)
Sept. 30	$1.39	. . .	1.41 (1 month)

Rossington Sales has a December 31 year-end and does not want to make any unnecessary adjusting entries through the year.

Atlantic Provinces Association of Chartered Accountants, adapted

Symms's bookkeeper is confused by this transaction, and has consulted you, Rossington's auditor. You have promised to provide journal entries for the sequence of events.

Also in 1989, Symms entered into a new venture with a manufacturer in London, England. The operation was established to make stuffed toys for Rossington to sell in the North American market. The manufacturer provided his facilities and expertise, Symms provided a certain amount of capital and his design and marketing expertise. The investment was made through Rossington Sales Ltd., which then owned 60 percent of the shares of the venture, called London Exports Ltd. Condensed financial statements for the first year of the operation are shown in Exhibit 1. In this first year, Symms has been to England four times to assist in setup and design. He has found it very time consuming and is hoping it will become less so in the future.

Symms knows that there are two different alternatives to convert the financial statements into Canadian dollars for inclusion in the Rossington financial statements. He has asked for a review of all the factors and an opinion as to the correct decision in his case. He has asked the auditor to calculate the net income that would be reported under the recommended method.

Required

As Rossington's auditor, respond to the requests of Phil Symms.

EXHIBIT 1

LONDON EXPORTS LTD.
Condensed Financial Statements
For the Year Ended December 31, 1989
(in British pounds)

	Opening Balances March 31, 1989	*December 31, 1989*
Balance sheet:		
Assets:		
Cash	£100,000	£ 8,000
Inventory	—	75,000
Receivable from Rossington. . . .	—	180,000
Fixed assets	120,000	102,000
	£220,000	£365,000
Liabilities:		
Current liabilities	—	£120,000
Owners' equity:		
Invested capital	£220,000	220,000
Retained earnings	—	25,000
	£220,000	£365,000

Income statement:	
Sales.	£180,000
Cost of goods sold.	100,000
Gross profit.	80,000
Expenses (including £18,000 of depreciation)	55,000
Net income	£ 25,000

1. All purchases and expenses were made evenly over the period. Closing inventory was acquired in the last quarter.

2. Exchange rates:

	1 £ =		*1 £ =*
March 31, 1989	$1.80 Cdn.	2d quarter	$1.78 Cdn.
December 31, 1989 . .	$1.84 Cdn.	3rd quarter.	$1.83 Cdn.
1st quarter	$1.74 Cdn.	4th quarter.	$1.85 Cdn.
		Average, 1989	$1.82 Cdn.

3. The receivable of £180,000 from Rossington is on Rossington's books at $327,500. The sales are denominated in pounds (£).

Case 73

S Limited

S Ltd. is one of the wholly owned subsidiaries of R Ltd. All these companies are incorporated under the Canada Business Corporations Act. The shares and debt of R Ltd., which manufactures various types of electronic equipment, are publicly held in Canada. S Ltd. was incorporated about one year ago to help diversify the operations of R Ltd. S Ltd. arranges construction, then owns and leases commercial properties.

The first year-end of S Ltd. is rapidly approaching and accounting principles and policies must be chosen for the company. During the last three months of this first year, S Ltd. completed construction on its first two buildings; the first building is to be leased for 20 years to C Ltd., another subsidiary of R Ltd., slightly below market rates; and the second has 12 floors, 6 of which are under lease to the federal government on a 10-year basis with lessee options extending for a further 20 years. Only two other floors in the second building are presently under contract with occupancy to commence in six months.

Management of S Ltd. has proposed the following:

1. All buildings are to be depreciated on a 40-year life using the sinking fund method with an interest factor of 6 percent per annum. Depreciation is to commence when 60 percent of the building is occupied.
2. A present value of future lease payments less expected maintenance and similar costs will be computed annually, using a 6 percent after income tax rate. If this sum is less than S Ltd.'s carrying value of each building, the carrying value will be written down to the present value. If a building is not fully leased, the present value would be compared

Adapted, with permission from the *Uniform Final Examination Handbook,* (1979), © The Canadian Institute of Chartered Accountants, Toronto.

Changes to the original questions and/or suggested approaches to answering are the sole responsibility of the authors and have not been reviewed or endorsed by the CICA.

on a proportionate basis. (For example, if the building is 60 percent occupied the present value of lease payments would be compared to 60 percent of the carrying value to ascertain whether a write-down is necessary.)

3. Revenue recognition will be on a cash basis, being recorded on receipt of rental cheques from lessees.

4. Any public relations expenditures are to be capitalized as building costs.

5. Property taxes on land held for future buildings are to be capitalized as part of the cost of land.

6. Any building acquired by trading with other owners is to be recorded at fair market value at the date of exchange. (S Ltd. is presently considering trading building 2 for another building close to 1. The only cash to be exchanged is minimal, representing the difference between the mortgages outstanding on the two buildings.)

CA has obtained the audit of S Ltd. and for years has held the audit of R Ltd. R Ltd. depreciates its buildings and machinery on a straight-line basis over periods of up to 40 years.

The treasurer of R Ltd. and the controller of S Ltd. have arranged a meeting with CA to discuss these accounting policies, and they have informed CA that they consider the amounts involved material. They desire an unqualified audit report and want to discuss whether the above proposals are acceptable. Whether the proposals are acceptable or not, the client wishes to know CA's opinion, with reasons as to the most appropriate alternative in each case.

Required

Assume the role of CA and prepare a position paper on the matters to be discussed at the upcoming meeting.

Case 74

Scientific Delivery Corp.

Scientific Delivery Corp. (SDC) is a Canadian company founded in 1982; it went public in 1986 and acquired existing businesses in the United States and Great Britain. The founder and original president, Jonathan Claxon, retired in 1988 after developing a strong management team and training his successor.

SDC's product is laser beam technology. A laser is a beam of light whose energy can be directed onto small surfaces; laser technology is used for product labeling, coding of electronic components, welding, drilling, cutting, spectroscopy (identification of the atoms or molecules in an unknown substance), and delicate surgery (for example removal of cataracts and replacement of the lens). Different laser radiation wavelengths are required for different purposes; therefore there is a range of laser products (gas, solid state, dye, excimer). The difference among them is the material which produces the laser light. SDC's products are primarily in the scientific and components coding lines.

In 1989 the company's management realized that expansion of sales in the component coding area would continue only if more electronic components could be made laser markable; as a result, SDC began a program to develop new coating materials for the components. In 1989 several events affected SDC's results. One was the introduction by the company of a dye laser. SDC's sales of excimer lasers had been decreasing because the two types are usually purchased together, and it was hoped that the addition of the dye laser to the product line would help the company overcome a competitive disadvantage. Also in 1989 the effects of worldwide cutbacks in government funding for research were felt. In addition, all North American scientific instrument manufacturers had problems in pricing their export sales due to wide fluctuation of most European currencies.

The 1990 results showed continued effects of the 1989 setbacks; however, near the end of 1990 SDC received an order for $1.2 million in solid state lasers for use in surgery. The company was also in the process of developing applications of gas laser technology for use in military defence.

In 1988 management changed the policy for capitalization and amortization of research and development costs. Below are extracts from SDC's most recent financial statements:

Research and Development Costs

Development costs relating to specific products that in the company's view have a clearly defined future market are deferred and amortized on a straight-line basis over three years, commencing in the year following the year in which the new-product development was completed.

Provision for Income Tax

The company uses the tax allocation method of accounting for taxes.

Details from the past five financial statements, as originally issued, are as follows (in thousands):

	1990	1989	1988	1987	1986
Sales	3,000	4,300	3,500	3,200	3,500
Net income (loss) before tax	(475)	450	400	350	650
Expenditure on research and development*	1,625	1,425	900	1,200	1,125
Current year's R & D expensed*	0	0	0	1,200	1,125
Previously deferred development costs expensed	1,175	1,075	925	0	0
Deferred development balance at year-end	2,875	2,425	2,075	0	0
Total assets	5,700	6,000	4,800	3,800	3,000
Tax rate	.48	.48	.48	.48	.48

* 1982–85: $450 per year.

Required

Comment on SDC's accounting policies for research and development and income taxes. Include in your discussion your recommendations for the measurement and disclosure of the taxable loss carryforward in 1990.

Case 75

Sherrard and Walsh Ltd.

Sherrard and Walsh Limited was incorporated in 1967 and established a formal pension plan on July 1, 1983, to provide retirement benefits to all employees. The plan is (benefits based on the five highest years' salary) noncontributory and is operated by a trustee, the Bank of Newfoundland, which invests all funds and will pay benefits when they come due. There have been no amendments to the plan since its inception.

Dave Walsh, the controller, has called you, an independent accountant, concerning the most recent Actuarial Report, as of June 30, 1989. He would like you to review this report with reference to the requirements of Section 3460 of the *CICA Handbook,* to determine its acceptability for financial reporting purposes. Up to now, Sherrard and Walsh Ltd. has always simply expensed the amount paid to the actuary.

He has also asked you for an indication of how pension expense would be calculated using the *CICA Handbook* rules. Therefore, he has suggested that you use the figures in the actuary's report to calculate pension expense, so he can have a model to follow in the future. At this point, Walsh is not concerned about any cumulative balance or retroactive treatment, just the calculation of current pension expense. Walsh would also like you to draft any notes to the financial statements that would be required. You know from past experience that Sherrard and Walsh are not enthusiastic about any disclosure and will only include minimum requirements.

Required

Respond to the requests of Dave Walsh.

Basic Noncontributory Pension Plan Actuarial Report as of June 30, 1989—Sherrard and Walsh Limited

---

1. *Funding Requirements:*
   Current service cost (before adjustment for experience gains)
   computed under an accumulated benefit method . . . . . . $ 34,150
   Experience gains . . . . (20,500)
   Experience losses 350
   Interest on accrued benefits 9,916
   Interest on pension fund assets . . . . (8,410)
   Funding of past service cost (principal only; over 20 years) . . 5,000
   Funding requirement . . . . $ 20,506

2. *Fund Assets:*
   Cash . . . . $ 4,200
   Dividends receivable 1,525
   Investment in common shares, at cost (market, $177,800) . . 162,750
   $168,475

3. *Actuarial Liabilities:*
   Number of employees 46
   Number of employees retired 0
   Yearly earnings of employees $598,000
   Actuarial liability, at year end, as calculated by actuary . . . $145,000

4. *Actuarial Assumptions:*
   Interest 7%
   Mortality . . . . 1951 Group Annuity Tables
   Retirement . . . . age 65
   Average remaining working lives of
   employees at June 30, 1989 . . . . 22.5 years
   (at July 1, 1983, 30 years)

Silverado Investments Limited

Silverado Investments Limited (SIL) began operations in 1978 when Eldon Silver left his job as head project engineer for Alis-Dan Construction and started his own real estate development company. The company was an immediate success resulting from a combination of Silver's entrepreneurial skills and the significant demand for Multiple-Unit Residential Buildings (MURBS), the flagship project of the operation.

Between 1978 and 1983 all of the projects completed by SIL were successful, usually resulting in a 10 to 15 percent before tax profit. The company was fortunate enough to have several foundations in place when the 1981 federal tax budget eliminated MURBS, and they were able to continue these projects without undue delay. The last MURB project was completed in October 1985.

The normal processes for a MURB project consisted of an outside promoter syndicating the project and setting up a limited partnership. SIL would then find a site, arrange for interim and mortgage financing, and construct the building (usually employing subcontractors). Mortgage advances approximating 85 percent of the total cost were made to SIL as the building progressed. Upon project completion, SIL would receive the final payment of approximately 15 percent from the promoter and would then turn the project over to an independent property manager.

Since 1985, SIL has continued to develop residential real estate. However, with the demise of the MURB tax incentive, the attractiveness of rental projects to investors has declined. To sell an investment syndication now, the developer must play a much more active role.

Adapted, with permission from Manfred Schneider.

Accounting policies for various aspects of these post-MURB real estate projects have yet to be established. (See Exhibit 2.) Silver is concerned that these policies should be the correct ones and that they can be consistently applied to future projects. His concern is magnified by the fact that bank and securities commissions (under whose jurisdictions these limited offerings are promoted), now want audited statements for the corporation as a whole.

Silver has contacted you, a professional accountant, to provide a complete analysis of the issues and to give recommendations for policies. The company's 1986 draft financial statements (Exhibit 1) and description of current projects (Exhibits 2 and 3) have been provided.

Required

Respond to Silver's request.

EXHIBIT 1

SILVERADO INVESTMENTS LIMITED
Balance Sheet (unaudited)
at September 30
(in thousands)

	1986 (DRAFT)	1985
Assets		
Properties:		
Income-producing	$ 1,400	$ 1,500
Held for future development	1,500	800
	2,900	2,300
Projects under construction with sales agreements net of		
mortgage advances	4,100	6,500
Cash	1,650	—
Due from joint venture	863	754
Mortgage advances receivable	2,900	4,875
Investment in joint venture, at cost	1,000	1,000
Other assets.	800	780
	11,313	13,909
	$14,213	$16,209
Liabilities		
Accounts payable related to projects under		
construction.	$ 7,280	$10,610
Accounts payable—other.	2,175	1,610
	9,455	12,220

EXHIBIT 1   (*concluded*)

	1986 (DRAFT)	1985
Shareholders' Equity		
Capital stock	$ 1	$ 1
Retained earnings	4,757	3,988
	4,758	3,989
	$14,213	$16,209

**Statements of Income and Retained Earnings
for the Year Ended September 30**

Revenue:		
Residential project sales	$15,000	$19,000
Rental and other.	154	145
	15,154	19,145
Expenses:		
Cost of projects sold	12,756	16,250
Rental	142	130
General and other	1,125	830
	14,023	17,210
Net income for the year	1,131	1,935
Retained earnings at beginning of year	3,988	2,053
Dividends.	362	—
Retained earnings at end of year	$ 4,757	$ 3,988

EXHIBIT 2   Current Projects—Silverado Investments Limited

1. *Income-Producing Properties*—consists of a 40-unit apartment building owned and operated by SIL since 1981. The building is in the rapidly developing harbourfront area. SIL has applied to the municipality to obtain approval for condominium status. If the approval is granted, it is expected that the units could be sold for $100,000 each. Approximately $1.1 million would be needed for improvements at that time. The company has stopped depreciating the building because the site is already undervalued on the books.

2. *Held for Future Development Properties*—consists of a 15-acre site on the outskirts of Montreal. SIL has subdivided the land in Phase 1 and since August 1986 they have been selling the individual lots. Additional information with respect to this project follows:

EXHIBIT 2   (*concluded*)

---

    a. Phase I—Consists of 25 single-family lots on four acres and a one-acre lot suitable for 25 multiple-unit dwellings (i.e., duplexes, town-houses, and so on).

        Phase II—Plans have not been finalized on this 10-acre parcel. The mix of units is expected to be similar to Phase I.

    b. Development costs of $300,000 have been incurred to construct roads and water mains. These costs are expected to benefit each phase equally.

    c. The sales prices are estimated to be $25,000 each for the single-family lots and $15,000 per unit for the multiple-dwelling lots in Phase I. In Phase II, prices will be $30,000 and $20,000, respectively.

    d. Five single-family lots have been sold since September 30, 1986 and 15 more are expected to be sold soon. It is expected that 10 multiple-dwelling units will also be sold by the end of December.

    e. Revenue from lots sold has been recorded but no cost has yet been expensed.

  3. *Projects under Construction*—consists of a major development project (255 units) for which an agreement has been signed with a group of limited partners. When the project is completed, in July of 1987, the building will be sold to the partners, who will pay SIL as follows:

Cash, provided by first mortgage from Confidential Insurance .	$11,000,000
Cash, payments by the investors to SIL.	1,000,000
6% notes receivable to SIL from the investors, payable in four equal installments on the anniversary of the turnover date.	2,000,000
Five-year 18% second mortgage provided by SIL	1,500,000
	$15,500,000

The estimated total costs of the project are $12,300,000. SIL plans to record the profit ($3,200,000) in July 1987, when the building is completed. The assets received in consideration (listed above) would be recorded at that time.

EXHIBIT 3   Information on Development Project under Construction—Silverado Investment Limited

---

SIL is currently constructing a 255-unit luxury apartment complex, which will be completed by July 1987. (See item 3, Exhibit 2.) This project differs from the former MURB projects in both the manner of financing and in the number of indemnities and covenants that SIL must provide. The turnover date, referred to below, is the date the Limited Partnership assumes ownership of the project. It occurs when the project is finished and 90 percent leased.

EXHIBIT 3 *(continued)*

EXTRACTS FROM OFFERING MEMORANDUM

SIL Second Mortgage. The SIL mortgage will be in the principal amount of $1.5 million and will bear interest at the rate of 18 percent after the turnover date.

The SIL mortgage will be for a five-year term beginning on the turnover date. The mortgage will include the following terms:

1. The mortgage will be without recourse to the limited partners.
2. Payment of principal and accrued interest at maturity only to the extent that proceeds are available from the refinancing of the first mortgage; and the mortgage to be renewed for any unpaid balance for a further term, without interest.
3. The Limited Partnership will have the right to set off amounts owing by it under the SIL mortgage against amounts by which SIL is in default under the Purchase and Development Agreement.

Initial Leasing Period Indemnity

The Purchase and Development Agreement provides that SIL will operate the project on behalf of the Limited Partnership and will indemnify the Limited Partnership for all losses incurred in operating the project during the initial leasing period which ends on the turnover date.

Cash Flow Guarantee

SIL has covenanted to provide interest-free loans to the Limited Partnership for the following purposes:

i. To fund, as required, for a period of 10 years from the turnover date, the amount, if any, by which the total operating expenses of the project (including payments on account of principal and interest due on the mortgages, but excluding noncash items such as depreciation and reserves for replacement of equipment and chattels) exceed the aggregate gross income receipts from the project.
ii. To fund, during the period commencing on the turnover date and ending on December 31, 1987, the amount (the "Guaranteed Amount"), if any, by which the actual net cash flow is less than the amounts set forth opposite "Net Distributable Cash Flow" contained in the "Forecasts."

The "Forecasts," which are not contained in these exhibits are cash flow predictions outlining the expected positive cash flow available for distribution to the partners.

Management of the Project

SIL will be appointed manager of the project for a term of 10 years, and will be paid 5 percent of the monthly gross income receipts.

EXHIBIT 3 *(concluded)*

The management agreement will provide that SIL will be responsible for the ongoing leasing of apartment units comprising the project, maintenance and repairs, collection of rents, payment of all expenses properly incurred in connection with such duties out of revenues received from the project including all amounts payable under the mortgages, the maintenance of fire and liability insurance on the project, the preparation of a budget for each fiscal year for the project and the annual remittance of cash surpluses to the Limited Partnership.

Case 77

Smith Wesley Ltd.

Smith Wesley Ltd. is a manufacturer and supplier of paper products. It specializes in a broad range of office needs, including photocopier paper and stationery, as well as corrugated (paperboard) boxes for packaging, newsprint, and so forth. The company is fully integrated, owning timberland, milling and manufacturing facilities, and sale and distribution centers.

Smith Wesley is 29 percent owned by a large American multinational company. The remaining common shares are widely held and traded on the Toronto Stock Exchange. Recently, the company has suspected that shares are being quietly accumulated by a group of investors interested in a takeover bid.

Smith Wesley's operating results have not met its own or analyst's expectations over the last three years. This was due to two factors: a softening of product prices in reaction to increased competition, and increased production costs. Smith Wesley recently completed an aggressive capital expansion program, resulting in state-of-the-art, highly efficient production facilities. Unfortunately, the facilities are only highly efficient if run at peak capacity, which sales volume has not been able to support. Product costs, therefore, have exceeded expectations.

Smith Wesley is concerned that its seemingly poor operating results will encourage existing shareholders to divest, and make the company an easy target for a takeover attempt. Accordingly, it is examining its reporting practices to see if its financial position is being well represented.

Currently, inventories are valued on the last-in, first-out (LIFO) method, to facilitate performance evaluation by their major American shareholder. The first-in, first-out (FIFO) system has been used for tax purposes. The following values (in thousands) have been calculated:

Inventory	LIFO	FIFO
December 31, 1989.	$115,398	$162,998
December 31, 1988.	$111,261	$150,861
December 31, 1987.	$106,419	$140,421

Management is considering changing their inventory costing system from LIFO to FIFO to make their statements more comparable to other Canadian companies.

Required

1. Recast the 1989 and 1988 income statement (only) using FIFO as an inventory costing policy. The tax rate is 43 percent.
2. Comment on the desirability of the proposed change. Your analysis should include the probable reaction of the stock market to the change.

EXHIBIT 1

SMITH WESLEY LTD.
Statement of Income and Retained Earnings
for the Year Ended December 31
(in thousands)

	1989	1988
Sales	$1,673,250	$1,840,360
Costs and expenses:		
Cost of sales.	1,316,260	1,330,040
Selling and general	293,740	306,670
Financing costs	175,090	157,760
	1,785,090	1,794,470
Income (loss) before tax.	(111,840)	45,890
Provision for tax (recovery)	48,090	19,730
Net income (loss).	(63,750)	26,160
Retained earnings, beginning of year	$ 247,830	$ 221,670
Retained earnings, end of year	$ 184,080	$ 247,830

Sousa Ltd.

Sousa Ltd. is a small, privately owned company, engaged in the plastic molding industry. Audited financial statements are prepared annually, and the year-end is December 31.

Recently, it leased three pieces of manufacturing equipment from the leasing subsidiary of a major chartered bank. It could have borrowed money from the same bank, using the equipment as collateral, at prime plus 3 percent, or about 10 percent interest. Management decided to use leases as the financing method. The lease contracts are showing in Exhibits 1–3.

All the leased manufacturing equipment has an approximate useful life of seven years. Other such equipment is depreciated using the straight-line method.

You, a member of Sousa's accounting department, have been asked by the controller to do an analysis that will show the impact each *separate* lease will have on net income, the balance sheet, and the notes to the financial statements.

Required

Prepare the requested analysis for each lease individually.

EXHIBIT 1

Equipment Lease

Alberta Lease Co.

LESSEE NO	LEASE NO
1426	4921

ALWAYS REFER TO THESE NUMBERS

LESSEE NAME Sousa Ltd.	SUPPLIER OF EQUIPMENT NAME X Machinery Co.
ADDRESS 100 Any Street	ADDRESS 400 Main Street
CITY Metropolis PROV. Alta.	CITY Metropolis PROV. Alta.
POSTAL CODE A1A 2B3 TELEPHONE NO. 991-9999	POSTAL CODE A2A 7B9 TELEPHONE NO. 997-1111
CONTACT Mr. Smith	SUPPLIER REPRESENTATIVE Mr. Jones

EQUIPMENT LOCATION IF OTHER THAN ABOVE: n/a ADDRESS CITY COUNTY PROV.

LANDLORD: n/a ADDRESS

NO OF UNITS	MODEL NO	YEAR	DESCRIPTION	LIST PRICE	SERIAL NO
1	40902	1988	Molding Equipment	$72,000	

TERMS OF PAYMENT (total subject to any provincial sales tax % changes)

TERM IN YEARS	NO OF RENTAL PAYMENTS	PAYMENTS WILL BE MADE	FIRST RENTAL DUE DATE M D Y	AMOUNT OF EACH RENTAL PAYMENT EXCLUDING SALES TAX	INSURANCE COSTS	TOTAL AMOUNT EACH PAYMENT	SECURITY DEPOSIT	PURCHASE OPTION PRICE AND DATE
3	3	☑ YEARLY ☐	07 01 88	$19621	$1,175	$20,796	$	$ n/a AT END OF OF THE LEASE TERM

TERMS AND CONDITIONS OF LEASE

For and in consideration of the covenants and agreements by the Lessee to pay the total rental payment herein provided for and to perform the terms, covenants and conditions on the Lessee's part herein contained, the Lessor hereby leases, and lets unto the Lessee, and the Lessee hereby leases and takes from the Lessor, each unit of equipment described above and hereinafter referred to as "said equipment", for the term set forth above (commencing on the date of the first delivery of any of the said equipment to the Lessee) and upon and subject to the covenants, conditions and provisions hereinafter set forth. Notwithstanding the foregoing, in the event that such first delivery takes place before the First Rental Due Date the term of this Lease shall be extended by the number of days from and including the date of the first delivery of any part of the said equipment and the First Rental Due Date.

1. RENTAL. For the use of said equipment, the Lessee shall pay to the Lessor at the Lessor's office, at 100 Main Street, Metropolis, Alta a total rental payment equal to the amount of each rental payment specified above multiplied by the number of rental payments specified above. The first rental payment and Security Deposit shall become due on the First Rental Due Date indicated above. Subsequent rental payments shall become due in every consecutive month or period, as the case may be, thereafter on the same date of each such month or period as the First Rental Due Date indicated above, or in the event that there is no such corresponding date, the last date of the said month. Rental payment hereunder is payable without abatement.

2. EQUIPMENT DESCRIPTION. The Lessee authorizes the Lessor to complete the description of said equipment above with the insertion of serial numbers and other details specifically identifying said equipment.

3. REPRESENTATIONS AND WARRANTIES. Each unit of said equipment leased

hereunder is of a size, design and capacity personally chosen and selected by the Lessee and the Lessee is satisfied that the same is suitable for its purposes and the Lessor has made no representation or warranty with respect to the suitability or durability of any such unit for the purposes or uses of the Lessee, or any other representation or warranty express or implied with respect thereto.

The Lessee acknowledges that said equipment hereby leased was personally chosen and selected by the Lessee for business purposes, and purchased at the Lessee's request from a supplier designated by the Lessee. Consequently, the Lessee takes full responsibility for the choosing and the selection, and will look only to the supplier for warranty against latent defects or other matters, the Lessor hereby conveying expressly and without reserve to the Lessee all warranties, if any, resulting from the sale of said equipment entered into with the supplier. The Lessee renounces the right to any claim or defence against the Lessor relating to said equipment. In the event of an action brought by the Lessor for default under the provisions of this Lease, the Lessee waives all defences predicated on the failure of said equipment to perform the function for which it was designed and further acknowledges and agrees that such failure shall not be deemed to be in breach of this Lease.

4. GOVERNING LAW. This lease shall be interpreted and enforced in accordance with the laws of the Province wherein said equipment is to be located according to the terms hereof. Lessor and Lessee hereby acknowledge that they have required this Lease and all related documents to be drawn up in the English language. Le Locateur et le Locataire reconnaissent avoir exigé que le présent crédit-bail et les documents qui s'y rattachent soient rédigés en anglais.

The Undersigned Agree to All Terms and Conditions Set Forth Above and in Consideration Thereof Hereby Execute This Lease.

Date June 15 19 88
Lessor

By Alberta Lease Co.
Authorized Signature

Name of Lessee SOUSA LTD.
(Legal Name of Firm)

By _____
Authorized Signature and Title

By _____
Authorized Signature and Title

LESSEE COPY

EXHIBIT 2

Equipment Lease

Alberta Lease Co.

LESSEE NO	LEASE NO
1426	4922

ALWAYS REFER TO THESE NUMBERS

LESSEE NAME Sousa Ltd.	SUPPLIER OF EQUIPMENT NAME X Machinery Co.
ADDRESS 100 Any Street	ADDRESS 400 Main Street
CITY Metropolis PROV. Alta.	CITY Metropolis PROV. Alta.
POSTAL CODE A1A 2B3 TELEPHONE NO. 991-9999	POSTAL CODE A2A 7B9 TELEPHONE NO. 997-1111
CONTACT Mr. Smith	SUPPLIER REPRESENTATIVE Mr. Jones

EQUIPMENT LOCATION IF OTHER THAN ABOVE	ADDRESS	CITY	COUNTY	PROV.
n/a				

LANDLORD	ADDRESS
n/a	

NO. OF UNITS	MODEL NO	YEAR	DESCRIPTION	LIST PRICE	SERIAL NO.
1	40170	1988	molding equipment	$115,000	

TERMS OF PAYMENT (total subject to any provincial sales tax % changes)

TERM IN YEARS	NO. OF RENTAL PAYMENTS	PAYMENTS WILL BE MADE	FIRST RENTAL DUE DATE M D Y	AMOUNT OF EACH RENTAL PAYMENT EXCLUDING SALES TAX	INSURANCE COSTS	TOTAL AMOUNT EACH PAYMENT	SECURITY DEPOSIT	PURCHASE OPTION PRICE AND DATE
5	5	☑ YEARLY ☐	07 01 88	$28,484	$1,300	$29,784	$	$ n/a AT END OF OF THE LEASE TERM

TERMS AND CONDITIONS OF LEASE

For and in consideration of the covenants and agreements by the Lessee to pay the total rental payment herein provided for and to perform the terms, covenants and conditions on the Lessee's part herein contained, the Lessor hereby leases, and lets unto the Lessee, and the Lessee hereby leases and takes from the Lessor, each unit of equipment described above and hereinafter referred to as "said equipment", for the term set forth above (commencing on the date of the first delivery of any of the said equipment to the Lessee) and upon and subject to the covenants, conditions and provisions hereinafter set forth. Notwithstanding the foregoing, in the event that such first delivery takes place before the First Rental Due Date the term of this Lease shall be extended by the number of days from and including the date of the first delivery of any part of the said equipment and the First Rental Due Date.

1. RENTAL. For the use of said equipment, the Lessee shall pay to the Lessor at the Lessor's office, at 100 Main Street, Metropolis, Alta a total rental payment equal to the amount of each rental payment specified above multiplied by the number of rental payments specified above. The first rental payment and Security Deposit shall become due on the First Rental Due Date indicated above. Subsequent rental payments shall become due in every consecutive month or period, as the case may be, thereafter on the same date of each such month or period as the First Rental Due Date indicated above, or in the event that there is no such corresponding date, the last date of the said month. Rental payment hereunder is payable without abatement.

2. EQUIPMENT DESCRIPTION. The Lessee authorizes the Lessor to complete the description of said equipment above with the insertion of serial numbers and other details specifically identifying said equipment.

3. REPRESENTATIONS AND WARRANTIES. Each unit of said equipment leased

hereunder is of a size, design and capacity personally chosen and selected by the Lessee and the Lessee is satisfied that the same is suitable for its purposes and the Lessor has made no representation or warranty with respect to the suitability or durability of any such unit for the purposes or uses of the Lessee, or any other representation or warranty express or implied with respect thereto.

The Lessee acknowledges that said equipment hereby leased was personally chosen and selected by the Lessee for business purposes, and purchased at the Lessee's request from a supplier designated by the Lessee. Consequently, the Lessee takes full responsibility for the choosing and the selection, and will look only to the supplier for warranty against latent defects or other matters, the Lessor hereby conveying expressly and without reserve to the Lessee all warranties, if any, resulting from the sale of said equipment entered into with the supplier. The Lessee renounces the right to any claim or defence against the Lessor relating to said equipment. In the event of an action brought by the Lessor for default under the provisions of this Lease, the Lessee waives all defences predicated on the failure of said equipment to perform the function for which it was designed and further acknowledges and agrees that such failure shall not be deemed to be in breach of this Lease.

4. GOVERNING LAW. This lease shall be interpreted and enforced in accordance with the laws of the Province wherein said equipment is to be located according to the terms hereof. Lessor and Lessee hereby acknowledge that they have required this Lease and all related documents to be drawn up in the English language. Le Locateur et le Locataire reconnaissent avoir exigé que le présent crédit-bail et les documents qui s'y rattachent soient rédigés en anglais.

The Undersigned Agree to All Terms and Conditions Set Forth Above and in Consideration Thereof Hereby Execute This Lease.

Date June 15   19 88

Lessor

By Alberta Lease Co.

Authorized Signature

Name of Lessee SOUSA LTD.
(Legal Name of Firm)

By _____
Authorized Signature and Title

By _____
Authorized Signature and Title

LESSEE COPY

EXHIBIT 3

Alberta Lease Co.

Equipment Lease

LESSEE NO	LEASE NO
1426	4923

ALWAYS REFER TO THESE NUMBERS

LESSEE NAME	Sousa Ltd.	SUPPLIER OF EQUIPMENT NAME	X Machinery Co.
ADDRESS	100 Any Street	ADDRESS	400 Main Street
CITY	Metropolis PROV. Alta.	CITY	Metropolis PROV. Alta.
POSTAL CODE	A1A 2B3 TELEPHONE NO. 991-9999	POSTAL CODE	A2A 7B9 TELEPHONE NO. 997-1111
CONTACT	Mr. Smith	SUPPLIER REPRESENTATIVE	Mr. Jones

EQUIPMENT LOCATION IF OTHER THAN ABOVE: n/a   ADDRESS   CITY   COUNTY   PROV.

LANDLORD: n/a   ADDRESS

NO. OF UNITS	MODEL NO.	YEAR	DESCRIPTION	LIST PRICE	SERIAL NO.
1	1724	1988	molding equipment	$179,000	

TERMS OF PAYMENT (total subject to any provincial sales tax % changes)

TERM IN YEARS	NO. OF RENTAL PAYMENTS	PAYMENTS WILL BE MADE	FIRST RENTAL DUE DATE (M D Y)	AMOUNT OF EACH RENTAL PAYMENT EXCLUDING SALES TAX	INSURANCE COSTS	TOTAL AMOUNT EACH PAYMENT	SECURITY DEPOSIT	PURCHASE OPTION PRICE AND DATE
4	4	☑ YEARLY ☐	07 01 88	$52,600	$2,500	$55,100	$	$100 AT END OF 4th. OF THE LEASE TERM

TERMS AND CONDITIONS OF LEASE

For and in consideration of the covenants and agreements by the Lessee to pay the total rental payment herein provided for and to perform the terms, covenants and conditions on the Lessee's part herein contained, the Lessor hereby leases, and lets unto the Lessee, and the Lessee hereby leases and takes from the Lessor, each unit of equipment described above and hereinafter referred to as "said equipment", for the term set forth above (commencing on the date of the first delivery of any of the said equipment to the Lessee) and upon and subject to the covenants, conditions and provisions hereinafter set forth. Notwithstanding the foregoing, in the event that such first delivery takes place before the First Rental Due Date the term of this Lease shall be extended by the number of days from and including the date of the first delivery of any part of the said equipment and the First Rental Due Date.

1. RENTAL. For the use of said equipment, the Lessee shall pay to the Lessor at the Lessor's office, at 100 Main Street, Metropolis, Alta a total rental payment equal to the amount of each rental payment specified above multiplied by the number of rental payments specified above. The first rental payment and Security Deposit shall become due on the First Rental Due Date indicated above. Subsequent rental payments shall become due in every consecutive month or period, as the case may be, thereafter on the same date of each such month or period as the First Rental Due Date indicated above, or in the event that there is no such corresponding date, the last date of the said month. Rental payment hereunder is payable without abatement.

2. EQUIPMENT DESCRIPTION. The Lessee authorizes the Lessor to complete the description of said equipment above with the insertion of serial numbers and other details specifically identifying said equipment.

3. REPRESENTATIONS AND WARRANTIES. Each unit of said equipment leased

hereunder is of a size, design and capacity personally chosen and selected by the Lessee and the Lessee is satisfied that the same is suitable for its purposes and the Lessor has made no representation or warranty with respect to the suitability or durability of any such unit for the purposes or uses of the Lessee, or any other representation or warranty express or implied with respect thereto.

The Lessee acknowledges that said equipment hereby leased was personally chosen and selected by the Lessee for business purposes, and purchased at the Lessee's request from a supplier designated by the Lessee. Consequently, the Lessee takes full responsibility for the choosing and the selection, and will look only to the supplier for warranty against latent defects or other matters, the Lessor hereby conveying expressly and without reserve to the Lessee all warranties, if any, resulting from the sale of said equipment entered into with the supplier. The Lessee renounces the right to any claim or defence against the Lessor relating to said equipment. In the event of an action brought by the Lessor for default under the provisions of this Lease, the Lessee waives all defences predicated on the failure of said equipment to perform the function for which it was designed and further acknowledges and agrees that such failure shall not be deemed to be in breach of this Lease.

4. GOVERNING LAW. This lease shall be interpreted and enforced in accordance with the laws of the Province wherein said equipment is to be located according to the terms hereof. Lessor and Lessee hereby acknowledge that they have required this Lease and all related documents to be drawn up in the English language. Le Locateur et le Locataire reconnaissent avoir exigé que le présent crédit-bail et les documents qui s'y rattachent soient rédigés en anglais.

The Undersigned Agree to All Terms and Conditions Set Forth Above and in Consideration Thereof Hereby Execute This Lease.

Date June 15 19 88

Lessor

By Alberta Lease Co.
Authorized Signature

Name of Lessee SOUSA LTD.
(Legal Name of Firm)

By _____
Authorized Signature and Title

By _____
Authorized Signature and Title

LESSEE COPY

Case 79

Specialty Meat Products Ltd.

Specialty Meat Products Ltd. (SMPL) is a wholly owned subsidiary of a public Canadian corporation. SMPL prepares and packages meat, primarily beef and chicken, which is sold in bulk to consumers and in larger shipments to grocery chains in central Ontario.

In January 1989, SMPL's top management were finalizing the acquisition of machinery for a new packaging line, which could be acquired outright by a purchase with debt financing or leased through a financial institution. The decision has been made to acquire the machinery. The issue now is how it should be financed.

All members of SMPL's management participate in an incentive plan which the parent company has established in its subsidiaries. The main component of the plan is subsidiary return on capital, defined as net operating pretax profit divided by total subsidiary active assets excluding cash.

SMPL's management team has always considered their annual bonus to be an important part of their total compensation package. Typically, individuals received a bonus of 20 to 25 percent of their base salary. The bonus had been growing, as has SMPL's return on capital, at about 10 percent per year. This is expected to level off in 1989, as capacity has been reached.

Excerpts from the annual report, dated December 31, 1988, are shown in Exhibit 1. The report is currently being audited, but no major changes are expected from the audit examination. Details about the various financing options are outlined in Exhibit 2. SMPL's marginal tax rate is 35 percent.

Required

Undertake analysis to answer the following:

1. Which of the financing options is "best" for SMPL?
2. How will each option affect the 1989 return on capital calculation? Assume that 1988 results predict the 1989 figures.
3. How should SMPL finance the acquisition? Explain your recommendation.

EXHIBIT 1   Excerpts from SMPL's 1988 Annual Report

	Year Ended Dec. 31, 1988 (000s)
Income statement:	
Sales	$24,699
Cost of sales	20,564
	4,135
Selling, general, and administrative expenses	1,760
Interest expense	503
Depreciation	621
	2,884
Net income before the following	1,251
Share of affiliated companies profits	100
	1,351
Provision for income taxes*	434
	917
Extraordinary item (net of applicable income tax)	120
Net income	$ 1,037

	December 31, 1988 (000s)
Balance sheet:	
Assets:	
Current†	$ 7,090
Fixed (net of straight-line depreciation)	5,451
Other:	
Investment in shares of affiliates	778
Advances to affiliates	165
	$13,484

* The deferred portion is $203,000.
† Includes cash of $91,000.

EXHIBIT 2   Alternative Financing Arrangements

Project details:
  Cost: $3,000,000
  Economic life: 10 years, no salvage value
  CCA rate: 20% (10% in year 1).
Alternative financing arrangements:
  1. Lease no. 1
      Lease term: 1 year, renewable at SMPL's option
      Annual lease payment, paid in advance: $535,000
  2. Lease no. 2
      Lease term: 5 years with option to renew for a second 5-year term
      Annual lease payment, paid in advance: $750,000, first term; $33,200,
        second term
  3. Purchase with debt financing:
      Loan amount: $3,000,000
      Term: 10 years
      Interest rate: 12%, fixed rate
      Payments: Blended, level, end of year

Sunbeam Iron Mines Ltd.

The partner in charge of the Sunbeam Iron Mines Ltd. audit has just briefed you on an accounting problem that has developed in the company. You have worked on this audit client for the last two years, and are reasonably familiar with the operation. The mining industry is highly cyclical, and the company's fortunes have waxed and waned with fluctuating ore prices. They have been reasonably profitable recently, but are keen to minimize fluctuations in income.

At this point in time, the 1989 fiscal year has ended, and the audit work is complete. The statements have yet to be issued, as a few final issues have yet to be ironed out.

The partner informed you that there now appears to be a major problem with the deferred development expenses (DDEs).

DDEs are a basic principle in accounting for mine operations. When initial development costs are incurred, they are not immediately expensed, but rather deferred as an asset on the balance sheet, to be amortized as the mine property generates revenue in future years. The amortization rate is based on expected future revenues from total ore reserves.

The 1989 draft financial statements currently show $75 million of DDEs on the balance sheet. In previous years, the DDEs had been amortized at the rate of $500,000 to $800,000 per year, and ore reserves appeared vast.

The partner has just seen revised geological reports, prepared by Sunbeam Iron Mines' geologists, that showed a significant drop in proven reserves, down to 20 million tons. Based on this estimate, the partner did an analysis that showed that $55 million of the DDEs should be written off. Net of deferred tax, the write-off would be $35,475,000.

After the partner raised this issue with the company, Sunbeam produced another report, also prepared by their geologists. While it had the same conclusions about proven reserves, it estimated the presence of 74 million tons of inferred ore reserves recoverable by underground mining techniques. The partner felt that this report had been hastily assembled to counteract the effect of the first report on financial markets.

The company told the partner that they prefer to simply disclose the decline in their proven reserves in a note to the financial statements and increase the rate of future amortization. They do not feel a write-down is required as this is a change in estimate, to be accounted for prospectively. This became a major difference of opinion between the partner and the company's management. They also informed the partner that, should a write-down have to be made, it should be presented as a prior period adjustment, not as an unusual or extraordinary item (the alternatives the partner suggested).

A meeting of the Audit Committee has been scheduled for next week, and the partner has asked you to prepare a report for him to use in this meeting. He has specifically asked you to evaluate both sides of the argument, as he wants to ensure that he has given the company's side the consideration it deserves. The report should include your recommendations.

Before starting your report, you did some research into the area of "inferred reserves." The concept of inferred reserves rests on implication. If ore has been found, or regularly found, in one geological formation, then the presence of that same formation in another area has the possibility of ore reserves as well. These are called *inferred reserves*. These types of reserves are not normally included in amortization calculations by other companies in the industry.

Further, you discovered that the underground mining techniques necessary to mine Sunbeam's inferred reserves have yet to be fully established. The company currently has commissioned a $2 million study to investigate the feasibility of the techniques.

Required

Respond to the request of the partner and prepare the report.

Case 81

Sunrise Enterprises Limited

Sunrise Enterprises Ltd. is a small manufacturer of pipe fittings with a December 31 year-end. The company is privately owned by Greg Lai, the president and general manager. An annual audit is performed, primarily to satisfy the chartered bank that provides financing for fixed assets and working capital.

Mr. Lai has raised the following concerns with reference to the depreciation charges on assets:

1. If possible, he wishes to change the depreciation method for his manufacturing equipment from declining-balance to "units-of-production," or usage. Details are in Exhibit 1.
2. He does not wish to depreciate his factory building at all, as he is confident that the building has actually appreciated in value, not depreciated, over the last year. Sunrise Enterprises is located in a major urban center where appreciation of residential real estate is well documented. Lai has watched several commercial properties around him sell for "fabulous" prices in the past 18 months.

Lai has also asked for an explanation of depreciation in general, as he feels it is a "waste of time." He points out that all the bankers seem to be interested in is cash flow, and Sunrise having enough cash to make loan and interest payments. Lai cannot decide what is the "right" way to depreciate, as everyone he talks to seems to do it differently.

Required

Draft a response to Mr. Lai.

EXHIBIT 1   Sunrise Enterprises—Fixed Asset Data

- Manufacturing Equipment, balance per G/L, December 31, 1989, at cost. $2,700,000

- Accumulated Depreciation, Manufacturing Equipment, balance per G/L, December 31, 1989. (Depreciation has not yet been booked for 1989.) $1,210,000

- Machinery lasts 12–15 years, on average, and is being depreciated straight line over this period.

- 1989 depreciation, straight-line method. $ 240,000

- Machinery was used for a total of 1,700 hours in 1989. Total available machine-hours (excluding overtime) in this period were 1,950. The plant was idle due to lack of orders for several weeks during the year. Estimated machine-hours over the remaining life of all manufacturing equipment, approximately 14,700 (Lai's estimate).

- Usage of machine-hours is not available for 1988 or prior years as data was not kept by the company.

Tasty Pizza Limited

Tasty Pizza Limited is a well-established local pizzeria which has expanded into franchising pizza outlets throughout Canada. The company has developed a new technique for making dough. This technique was successfully refined during 1989, and the company intends to acquire the necessary specialized equipment to supply all of the franchise outlets with dough manufactured at the head office.

Each franchisee receives the right to use the company's name and to benefit from training and advertising programs. The franchisee agrees to pay $60,000 for exclusive franchise rights in a given city. This initial franchise fee is payable on the following terms: $10,000 down and the remainder payable in five annual noninterest-bearing installments of $10,000 each. Franchisees expect to be able to pay their installments out of cash flow generated by the franchise.

The life of a standard franchise agreement is 15 years. Each year, the franchisee will pay the company a certain percentage of outlet sales to cover the cost of advertising and other services in addition to paying for dough purchased from the company.

In 1989, Tasty Pizza sold 10 franchises while none was sold in the previous year. Prior to 1989, the company prepared financial statements solely for the purpose of filing with Revenue Canada. As a newly hired controller, one of your responsibilities is to recommend appropriate accounting policies to be followed in 1989 and subsequent years.

The date is December 1, 1989, and the fiscal year-end is December 31, 1989. The company is about to meet with its banker to renew its line of

Society of Management Accountants, adapted.

credit, secured by its land and building. The banker has indicated that he will require audited financial statements in order to consider the loan request.

In preparation for the meeting with the banker, the company's president has asked you for a report concerning the following matters:

1. The appropriate accounting treatment and financial statement presentation for the initial franchise fees and related receivables. Prior to an overall recommendation, the president wants you to consider alternatives and the impact of each alternative on the banker's likely decision to grant the loan. A draft balance sheet, prepared by the company's bookkeeper before your arrival and dated December 31, 1989, contains an amount of $500,000 for franchise fees receivable.

2. The accounting implications and appropriate financial statement presentation of a lease versus buy decision relating to dough-making equipment which the company will acquire on December 31, 1989. If the company decides to lease, it will sign a 10-year, noncancellable lease. Annual lease payments of $20,000 would be payable at the end of each year for 10 years starting on December 31, 1990. The estimated useful life of the equipment is 15 years. The lessee has the option to purchase the equipment at the end of the 10-year lease term for $10,000.

    If the company decides to purchase, it will finance the purchase with long-term debt. The loan principal would be repayable in 10 equal annual installments. Interest would be computed at the rate of 12 percent on the principal outstanding during the year and paid annually. The purchase price of the equipment would be $110,000.

    The president tentatively favors the leasing option because he perceives that the company's debt to equity ratio will look more favorable if this option is chosen.

    In an advance ruling, Revenue Canada has indicated that the lease would be treated as a capital lease for income tax purposes. The president wonders how this will affect the lease versus buy decision, especially given the company's tax-loss carryforwards incurred in prior years as a result of the deduction of development costs for tax purposes.

3. The appropriate accounting treatment for certain assets. The company records depreciation on the building and equipment in an amount equal to the capital cost allowance claimed. In addition, a line item called deferred product development cost appears on the balance sheet. This item consists of costs (wages and materials) directly related to the development of the new dough-making techniques. These costs were incurred in 1989 and prior years, and are being amortized on a straight-line basis over five years, commencing in 1989.

4. A brief outline of any other information (besides that discussed in items [1] to [3] above) which you believe should be prepared for the banker.

Required

Prepare the report requested by the president.

Case 83

Tom's Outdoor Experience

Tom's Outdoor Experience (TOE) is a sporting goods store owned by Tom Dennison. Tom handles limited product lines. Summer sales centre on bicycles, camping gear, and clothing for both activities. Cross-country skis and related equipment and clothing are the major winter lines. The store is a year-round centre for running enthusiasts because better footwear and clothing for this sporting activity are featured. The store is situated in a small city in Ontario.

Operations began in 1973 when Tom purchased the building that houses the store. The business provided adequate cash flow to raise a family of three children. Now that the children are grown, Tom's wife has resumed her career. Tom has decided to open a new store in a nearby city as he is certain there is an available market.

Tom has been a close friend of your family for many years. In April 1986 he telephoned to ask your advice about preparing a presentation to his banker so that he could proceed with his expansion plans.

The conversation proceeded as follows:

Tom:

I spoke to the bank manager about borrowing $200,000 to buy that building, clean it up a little, and install some equipment. The building, at $175,000, is a good buy according to the real estate agent. I got a $15,000 quote from a contractor to do the renovations it requires. I think that $10,000 is enough to buy a cash register, display racks, and the little pieces of equipment needed to repair bikes and skis.

You:

I guess the banker needs some collateral and some indication that you'll be able to repay the loan.

Institute of Chartered Accountants of Ontario, adapted.

Tom:

That's right. And that's where I thought you might be able to help. Tell me what he wants and how to put it together.

You:

He probably wants to see cash flow statements, some ratio analysis, and anticipated results for the new locations. Do you have financial statements prepared?

Tom:

Yes, the January 31, 1986 year-end balance sheet and income statements are done (Exhibits 1 and 2). I also have written a list of things that I expect will happen with the new store (Exhibit 3).

You:

Good. Have you borrowed money from this bank before?

Tom:

Yes, I have a line of credit with them, and I'm still paying the $386 per month on the mortgage of the old store. The banker says my credit rating is good, and that I could probably get both long- and short-term money at 12 percent. I asked·him if a working capital loan of $20,000 for the new store would be possible. He said that he would consider it at the same time as the new building package.

You:

You seem to have thought this out thoroughly.

Tom:

If I brought over the documentation, could we put something together to-night? I'm seeing the banker tomorrow morning. If you can do the numbers, I can justify the marketing aspects. I'd really like to know what you think about this new venture.

You:

Sure Tom. I'll see you about 7:30.

Tom arrived with his documentation and financial statements. He assured you that he could have the presentation typed in the morning before his meeting with the banker.

Required

Prepare the necessary quantitative and qualitative analyses that would help Tom present his request to his banker. State any assumptions you make.

EXHIBIT 1

TOM'S OUTDOOR EXPERIENCE
Tom Dennison, Proprietor
Balance Sheet
As at January 31

	1986	*1985*	*1984*
Assets			
Current assets:			
Cash	$ 2,570	$ 2,400	$ 1,500
Accounts receivable	840	1,160	950
Inventory	49,130	44,760	38,950
Prepaids	2,010	1,860	1,400
Total current assets	54,550	50,180	42,800
Fixed assets:			
Equipment	8,500	8,500	6,000
Building	40,000	40,000	40,000
Land	6,000	6,000	6,000
	54,500	54,500	52,000
Less: accumulated depreciation	24,700	21,450	18,200
	29,800	33,050	33,800
Total assets	$84,350	$83,230	$76,600
Liabilities and Owner's Equity			
Current liabilities:			
Bank indebtedness	$ 7,000	$ 9,300	$ 4,700
Accounts payable	24,410	28,580	27,700
Accrued liabilities	1,450	1,950	1,700
Total current liabilities	32,860	39,830	34,100
Mortgage payable	30,830	32,300	33,600
Owner's equity:			
Tom Dennison, capital	20,660	11,100	8,900
Total liabilities and owner's equity.	$84,350	$83,230	$76,600

EXHIBIT 2

TOM'S OUTDOOR EXPERIENCE
Tom Dennison, Proprietor
Statement of Income and
Owner's Equity
For the year ended January 31

	1986	1985	1984
Sales	$265,360	$233,800	$203,100
Cost of goods sold	171,690	147,360	125,860
Gross profit	93,670	86,440	77,240
Expenses:			
Selling and administrative	43,120	44,580	35,130
Depreciation	3,250	3,250	3,000
Interest on long-term debt	3,160	3,330	3,400
Interest on short-term debt	1,180	980	1,360
	50,710	52,140	42,890
Net income for the year	42,960	34,300	34,350
Owner's equity, beginning of year . .	11,100	8,900	6,400
Drawings	(33,400)	(32,100)	(31,850)
Owner's equity, end of year	$ 20,660	$ 11,100	$ 8,900

EXHIBIT 3   Basis of Projections for New Store (prepared by Tom Dennison)

1. The deal for the store will close May 31 if financing is secured. This will allow time for renovations and inventory stocking. Projected opening date: August 1, 1986.
2. Sales in the old store are expected to increase by a minimum of 15 percent per year during the next few years since fitness is becoming an essential part of many lifestyles.

   Sales in the new store in the first six months will be about 80 percent of the projected results in the old store, then will equal or better the level of the old store. I expect better sales because the new store is in a larger community and the store area is larger.
3. Profit margins in the old store have slipped slightly in past years because of pressure from the chain stores. With two stores, purchasing economies will ensure that my profit margin won't slip more than 1 percent per year. I am even expecting a slight recovery because we provide excellent service on all equipment. Customers appreciate that and are willing to pay for it.
4. Selling and administration expenses have leveled off because we are using more part-time staff. I expect that in addition to the regular costs, I'll have to pay about $5,000 per year more for one of the staff to act as a manager.
5. Drawings can be reduced to $15,000 per year. My wife's income is more than sufficient for living expenses since our house mortgage has been paid.

Total Beauty Ltd.

Total Beauty Ltd. was founded in Windsor, Ontario, almost 50 years ago. The company sells skin care, fragrance, makeup and glamour products to women through "Network Presentations," private parties held for half a dozen people by a hostess who may also be a Total Beauty counsellor. There are currently 10,000 Total Beauty counsellors located across Canada.

To service these sales, the company owns a plant, Helden Laboratories, which handled $741,000 sales volume in 1984; this increased to $1.6 million during 1985 and required expansion of the plant's capacity. By the end of 1985 the board of directors was planning an expansion into the American market through the acquisition of a small cosmetics company; this would require additional funding. If the move into the United States proved successful, the board intended to enter the European market at a later date.

Total Beauty's earnings history has been erratic. In the 1950s and 1960s the company was a household name throughout the country. In the late 1960s the company was purchased by a public corporation; the fit was not a comfortable one, and Total Beauty's image was harmed. By the mid-1970s the company was unknown. It was at this time that Thomas Elder, a wealthy entrepreneur, purchased a controlling interest in Total Beauty. By 1980 Elder's management had restored the company's national reputation, and Elder and a close group of friends owned all the shares. Just after the 1984 year-end, the current structure of Total Beauty Ltd. was created through a reverse takeover and the company was listed on the Toronto Stock Exchange.

It is now September 1985, and Thomas Elder has just reviewed the draft financial statements for the year ended August 31. He is not pleased with several of the requirements of Total Beauty's auditors, which he feels present the company in a bad light. He would like to hear some justification of, for example, the requirement that all the reorganization costs be expensed immediately. The reorganization costs represent salaries paid to employees who spent most of the year working on the changes to the company's methods of sales and distribution. Expensing them totally in 1985 seems to be unduly harsh, particularly for a company where items such as working capital are so strong and which has such a promising future.

Required

Revise Total Beauty Ltd.'s Statement of Changes in Financial Position to comply with Section 1540 of the *Handbook,* issued in 1985. Do not make any changes to estimates, policies, or classifications before you recast the statement. Analyze the financial health of the company and present your recommendation for the treatment of the reorganization costs.

TOTAL BEAUTY LTD.
Consolidated Income Statement (draft)
For the Year Ended August 31, 1985
(in thousands)

	1985	1984
Sales	$5,481.0	$4,824.7
Costs and expenses, including depreciation		
and amortization of $125.6 (1984: $74.7) . . .	5,439.4	4,530.9
Interest expense on long-term debt		
and capital leases	187.7	125.7
Other interest	77.5	10.2
Operating income (loss) before nonrecurring		
reorganization costs	$ (223.6)	$ 157.9
Nonrecurring reorganization costs	885.3	
Income (loss) before income taxes	$(1,108.9)	$ 157.9
Provision for (recovery of) income taxes	$ (117.0)	$ 86.0
Net income (loss)	$ (991.9)	$ 71.9

TOTAL BEAUTY LTD.
Consolidated Balance Sheet (draft)
August 31, 1985
(in thousands)

	1985	1984
Assets		
Current assets:		
Accounts receivable	$ 184.0	$ 558.1
Due from shareholder	30.0	250.0
Inventories	2,036.8	1,424.6
Income taxes recoverable (Note J).	113.0	
Deferred income taxes (Note J)		8.0
Total current assets	$2,363.8	$2,240.7
Fixed assets:		
Land	$ 533.8	$ 533.8
Building.	1,415.9	1,386.5
Furniture and equipment	46.0	21.2
Computer software.	53.8	
	$2,049.5	$1,941.5
Less accumulated depreciation	149.8	69.7
	$1,899.7	$1,871.8
Equipment under capital leases	258.1	
Less accumulated amortization	34.7	
	$ 223.4	
Deferred income taxes (Note J)	34.0	26.0
Other assets:		
Goodwill (Note C)	224.8	
Patents and trademarks.	39.9	45.0
Total assets	$4,785.6	$4,183.5
Liabilities and Shareholders' Equity		
Current liabilities:		
Bank indebtedness	$ 998.4	$ 540.6
Accounts payable and accruals	932.4	1,186.9
Due to shareholder.	15.0	
Current portion of capital lease	38.8	
Income taxes payable		120.0
Total current liabilities	$1,984.6	$1,847.5
Long-term debt (Note E)	1,621.7	1,064.1
Capital lease obligation (Note G)	210.3	
Deferred revenue	44.5	
Shareholders' equity:		
Common shares (Note F)	644.6	.1
Appraisal increment	1,113.8	1,157.0
Retained earnings (deficit)	(833.9)	114.8
Total liabilities and shareholders' equity . . .	$4,785.6	$4,183.5

TOTAL BEAUTY LTD.
Consolidated Statement of Changes in Financial Position (draft)
For the Year Ended August 31, 1985
(in thousands)

	1985	1984
Source of funds:		
Increase in long-term debt	$ 700.0	$1,064.1
Issuance of capital stock	644.5	.1
Increase in capital lease obligation.	210.3	
Proceeds on disposal of equipment	81.9	
	$1,636.7	$1,064.2
Application of funds:		
Net income (loss)	(991.9)	71.9
Charges to operations not affecting working capital:		
Depreciation and amortization.	125.6	74.7
Deferred income taxes	(8.0)	(26.0)
Deferred revenue recognized	(12.2)	
Total to (from) operations	886.5	(120.6)
Additions to fixed assets under capital leases	378.0	741.6
Acquisition of business (Note C)	209.5	
Working capital deficiency of acquired business	21.0	
Acquisition of patents and trademarks		50.0
Repayment of long-term debt	142.3	
Increase in deferred revenue	13.4	
	$1,650.7	$ 671.0
Increase (decrease) in working capital	$ (14.0)	$ 393.2

TOTAL BEAUTY LTD.
Extracts from the Notes to the
Consolidated Financial Statements (draft)
August 31, 1985

Note B: Summary of Significant Accounting Policies

Patents and Trademarks

Patents and trademarks are stated at cost less accumulated amortization. Amortization is computed on the straight-line method at 10 percent per annum.

Appraisal Increment

Appraisal increments are transferred to retained earnings on the straight-line method at a rate which approximates but does not exceed the realization on the related assets through depreciation or sale.

(continued)

Note C: Business Combination

Pursuant to an agreement dated September 1, 1984 Total Beauty Ltd. issued 3 million common shares in exchange for the outstanding shares of Total Beauty Canada ("Canada"), a private Canadian company. As a result of this transaction, control of the combined companies passed to the former shareholders of "Canada" as a group. Legally, Total Beauty Ltd. would be regarded as the parent or continuing company. However, since the former shareholders of "Canada" control Total Beauty Ltd. after the acquisition, "Canada" is identified as the acquirer and Total Beauty Ltd. is treated as the acquired company. The value of the shares issued has been determined to be $209,500 which represents the portion of the equity of Total Beauty Canada which was given up by the individuals who held the shares of Total Beauty Ltd. immediately prior to the combination.

Being the acquiring company, the net assets of "Canada" are included in the balance sheet at book value and the net assets of Total Beauty Ltd. have been recorded at fair market at the date of acquisition.

The acquisition is summarized as follows:

Assets and liabilities of Total Beauty Ltd. as at September 1, 1984:

Current assets	$ .9
Current liabilities	21.9
Working capital deficiency and net book value acquired	21.0
Assigned purchase value	209.5
Goodwill	$230.5

*   *   *   *   *

Note E: Long-term Debt

Mortgage payable, bearing interest at the mortgagee's prime lending rate, secured by the building and certain of the company's insurance policies, due on June 1, 1985 and extended on a monthly basis since that date.	$ 921.7
Debenture maturing November 30, 1989 bearing interest at 10% per annum.	300.0
Debenture maturing May 3, 1990 bearing interest at 10% per annum.	400.0
	$1,621.7

Subsequent to the year-end the mortgage payable has been renewed until August 31, 1986 with interest at 11.25 percent per annum. Although the mortgage is due within one year of the balance sheet date it has been classified as a long-term liability as management intends to renew the mortgage or refinance the amount with other long-term borrowings.

(continued)

Note F: Capital Stock

	Number Authorized	Number Issued
Opening balance	10,000,000	591,666
Issued to effect the business combination . . .		3,000,000
Issued through private placements		435,000
Issued to employees.		5,340
	10,000,000	4,032,006

The value assigned to the issued shares is calculated as follows:

Balance of Total Beauty Canada capital stock account immediately prior to the business combination	$ .1
Assigned purchase value of Total Beauty Ltd.	209.5
Shares issued through private placements.	435.0
Shares issued to employees	0
	$644.6

Note G: Commitments

The company leases office space, warehouse vehicles, and equipment under the terms of various operating and capital leases. Annual rentals under lease agreements presently outstanding are as follows:

	Capital Leases	Operating Leases	Total
1986.	$ 75.3	$113.8	$189.1
1987.	75.3	86.3	161.6
1988.	75.3	86.3	161.6
1989.	75.3	71.9	147.2
1990.	41.9	0	41.9
	343.1	$358.3	$701.4
Amount representing interest.	94.0		
Present value of minimum lease payments . . .	249.1		
Less current portion	38.8		
	$210.3		

*   *   *   *   *

Note I: Related Party Transactions

A shareholder and director of the company owns the $400,000 debenture maturing May 3, 1990 referred to in Note E.

The same shareholder and director receives a fee for providing personal guarantees against the mortgage payable and the bank loan of the company. Such fees amounted to $41,000 during the year.

(continued)

Note J: Income Taxes

Deferred income taxes arise principally from timing differences in reporting depreciation expense for tax and financial reporting purposes and from accounting for certain lease agreements as capital leases for financial reporting purposes.

The company has tax loss carry-forwards in the amount of $800,000 which expire in 1992.

Case 85

Toystore

Recently, a small group of business people contacted your CA firm in connection with a new venture. They had decided to open a retail toy and craft operation in an historic redeveloped section of the busy downtown retail area of a large city. One of the people involved, Marg Froese, had had similar experience in such a store in another city. She is the one who initially became aware of this opportunity, but did not have the financial resources to buy or develop the new location by herself.

The group has bought a rundown, historic building in the redevelopment section, renovated it within the city's constraints for the area, and established a retail operation. Various government grants and incentives are available to assist the merchants, and there has been enthusiastic response to the volume of retail traffic in the area and the investment value of the real estate.

Four people are involved in the venture: three "silent partners" will put up $300,000 of the funds required (see Schedule 1), and Mrs. Froese will contribute the balance. In exchange, she will get a 35 percent share of the voting stock of the resulting company. The remainder of the stock will be evenly divided between the three other investors. Mrs. Froese is the only investor active in the day-to-day management of the company, although the four of them together comprise the board of directors.

A buy-sell agreement has been formulated whereby Mrs. Froese has first refusal on any shares the other owners wish to sell, at a price determined by reference to the audited financial statements. New owners must be approved unanimously by the remaining shareholders.

The inventory is financed by a chartered bank. A line of credit of $250,000 has been approved, to be backed by personal guarantees from all four investors. The bank requires quarterly statements and audited yearly statements.

The investor group has asked your firm of independent accountants to give your recommendations concerning appropriate financial accounting policies. You have been asked to carry out this assignment.

You have been able to learn the following:

1. The city previously owned the building to be purchased. Its appraised value was approximately $350,000.
2. Structural renovation costs can be recovered from the provincial government in the amount of $75,000, or 50 percent of monies spent, whichever is less. A 20-year life seems reasonable for the building, 10 years for fixtures.
3. No property taxes will be payable for five years (this would represent approximately $7,000 per year).
4. Mrs. Froese is to be paid $42,000 per year, plus 10 percent of Before Tax Income.
5. As part of the purchase agreement with the city, the operation must be kept open for at least five years. The property may not be used for other than a retail operation. Resale of the property within 10 years requires city approval.
6. All sales are by cash or credit card.
7. Some shop fixtures, including the cash registers, are to be leased on short-term lease contracts.
8. A heavy promotion effort is planned (see Schedule 1) to make people aware of this new operation.
9. The toy business is heavily seasonal, with most sales occurring in the two months before Christmas. Mrs. Froese is hoping that the summer months will be almost as busy in this location, as the tourist traffic is expected to be very heavy.

Required

Carry out the assignment.

SCHEDULE 1 Costs of New Operation

Acquisition of land and building	$200,000
Structural renovation costs	125,000
Other renovation costs	60,000
Advertising and promotion	50,000
Store fixtures (excluding leased items)	40,000
Inventory, toys and crafts.	150,000
Preopening wages and other costs	25,000
Financing required	$650,000
Less bank loan	250,000
Net financing required from owners*	$400,000

* Note: Financing requirements are net of expected trade support (Accounts Payable, etc.).

Case 86

Triple A Contractors Ltd.

Triple A Contractors Ltd. was incorporated in 1919 as a Canadian entity. Its parent company, ESC Ltd., is located in England and carries on business principally as electrical subcontractors on commercial projects. The Canadian subsidiary generally subcontracts in large commercial building projects as electrical contractors but has also successfully bid and completed electrical subcontracts in mining installations, the DEW line and other significant Canadian ventures. It operates through 14 branches in all of the provinces except Prince Edward Island. While the parent company has provided guidance and review to Triple A, its management team and work force are Canadian and operate independently from the parent company. ESC Ltd. has subsidiaries in a number of European countries as well as the United States and Australia.

In early 1989 ESC Ltd. was acquired by a UK multinational public company, Acquisitors Ltd., which has several subsidiaries in various industries. The purchase of ESC Ltd. marked Acquisitors Ltd.'s entry into the construction business as well as the North American market.

Mr. J. E. de Courcey Thompson, FCA, educated at Eton and Oxford, qualified 20 years ago as an ACA with one of the reputable international public accounting firms and afterward joined Acquisitors Ltd. As the current financial director, he holds the strong conviction that all subsidiaries should follow the same accounting principles contained in the firm's *Accounting Manual,* and he will not tolerate deviations.

Mr. de Courcey Thompson was highly critical of ESC Ltd.'s financial director who permitted each subsidiary to use local accounting principles, if they were reasonable, and then prepared ESC Ltd.'s consolidated financial statements with only minor adjustments at head office.

Mr. de Courcey Thompson only grudgingly accepted *SSAP 15* on deferred taxes when it was issued by the Accounting Standards Committee.

Institute of Chartered Accountants of Ontario, adapted.

After reviewing the December 31, 1988 financial statements of the Canadian and U.S. subsidiaries he declared to his assistant that during his trip to North America he would certainly instruct the local vice presidents on the proper way to account for deferred income taxes and would not permit the methods described in the accounting policy notes to continue.

Mr. Henry Chan, the vice president of finance of Triple A, had been forming a mental picture of Mr. de Courcey Thompson based on correspondence between him and the recently removed former finance director of ESC Ltd. He also heard about Mr. de Courcey Thompson's criticism of Triple A's financial statements and his pending trip to North America when, among other things, he intended to insist that partial allocation be used when calculating tax expense.

As Mr. Chan was becoming nervous about the upcoming visit, he called Mr. Andrew McGowan, Triple A's audit partner, for assurance and support. Mr. McGowan agreed that Triple A's financial statements, which were filed annually with the Department of Consumer and Corporate Affairs, properly complied with the disclosure requirements of the *Handbook*. He concurred with Mr. Chan's understanding that all the requirements contained in the *Handbook* were carefully considered before being issued and represented good financial reporting. In response to Mr. Chan's enquiry, he pointed out that all countries do not follow similar accounting principles, and he promised to help Mr. Chan prepare for his meeting with Mr. de Courcey Thompson.

Mr. Chan agreed that Mr. McGowan would prepare draft financial statements as at December 31, 1989, without adjustments for taxes, based on Triple A's latest budgeted figures.

Required

Using the information presented in Exhibit 1, calculate the budgeted income tax expense for Triple A as at December 31, 1989. Prepare a memorandum to equip Mr. Chan for his meeting with Mr. de Courcey Thompson.

EXHIBIT 1

---

1. Extracts from the notes to the December 31, 1987 financial statements of Triple A Contractors Ltd.

   a. Contract revenue and cost recognition:

   Generally the Company uses the completed contract method of accounting for contracts under which billings and costs are accumulated until the contracts are completed. Under this method no profits are recorded until the contract is completed, but losses are provided for as soon as they become

---

EXHIBIT 1   *(concluded)*

---

evident. For longer-term contracts involving a number of phases, the Company records revenue and profits on the percentage of completion basis as work on each phase is completed.

  b. Income taxes:

  The provision for income taxes is computed in relation to accounting income for the year. Deferred income taxes are recorded for timing differences caused by reporting certain types of income and expense for income tax purposes in periods different from those in which they are reported for financial statement purposes.

2. In 1977 Triple A completed a thorough review of its accounting system with the aid of a management consulting firm. By the end of 1978 it had installed a completely integrated EDP system using IBM 360 hardware. With much more timely information, management was better able to predict and control costs on each contract; the time to close out and final bill a completed contract was reduced to one month after the work was finished; and the outstanding receivables were greatly reduced. The company's profit improved significantly over the next three years and Triple A was better able to price its bids in its highly competitive market.

3. In 1982 Revenue Canada reassessed Triple A for the years 1978–1981, claiming that Triple A should have included the profits on contracts closed out and billed in each January as part of the immediately preceding operating year. Triple A did not dispute the assessment and paid the interest on late payments.

4. For the year ended December 31, 1988 Triple A earned $7,236,000 before taxes. The effective tax rate was 47 percent.

5. The NBV/UCC timing difference at December 31, 1988 was $1,568,750 and a deferred tax credit was recorded at an effective accumulation rate of 48 percent. The net book value of fixed assets excluding land was $4,232,000. The profit on contracts closed out in January 1989 was $2,777,500 and in January 1988 was $218,000. The company had total assets of $36,300,000 and no long-term debt.

6. The company has an established policy of continually expanding and upgrading its fixed assets. At the end of 1989 it anticipates that the net book value of its depreciable assets will be $4,647,000 and its undepreciated capital cost will be $2,826,250.

7. The company has projected an effective tax rate of 45 percent and profits before tax of $6,703,000. It expects the contracts closed out in January 1990 to have profits of $589,600.

Case 87

Truro Development Ltd.

Truro Development Ltd., a Canadian public corporation, was founded in 1978 by entrepreneur Tommy Wilson. The company is a developer and marketer of packaged computer software. By 1983 Truro was experiencing severe cash flow problems due to rapid expansion. In the year ended March 31, 1984 the company was required by its auditors to write off all previously deferred start-up and research and development costs. These write-offs were classified as unusual items; the company already had a loss from operations of over $3 million so the reported net loss exceeded $16 million. Note 23 was included in the 1984 statements (Exhibit 1).

Tommy Wilson was not only a computer entrepreneur but he also had a good knowledge of Canadian tax shelters. In 1983 a change to the Income Tax Act came to his attention, and Truro's cash flow was able to benefit from Wilson's expertise.

The change to the Act helped companies which were in a loss position and were thus unable to take advantage of cash flow assistance to their business via reduced taxes. The Act permitted these companies to sell deductions which they were not able to use. Thus the loss company received cash from the sale of the deductions, and the purchaser claimed the deductions on his own tax return.

In 1983 Wilson negotiated a contract with Company X under which Truro would incur research and development expenditures qualifying for tax credits. As Truro would not be able to use these credits, Wilson sold them to Company X for net proceeds of $4 million. Note 21 describes the transaction.

On the day the contract was signed Wilson correctly made the following journal entries:

Dr. Deferred loss on sale of SRTC's $1,000,000
Dr. Cash   4,000,000
    Cr. Accrued expenses $5,000,000

To record the sale of tax deductions and the liability to incur qualifying research and development expenses.

Dr. Research and development expense $5,300,000
    Cr. Tax payable. $5,300,000
To record the liability for tax on sale of deductions.

Required

1. Present the remaining journal entries to year-end for the sale of the SRTC's, based on the information found in Note 21.
2. Recast the Statement of Changes in Financial Position on a cash equivalents basis, and compare the usefulness of information received in the Statement of Changes in Financial Position presented on a working capital basis to a cash equivalents basis.

EXHIBIT 1

TRURO DEVELOPMENT LTD.
Consolidated Balance Sheet
March 31

	1984	1983
Assets		
Current assets:		
Cash	$ 2,736,393	$ 3,638,929
Accounts receivable	3,575,811	4,145,160
Notes receivable.	1,051,332	—
Inventories	178,114	144,858
Prepaid expenses	273,289	181,421
Deferred loss on sale of SRTC's (Note 21) . .	550,000	—
Total current assets	8,364,939	8,110,368
Long-term receivables	1,689,908	2,537,146
Sundry investments	27,520	127,747
Purchased software	666,714	1,644,517
Fixed assets.	4,099,729	2,743,721
Goodwill	1,839,302	2,069,473
Total assets	$16,688,112	$17,232,972
Liabilities and Shareholders' Equity (Deficit)		
Current liabilities:		
Bank indebtedness.	$ 2,008,511	$ 343,496
Accounts payable and accrued expenses . . .	9,636,289	2,264,440

EXHIBIT 1   (*continued*)

	1984	1983
Taxes payable.	$ 2,780,000	$ 30,831
Deferred revenue	871,197	710,913
Total current liabilities	15,295,997	3,349,680
Deferred revenue	—	518,575
Long-term debt	183,500	460,956
Provision for future software purchase commitment.	1,529,399	—
Deferred taxes.	18,350	320,644
Shareholders' equity (deficit):		
Capital stock	19,413,345	15,257,400
Deficit	(19,752,479)	(2,674,283)
Total liabilities and shareholders' equity	$16,688,112	$17,232,972

TRURO DEVELOPMENT LTD.
Consolidated Statement of Loss and Deficit
Year Ended March 31, 1984

Revenue:	
Computer software packages	$ 2,618,767
Research and development fees	3,272,387
Contract consulting	6,094,163
Computer hardware	755,970
Other.	1,466,746
	14,208,033
Costs and expenses:	
Selling, administrative, operating	15,448,809
Depreciation and amortization	1,801,742
Interest.	290,389
	17,540,940
Loss before unusual items	3,332,907
Unusual items.	13,438,820
Loss before income taxes.	16,771,727
Income taxes (reduction)	(19,615)
Loss before minority interest	16,752,112
Minority interest in loss of subsidiary	(61,620)
Loss for the year	16,690,492
Cost of issuing shares	387,704
Deficit, beginning of year.	2,674,283
Deficit, end of year	$19,752,479

EXHIBIT 1 *(continued)*

TRURO DEVELOPMENT LTD.
Consolidated Statement of Changes in Financial Position
Year Ended March 31, 1984

Funds provided by:

Shares issued for cash	$ 3,768,241
Deferred revenue	480,317
Minority interest in subsidiary company	61,620
Total funds provided	4,310,178

Funds applied to:

Operations, net of nonfund amounts*	7,325,067
Acquisition of businesses	2,672,060
Less working capital at date of acquisition	(76,100)
Purchased software packages	3,484,846
Fixed assets	2,306,393
Increase in long-term receivables	2,158
Increase in sundry investments	10,044
Reduction in long-term debt	277,456
Total funds applied	16,001,924
Increase (decrease) in working capital	(11,691,746)
Working capital, beginning of year	4,760,688
Working capital deficiency end of year (Note 23) . . .	$ 6,931,058

* Note disclosure was made of the nonfund amounts. The note has not been reproduced here.

Notes to the Financial Statements

Note 21: Scientific Research Tax Credit ("SRTC") Financing

Income tax legislation was introduced in Canada during the year which, in effect, allows corporations to transfer to third parties their available deductions for expenditures incurred in carrying out qualified research and development since April 19, 1983. The rights to deduct the subject expenditures for income tax purposes and to claim related investment tax credits have been foregone. The company has entered into an agreement, toward which it has received $4 million, whereunder the company is to perform scientific research at a fixed price prior to March 31, 1985. Upon receipt of the funds under the aforesaid SRTC financing arrangement and designation of the amount of foregone expenditures, the company became liable for a refundable income tax under Part VIII of the Income Tax Act of Canada amounting to $5.3 million. As at March 31, 1984 the estimated liability for this tax had been reduced, based on research and development activities to that date, to $2,750,000 and will be further reduced as additional research and development expenditures are incurred at the rate of $1 for every $2 ex-

EXHIBIT 1 *(concluded)*

pended. As a result of having effected the aforesaid SRTC financing, the company incurred a deferred loss of $1 million which is being amortized over the term of its research agreement.

Note 23: Working Capital Deficiency

At March 31, 1984, the company has a consolidated working capital deficiency of $6,931,058. The most significant factors contributing to the decrease in working capital and the resulting working capital deficiency are the financing of the company's branch openings and start-up costs and the purchase of computer equipment and related facilities considered necessary for the continued growth of the company. A planned increase in marketing costs together with less than anticipated software package revenue resulted in a reduced operational cash flow from that planned. The combined impact of these factors has been to significantly impair the company's working capital. Accordingly, the company must obtain long-term financing by way of either equity or debt or generate sufficient cash flow from its future operations to reverse the company's present working capital deficiency. To this end, the company entered into a Scientific Research Tax Credit agreement. The amounts derived from this agreement have and will provide funds necessary for the company's ongoing research and development activities. In the event that the company is unable to finance its ongoing requirements on either a long-term basis or through operational cash flow or a combination thereof, its ability to carry on future operations may be impaired.

George Weston Limited

Consolidation of subsidiaries is required by Section 3050 of the *CICA Handbook*, "Long-term Investments." The Section, effective in January 1973, established a few rare circumstances that would dictate an exception to consolidation, which was established as the general rule.

In 1973, George Weston did not consolidate its 67 percent ownership interest in Loblaw Companies Limited. For the fiscal year ending March 31, 1973, Loblaw Companies Limited reported a loss of $14.8 million, or $1.40 per share of Loblaw stock.

In the circumstances, it can be assumed that none of the rare exceptions provided for in Section 3050 applied to Loblaw. This is apparently a valid assumption because George Weston Limited accepted a qualification from its auditors.

Extracts from Weston's 1973 financial statements are shown in Exhibit 1. In an address to the Toronto Society of Financial Analysts, G. E. Creber, president and managing director of George Weston Limited, argued that Weston's relatively small $31 million equity holding in Loblaw did not justify a consolidation that would double Weston's assets by adding those of Loblaw. Creber also argued that the fair disclosure provisions should override the recommendations contained in the *CICA Handbook*.

In the introduction to its accounting recommendations, the *CICA Handbook* states:

> . . . no rule of general application can be phrased to suit all circumstances or combination of circumstances that may arise, nor is there any substitute for the exercise of professional judgement in the determination of what constitutes fair presentation or good practice in a particular case. (p. 9, *CICA Handbook*.)

Adapted, with permission from John R. E. Parker.

Required

Discuss Weston's objections to consolidation thoroughly, examining both sides of the issue.

Your discussion should include a discussion and calculation of how Weston's financial statements would change (i.e., net assets, EPS, presentation, and so on) if Weston had consolidated Loblaw in 1973.

EXHIBIT 1   Extracts from Financial Statements—George Weston Limited
(December 31, 1973)

---

1. Summary of significant accounting policies:
   a. Basis of consolidation:
   The accompanying financial statements consolidate all subsidiary companies except Loblaw Companies Limited and its subsidiary companies ("Loblaw") which is carried at cost.

   George Weston Limited ("Weston") has voting control of Loblaw through ownership of 67.7 percent of that company's outstanding class B voting shares. The Weston holding of the combined Class A nonvoting shares and the class B voting shares represents 60.3 percent of the total participating shares outstanding. Because of the large minority interests in Loblaw, as well as the substantial minority interest in the Loblaw subsidiary companies themselves, management has felt that consolidation of the Loblaw accounts with those of Weston's would not be the most informative presentation.

   Effective January 1, 1973, the Canadian Institute of Chartered Accountants has recommended that, with rare exceptions, all subsidiaries should be fully consolidated. The effect of this recommendation is that the practice followed in the accompanying financial statements of carrying the investment in Loblaw at cost can no longer be said to be in accordance with generally accepted accounting principles.

   In view of this it is the company's intention to include the accounts of Loblaw in the Weston consolidated financial statements for the year commencing January 1, 1974, the earliest practicable period for which such a step could be taken. To provide a proper starting point for the consolidation, the fiscal year-end of Loblaw has been changed to coincide with that of Weston, effective December 31, 1973. The company proposes to first publish operating results on a fully consolidated basis commencing with the quarter ending March 31, 1974.

   The following information has been extracted from the audited consolidated financial statements of Loblaw for the 52 weeks ended March 31, 1973 (with comparative figures for the previous year as restated by Loblaw):

	1973	1972
	($000s)	
Working capital	$ 71,527	$ 99,588
Total assets	531,282	547,109

EXHIBIT 1   *(concluded)*

	1973	1972
	($000s)	
Minority interests in subsidiaries	$ 90,266	$ 111,267
Shareholders' equity	95,585	117,099
Sales	2,560,283	2,592,748
Income (loss) before special items	(6,539)	4,095
Net income	(14,764)	7,261
Weston's share of the above consolidated earnings (loss) of Loblaw (after eliminating an intercompany gain of $340,000 in 1973) is as follows:		
Net income (loss)—total	(9,097)	3,177
—per share of Weston common stock	(83)¢	(29)¢
Weston has reflected in its net income the dividends received from Loblaw as follows:		
Dividends received during the year ended December 31—total	2,510	2,274
—per share of Weston common stock	23¢	21¢

Weston's share of the undistributed earnings of Loblaw from date of acquisition to March 31, 1973 (after retained earnings adjustments) amounts to $19,705,000.

Wilfong Foods Ltd.

Wilfong Foods Ltd. (WFL) is a large Canadian supermarket chain, with common shares, preferred shares, and corporate debentures sold publicly.

Wilfong prides itself on the quality of its annual report, which has several times won awards for its informativeness. Accordingly, the controllers' department at WFL takes a serious interest in accounting trends and standard changes.

An analysis of the deferred tax account, and calculation for the latest year's "Provision for Tax" is contained in Exhibit 1. You, a junior accountant in the controllers' department, have been asked to prepare a brief summary of the financial statement impact of three independent scenarios:

1. A change to the accrual method from the deferral method, using the recently instituted Canadian methodology.
2. A change to partial tax allocation from full tax allocation. WFL defines partial tax allocation as considering only those timing differences expected to reverse in the next three years (accrual method).
3. A change to discounting deferred taxes from a nondiscounting system. A discount rate of 10 percent should be used (accrual method).

Required

Prepare the requested analysis.

EXHIBIT 1   Deferred Tax Data

---

a. Calculation of provision for tax:

	Accounting Income	Taxable Income	Effect on Deferred Taxes
Income before tax	$5,390,000	$5,390,000	
Plus:			
Depreciation		605,000	$ 605,000
Reserve for obsolete inventories		100,000	100,000
Club dues.	10,000	10,000	
Foreign advertising	20,000	20,000	
Less:			
Dividends from taxable Canadian corporations . .	(120,000)	(120,000)	
Capital cost allowance . . .		(1,750,000)	(1,750,000)
	$5,300,000	$4,255,000	$(1,045,000)
Tax rate, 42%	$2,226,000	$1,787,100	$ 438,900

b. Balance in deferred taxes, end of current year, including adjustment for above. . . . . $1,258,200 cr.

Consisting of:
1. Provision for obsolete inventory ($100,000 × .42) $ 42,000 dr.
   Provision in current year income
   Deductible for tax when incurred, expected next year

2. Net book value versus UCC

Net book value, end of year	$6,785,000	
Undepreciated capital cost, end of year	3,485,000	
Difference.	3,300,000	
Rate of accumulation	.394	1,300,200 cr.
		$1,258,200 cr.

c. Additional information:
1. Tax rates are expected to stay stable for the next two years, then increase by 1 percent per year for the next five years.
2. The net book value/UCC timing difference is expected to reverse as follows (1 is next year, 5 is fifth subsequent year, etc.):

Year	Amount
1	$ 430,000
2	475,000
3	500,000
4	540,000

EXHIBIT 1   *(concluded)*

Year	Amount
5	$ 560,000
6	795,000
Total . . .	$3,300,000

Current year's timing differences reverse in Year 3 ($400,000), Year 4 ($540,000), and Year 5 ($205,000).

Note: New originating timing differences are not considered in the above schedule, which shows how the $3,300,000 would reverse if no capital assets are acquired. If new capital assets are acquired on schedule, no reversals are expected after year 2.

Wylie International Ltd.

Wylie International Ltd. was founded in 1970 by the Hodge family of Regina. The initial share capital was $3 million, and the company remained family owned for the next 20 years. It is still run by family members.

Wylie International Ltd. is a marketing services company specializing in the distribution of consumer packaged goods to retailers in Canada and the United States. The company deals with more than 30,000 retailers, the majority of them located in Canada, and provides products and marketing assistance to smaller outlets such as convenience stores (as opposed to the national and regional supermarkets which warehouse and deliver to their own outlets and design and implement large-scale advertising campaigns). Initially the products distributed were tobacco and confectionery items; recently the product line has been expanded to include groceries, health and beauty aids, fast foods and general merchandise. Wylie now distributes more than 10,000 brand name items. Tobacco and confectionery items still comprise the majority of dollar sales, and the company is the largest distributor of these items in Canada.

The company not only offers product purchasing and storage services to the smaller outlet but is also able to assist in store design and layout. Sales representatives monitor the presentation and turnover of products and offer suggestions for substitutions or alternative display options.

Wylie International Ltd. grew over the 20 years to the organization it is today (Exhibit 1) by acquiring existing firms in the same line of business and consolidating small distribution centres into large semiautomated warehouses which cover a much larger geographical area. The company is currently focusing its attention on product mix—away from low-margin tobacco products into higher-margin health and beauty aids, groceries, and fast foods.

During most of the company's history the primary financial information required has been audited statements for the bank. However, during 1990 the company plans to become listed on the Vancouver Stock Exchange and to raise $60 million additional equity by the end of the year. The proceeds of the issue will be used as shown below. The excess of the purchase price over the fair value of the assets acquired is forecast to be approximately $6 million.

(millions)

Inventories	$24.0
Land	4.0
Building improvements	2.5
Equipment	9.0
Leasehold improvements	.5
Purchase of interest in the following companies: Ballantine Sales and Associates, a food broker, 84%; Carleton Merchandisers, a distributor of tobacco, confectionery, and health and beauty aids, 100%; Johnstone Enterprises Ltd., a fast-food distributor, 30%	20.0
	$60.0

In 1989 Wylie loaned funds to one of its investees to purchase two local food brokerage firms in Manitoba which were subsequently merged into one organization. Within months Wylie's board became aware that because of unforeseen competitive pressures the investee and the Manitoba firm were not compatible. By February of 1990 Wylie announced plans to sell its interest in the investee. The cost of the investment was $2.5 million and the loan amounted to $2.7 million, both of which were treated as long-term assets.

It is now March 1990 and Carl Hodge, the president of Wylie, has requested a meeting with the auditors. He wonders, despite the fact that previous statements have been audited, if in the past he has chosen the "best" accounting policies, given the company's plans to go public. He is requesting specific input on which policies might be changed before the prospectus is prepared. He would also appreciate receiving advice on specific accounting policies which may be relevant to Wylie in the future so that he knows his options and wishes to hear any other comments the auditors may have with regard to the preparation of the next set of statements.

Required

Assume the role of Wylie's auditor. Advise Carl Hodge on the most suitable accounting policies for his company, given his objectives. Include in your analysis any points which should be brought to Hodge's attention with regard to the next set of financial statements.

EXHIBIT 1 Organizational Chart, December 31, 1989

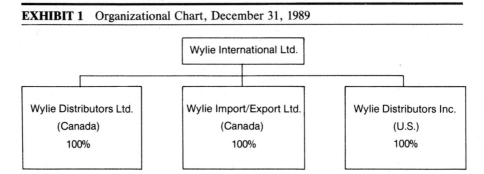

Wylie Distributors Ltd. (Canada) is engaged in the buying, warehousing, selling and delivery of cigarettes, cigars, tobacco, confectionery, health and beauty aids, general merchandise, and groceries. Currently it operates in British Columbia, Saskatchewan, and part of Manitoba. There are two warehouses in British Columbia serving that province, and a third warehouse in Manitoba which distributes to that province, Saskatchewan, and the Ontario lakehead.

Wylie Import/Export Ltd. distributes giftwares and sundries to gift shops and specialty stores throughout Canada. Drawing on merchandise from foreign manufacturers, the company handles a number of major brands exclusively for Canada. The head office and warehouse are located in Regina with sales offices in Calgary, Winnipeg, and Toronto.

Wylie Distributors Inc. (U.S.) conducts its operations virtually identical to its Canadian counterpart, although on a much smaller scale. The company has a very small office staff and one warehouse in Minneapolis; considerable effort is planned to increase distribution.